Pandemics, Politics, and Society

Pandemics, Politics, and Society

Critical Perspectives on the Covid-19 Crisis

Edited by
Gerard Delanty

DE GRUYTER

ISBN (Paperback) 978-3-11-071323-7
ISBN (Hardcover) 978-3-11-072020-4
e-ISBN (PDF) 978-3-11-071335-0
e-ISBN (EPUB) 978-3-11-071340-4

Library of Congress Control Number: 2020952254

Bibliographic information published by the Deutsche Nationalbibliothek
The Deutsche Nationalbibliothek lists this publication in the Deutsche Nationalbibliografie;
detailed bibliographic data are available in the Internet at http://dnb.dnb.de.

© 2021 Walter de Gruyter GmbH, Berlin/Boston
Cover image: Egon Schiele, The Family (Squatting Couple). 1918, oil on canvas, 150 x 160.8 cm.
Belvedere, Vienna, Inv. No. 4277. © Belvedere, Vienna, photo: Johannes Stoll
Printing and binding: CPI books GmbH, Leck

www.degruyter.com

Contents

Part 3: **The Social and Alternatives**

Preface

The idea for this volume took shape in Barcelona during the historic lockdown in spring 2020. I was on research leave and had just finished writing a book on critical theory and social transformation only to contemplate the onset of what is perhaps the most significant social transformation since the fall of communism. At the time, it was impossible to imagine anything like the severe lockdown that the Spanish state imposed, ostensibly to slow down the contagion in order to ease pressure on the health system. The suddenness of the suspension of liberties and normal life was as much a shock as the arrival of the pandemic itself. Initially, unsurprisingly, critical responses to the pandemic focused on the reactions of governments, which mostly acted too late and resorted to what were in many cases unprecedented lockdowns that led in turn to significant social and economic upheaval.

However, some months later it became apparent that a fuller analysis would need to address the reality of the pandemic itself beyond the restrictions to individual liberty and the failure of governance. And so the idea for a collaborative book emerged: in the need for a more comprehensive sociological assessment of the current situation and the prospects for the future. This volume is an early contribution to this goal.

It is becoming increasingly clear that the Covid-19 pandemic is a complex phenomenon, both epidemiologically and sociologically. It is, on one level, an illness that has truly global reach despite major regional differences in terms of its impact. So, as far as western societies are concerned, the health emergency marks a break with the historical experience of the past hundred years or so since the elimination of cholera. This was a time when the most deadly infectious diseases were concentrated in Europe's former colonies. However, the separation of metropole and colony has broken down with the pandemic. On another level, in terms of historical experience, the Covid-19 pandemic is not so exceptional in the history of infectious diseases. Indeed, the post-1945 period that saw the final eradication of smallpox and polio in western societies was exceptional. What we are now witnessing, at least since the late 1990s, is the spread of new infectious diseases, which, unlike smallpox and polio, are zoonotic diseases, i.e. they derive from viral infections in other animals. We can expect more.

Covid-19 is therefore a wake-up call for greater preparation, but it also calls for greater public understanding and debate on how democratic societies should respond to such pandemics, what kind of knowledge is required, and how they may be prevented. It is also particularly significant that the pandemic is occurring at a time of major societal crisis on many levels: the ecological crisis, the crisis of capitalism, and the crisis in democracy have all become entangled in the health crisis. The pandemic has intensified the sense of precariousness and anxiety that contemporary society engenders. It has exacerbated inequalities, xenophobia and racism. However, the current situation is ambivalent. On one side, there is a sense of catastrophe or regression, while on the other, there is the prospect of a transition to new times, or possibly we may just be in a state of perpetual transition to an unknown destiny. Perhaps the significance of the pandemic ultimately resides in the chances of a new model of society emerging from the debris of the present. But it is also possible that the pandemic simply entrenches changes that have already occurred. The chapters in this volume explore the ramifications of these problems and the sense of a historical moment of rupture.

In editing this volume, I have incurred many debts. I am especially grateful to the authors who enthusiastically responded to my invitation and contributed chapters at very short notice during what was for everyone a very unusual summer. It has been a pleasure to have worked with such an exceptional team. My thanks also go to the publisher at De Gruyter, Gerhard Boomgaarden, for instigating this volume and to Michaela Göbels for her assistance with its production. An anonymous reviewer of the proposal made some excellent suggestions to improve the original conception of the book. I am also grateful to Gordon Connell for his excellent copyediting of some of the chapters and to Neal Harris who provided additional assistance with the completion of the volume. I am grateful to my wife, Aurea Mota de Araujo, for suggesting the cover design, the painting by the Austrian expressionist artist Egon Schiele 'The Family' (1918). The painting depicts the artist, his wife and their unborn child shortly before their death in October 1918 of the devastating flu pandemic of that year. It appears to show resignation in the face of the inevitable, but also calm and perhaps even hope in the face of catastrophe. I am grateful to the Belvedere Gallery, Vienna for permission to use a photograph of the painting.

Gerard Delanty
Barcelona and Brighton, September 2020

Gerard Delanty
Introduction: The Pandemic in Historical and Global Context

For many people the world changed in the first half of 2020. The sudden arrival of Covid-19 and the declaration of a pandemic on 11th March by the World Health Organization changed social life in far-reaching ways.[1] The pandemic was a social and economic shock as well as a political crisis and a psychological trauma. There was an abrupt end to mobility as, one by one, states imposed lockdowns and quarantines with the result that normal life ceased. Death not life dominated the media for months. Capitalism itself was put on hold, or so it seemed for a brief moment.[2] What at first seemed possible only in a dictatorship became an increasingly accepted way to respond to the danger posed by the coronavirus. Almost a year later, it does not look like the pre-pandemic world will simply return, but a new world is also not in sight. The tensions resulting from the Covid-19 pandemic have become entwined in a range of other social and political issues, such as the Black Lives Matter [BLM] movement around racial injustice, the acceleration of post-democracy, and the problems already endemic to capitalism of major social inequalities.

The point of departure for this volume is that the pandemic presents many challenges for social and political science. To begin, the shock of the pandemic needs to be placed in longer historical perspective as well as in global context. The advanced western world had become accustomed to relative freedom from dangerous infectious diseases. But from a global and historical perspective this is a somewhat narrow view of historical experience. A re-contextualization of the pandemic does not detract from the fact that it has clearly become an event of considerable significance that has opened up a wide range of possible political epistemologies. Extreme right-wing groups, conspiracy theorists and American Pentacostalists, at one end of the political spectrum, are mobilizing as much as those at the other end, such as BLM and radical ecologists. Some-

---

1 A note on terminology may be helpful. SARS-CoV-2 is the virus classification that caused Covid-19. The former is one of a group of RNA based coronaviruses. It means 'severe acute respiratory syndrome coronavirus'. Other coronaviruses are MERS-CoV, which appeared in 2012 in Saudi Arabia, and SARS-CoV, which emerged in 2002 in Guangdong in China. Covid-19 is a classification of infectious diseases (Co for Coronavirus; vi for virus; 19 for 2019). Covid-19 was declared a pandemic by WHO in March 2020.
2 The reality of course is an economic crisis and a downturn in growth. It does not necessarily signal a crisis of capitalism.

https://doi.org/10.1515/9783110713350-001

where in the middle are libertarians campaigning against restrictions to individual liberty. Resistance is everywhere. But, as with most social and political phenomena, resistance does not take just one form.

An epidemic or pandemic is an event – a disease and illness – that projects a certain image around which rival interpretations compete. The image may be more terrifying than the disease, which will visit only some, but the consequences for all will be great.

The Covid-19 pandemic is increasingly attracting the attention of academics working in many fields across the social and human sciences. Social and political scientists have begun to explore the wider societal significance of the pandemic and the responses to it. The economic and social consequences will almost certainly outlive the pandemic itself. The analysis of the pandemic is not confined to the specialist fields of epidemiology and public health on how infectious diseases spread and how they can be controlled. This is as much a sociological question as it is a biological one, since viral infections are transmitted through social interaction. Communication makes possible the contagion of disease.[3] The health crisis touches on numerous aspects of social organization including the role of medical experts, as discussed by Stephen Turner and Jan Zielonka in this volume. In many ways, the pandemic also poses fundamental existential questions about social life as well as exposing many of the inequalities in contemporary societies. It also comes at a time of major social transformation on a global level as a deep sense of crisis and anxiety is felt everywhere, especially concerning environmental and economic sustainability. The problems of contemporary societies have become intensified as a result of the pandemic. It is possible to speak of a triple crisis: a health and medical crisis, an ecological one, and a crisis in capitalism and globalization.

Viruses and Globalisation

Infectious diseases have played a pervasive role in the shaping of human societies.[4] The history of infectious diseases demonstrates the fragility of the human body and social organization in face of major epidemics. It is arguably the case that throughout the history of civilization, the greatest danger to social

---

3 As Priscilla Wald argues in a remarkable work, 'Contagion is more than an epidemiological fact. It is also a foundational concept in the study of religion and of society, with a long history of explaining how beliefs circulate in social interaction (Wald: 2008: 2).

4 For some general overviews, see Harrison (2004), Hays (2009), Honigsbaum (2020), Oldstone (2010), McNeil (1998), McMillen (2016), Morse (1993) and Snowden (2020).

life has been the unrelenting presence of epidemics. The spread and control of disease, far from being incidental to social life has been as much a feature of human societies as war (Snowden 2020). The decline of war as the main cause of death, left infectious disease as the primary killer for much of the world. Epidemics are not just biological facts; they are deeply entwined in the social and political fabric of societies. They are also integral to much of human experience simply because they portend death.[5] But they also give rise to hope in face of catastrophe. As Bryan Turner shows in his chapter in this volume, epidemics and pandemics have been world-changing events and there are certain historical similarities between Covid-19 and previous pandemics in terms of the search for meaning in the face of catastrophe.

It is now widely recognised that epidemics must be located in the global context; contagion, by its nature, is not confined by national boundaries or borders. Even before the transoceanic European contacts with the Tropics and the New World, the dissemination of infectious disease across civilizations was ever present, as evidenced by the bubonic plague. In this context, there is a fuzzy line between an epidemic and a pandemic. The latter is by definition an epidemic that is global. Today most pandemics are influenzas. Pandemics recognised by the World Health Organization have all been influenza epidemics (1958, 1968, 2009) with the exception of Covid-19. The increasingly global scope of epidemic diseases also reveals another fact of human life: the pathogens that inflict suffering on humans are now connected with the planetary crisis of life itself. For at least these reasons it is questionable that globalization is threatened by the pandemic, though now global travel has decreased. Globalization constitutes the very conditions of the possibility of pandemics. The Covid-19 pandemic is also, as Daniel Chernilo says in his chapter in this volume, arguably the first global phenomenon in human history in which the majority of the world's population is experiencing a similar event at the same time. Of course, they are experiencing it in very different ways. For Frédéric Vandenberghe and Jean-Francois Véran in their chapter in this volume, the pandemic is what they call a global total social fact

Nonetheless, the immediate impact of a pandemic is local before it is global. Since the direct social effects of epidemics have always been demographic, their control became inevitably bound up with the historical formation of states. The control of populations and territory is the primary role of the state. Since antiquity, states have been faced with the fundamental problem of the survival of their citizenry as a result of devastation from disease. In the longer perspective

---

5 On this, see Fassin (2018).

of history, it is remarkable that until the late nineteenth century following major scientific breakthroughs with the work of Louis Pasteur in France and Robert Koch in Germany, there was little or no understanding of the causes of infectious diseases. Viruses[6] remained invisible with the early microscope and were not identified until the 1890s as separate from bacteria, but it was not until the 1930s with the invention of the electronic microscope that they were finally made visible. Consequently, before the advent of germ theory, the explanations found for most – if not all – infectious diseases were often religious or were attributed to the natural order of life or to some mysterious atmospheric entity such as 'miasma'.

In the absence of vaccines, immunity, the only real protection against infectious disease, takes a considerable time to develop and for the majority of diseases there is no immunity. For much of history, people had little or no protection against the spread of infectious diseases, which grew along with increased population density and mobility. The rise of capitalism and industrial society in the nineteenth century led to rapid population increase and urbanization. While this provided fertile ground for the spread of airborne infectious diseases, such as tuberculosis, and waterborne diseases, such as typhoid and cholera, the other side of the double-edged sword of modernity was the rise of science and secularization, which prepared the ground for significant progress in medicine and in public health. Sanitation and, later, inoculation was as central to the 'civilizing' project of modernity as was education, liberty, justice and democracy (see Harrison 2004). The Enlightenment proclaimed science to be the basis of progress, which included new conditions for human life itself. It cultivated the Eurocentric belief that Europe was – or could be – free of disease, while ignoring the fact that European imperialism was a major force in the spreading of disease. It was smallpox followed by measles that brought about the end of the Inca and Aztec civilizations in the 1530s following the Spanish conquest that was enabled by the incredible loss of 90 per cent of the Amerindian population. These viruses changed fundamentally the course of world history.

As Carl Zimmer wrote in *A Planet of Viruses:* 'Viruses are unseen but dynamic players in the ecology of Earth. They move DNA between species, provide new genetic material for evolution, and regulate vast populations of organisms. Every species, from tiny microbes to large mammals, is influenced by the actions of viruses' (Zimmer 2015: ix). Yet, despite this reality, the modern world gave rise to the dream of hygienic containment, the desire for contagion-free societies and the sovereign individual (see Bashford and Hooker 2014). The impossibility of re-

---

6 Most viruses are hundreds of times smaller than a bacterium.

alizing this dream led to anxieties of contagion, including the very idea of contagion. Fear of inflection and fear of others are closely connected. As the Italian philosopher Roberto Esposito explains in his book *Immunitas*, the category of life itself includes an element of its opposite, such that both the human and the social body are not pure or self-contained. The body is in continuous exchange with its environment (Esposito 2011). Eradication is a myth that rarely is achieved.

Modernity, Catastrophe and Disease

By the second half of the twentieth century, it seemed that modernity had conquered some of the worst infectious diseases. Despite what was perhaps the greatest catastrophe in human history, the 1918 flu pandemic, which led to the death of more than 50 million people, significant progress continued to be made against infectious diseases as the primary causes of major social transformations (Barry 2020; Spinney 2018). In Europe, at least, cholera, typhoid and smallpox became less important than tuberculosis as the main cause of mortality. The end of epidemics appeared to be in sight with the eradication of smallpox in the 1970s, the discovery of antibiotics and vaccinations for a range of infectious diseases such as polio, measles, tuberculosis, diphtheria, and whooping cough.

This book begins with the recognition that the apparent end of the major historical infectious diseases through their eradication or elimination and the victory of human power over natural pathogens must be questioned. The argument underlying this volume is that epidemics and pandemics have been, and will continue to be, part of human history. Their form will change and the specificity of pathogens will change, but they are not anomalies of the human condition. Human have established themselves as the masters of nature; they have positioned themselves, figuratively speaking, at the top of the food chain, but they have not gained control over the most primordial and smallest form of life, the virus to which they are in thrall. The longer perspective of history reveals that we are always between an epidemic or a pandemic. It is only a question of scale and timing. This is not to deny the tremendous success of the modern state and of science in its response to major epidemics, which are no longer the major causes of mortality. It is also incontrovertible that improved conditions of life as a result of diet, sanitation, vaccination and pest control are the most effective remedies against some of the most virulent diseases such as malaria, yellow fever and cholera that still persist in many of the less developed countries. Nonetheless, the great faith in scientific progress that came with modernity does not lead to one single future and nor does it offer protection against catastrophe. As Mark Harrison (2014) as shown, the rise and expansion of commerce was accompanied by the spread of infectious diseases. The entangled history of commence and contagion, reveal an interconnected world that does not lead inexorably in the direction of immunity against disease.

Histories of epidemics provide detailed and rich histories of the complex epidemiology of infectious diseases. Much is now known about the entangled history of viruses and human societies since William McNeill's seminal *Plagues and Peoples* in 1976. Major works by other historians of disease, such as Hays (2009) and Oldstone (2010), provide ample evidence that successful immunization has not given modern societies total protection from deadly microbes. This has also been affirmed by Frank Snowden (2020). As McNeill and others have shown, there are many historical examples of microbes instigating major historical transformations from Athenian society and the Roman Empire, to the pre-Columbian civilizations of the Incas and Aztecs (see also Price-Smith, 2008; Ranger and Slack 1992). Viruses and bacteria were also catalysts in bringing about the transformation of Europe from the Black Death to the 1918 flu. Societies, to be sure, adapt to changes in their environment, but no social or even human evolutionary or cultural response equals the capacity of viruses to adapt to their hosts. Viruses evolve and mutate more rapidly than any other organism (Wolfe 2011: 8 and 34). This is one of the reasons for their tremendous capacity to bring about major social changes (see also Diamond 1998). It is worth recalling that the three greatest catastrophes, in terms of the number of deaths, in human history were the Bubonic Plague in the 1340s, the devastation of the Inca and Aztec civilizations by smallpox and measles in the 1530s, and, as mentioned, the 1918 flu pandemic. It is a further question whether the cultural memory of these events was in relation to their historical importance as catastrophic events. The 1918 flu, for example, was overshadowed by the memory of the war that preceded it even though it caused more deaths. Perhaps the horror of the war and the mass death it produced de-sensitised war-torn societies to death.

Social and political scientists, unlike historians, have given insufficient attention to epidemics[7], with the single and notable exceptions of HIV/AIDS, on which there is now a large interdisciplinary literature. Perhaps because the age of the great historical pandemics in western societies appeared to have passed, social science has for the greater part given more attention to other prob-

---

7 Some exceptions are Davis (2005), Dingwall et al (2013), Opitz (2017), Weir and Mykhalovskiy (2010). It should be noted that sanitation and disease were taken seriously in early Chicago sociology. See Chapter 3 Wald (2008).

lems that emanate directly from human societies, such as technologically based risks from nuclear plants and nuclear weapons (Beck 1992). There is also the widespread recognition that death in the advanced western world is more likely to be due to degenerative diseases, such as cancer and heart disease than infectious diseases (see Aries 1974, 1991). There are several reasons to ask why what Ulrich Beck termed 'risk societies' are less prone to pandemics and major destabilizing forces deriving from viruses. This volume seeks to demonstrate the importance of redefining human societies in terms of vulnerabilities, suffering, susceptibility to catastrophe, and pathologies of both a biological and social nature.

After such catastrophes as Hurricane Katrina in August 2005 or the Asian Tsunami of 2004, we are now more sensitive to the vulnerability of human societies to natural catastrophe (see also Jones 2018). Such events are not simply natural, but also social events. To follow Tierney, disasters entail the juxtaposition of physical forces, which may be geological, atmospheric or technological forces, and other social and political relations in the context of vulnerable communities (Tierney 2019: 4–29). They are not a departure from normal life, but increasingly a part of normal life. From a critical perspective, disasters are not isolated events but part of the fabric of societies and are characteristic of the social contexts in which they occur as opposed to being external to those settings. So major events, such as Hurricane Katrina reveal that catastrophes are not exogenous but endogenous to the social order (see also Blaikie et al 1994; Elliott and Hsu 2016). As Tierney and others who research disasters show, the potential for disaster is growing as a result of the ever greater concentration or density of populations living in high-risk areas as well as the circulation of dangerous substances – as is also aptly illustrated by the catastrophic explosion in Beirut in August 2020. While many events are contained in a specific area, many are not, such as the Chernobyl explosion in 1986 or, as Jean-Luc Nancy argues, the explosion at the Fukushima nuclear power plant in Japan (Nancy 2015). More pertinent in the present context are the causes of epidemics, which can also be seen as the consequence of a local disaster taking on a global dimension.

The Social Construction of Disease

Since the tremendous impact of the work of Michel Foucault on health and medicine as well as on many other aspects of modern society, there has been a pervasive tendency in social science to emphasise the cultural dimensions of social phenomena, especially those concerning power and domination. While this has opened up an important critical perspective on the social construction of what had previously been seen as natural (the self, illness, identity, gender) it has led to an overemphasis on the cultural nature of disease, often to a point that the objectivity of the disease is reduced to its discursive existence.

Epidemics are both pathological realities as well as social constructions in that they are mediated by social and political conditions. Infectious diseases are neither entirely constructions nor objective realities. They are realities in themselves but are culturally mediated by being interpreted in particular ways in specific times and places. They have social significance and political implications arising from human responses to what we can call the objective event of the epidemic or pandemic.

For this reason, the claim made by the Italian philosopher Gorgio Agamben that the pandemic is an 'invention' is misleading.[8] It is clear though he meant that it has been the subject of political instrumentalization and that the political consequences may be greater than those of the virus. The initial shock for many people was less the virus and the disease that it caused than the lockdown. But viruses have a reality in themselves that often eludes what humans can do with them. Yet, they acquire meaning and significance from the ways in which they are known and interpreted. For example, as Charles E. Rosenberg (1989) has written in an insightful essay on AIDS, epidemics take on a dramaturgic form in that they are events that happen at a specific moment in time and which unfold around a narrative of increasing revelation and tension leading to individual and collective crisis. Of course, most people are spectators in these dramas, which concern universal themes and give expression to deep anxieties that are nurtured by uncertainty. Yet, while a drama has a moment of closure, the reality of disease is very often that there is no closure other than death.

Priscilla Wald has drawn attention to another aspect of the cultural fabric of disease outbreaks: the role story-telling and narrative: 'The outbreak narrative is a powerful story of ecological danger and epidemiological belonging, and as it entangles analyses of disease emergence and changing social and political formations, it affects the experience of both' (Wald 2008: 33). It makes possible, she argues, through the language of crisis new acts of imagining the social body and political community.

Looking to the future and the alarming prospect of new viruses, there is the more radical possibility, as Nathan Wolfe argues in his book *The Viral Storm*, that a pandemic – the global spread of a highly infectious disease – could exist without being detected because of the absence of symptoms (Wolfe 2011: 98–9). Such a virus, unless it were one of the many harmless ones, would be a time bomb in that when the symptoms became manifest it would be too late

---

8 See https://www.journal-psychoanalysis.eu/coronavirus-and-philosophers/

to do anything about it. This, in effect, was what happened with HIV, which circulated for half a century in human populations before becoming detected. HIV also reveals the tremendous capacity of viruses, especially RNA viruses, to mutate very quickly and thus resist effective vaccines. They are not stable entities but evolving and often rapidly.[9] Until now, many of the most virulent viruses were either conquered, such as smallpox and polio, or confined to animals, such as fowl, pigs, some species of monkeys, or retained in animals that are natural reservoirs, such as bats for whom they are not dangerous. What we are now witnessing is the fluidity of human and nonhuman viruses. For this reason, the modern myth of a disease free world must be questioned.

New Infectious Diseases

It is now widely recognised that the social and the natural worlds are not separated, but are entangled in each other. This is one of the most important insights in social science in recent years (see Labour 1993, 2017). It was one of the fundamental arguments in William McNeill's classic work *Plagues and Peoples*, which claimed that the age-old balance between host and parasite is a permanent feature of the human condition and that the way they constantly return shows we remain caught up in the 'web of life'. Such a view provides a context in which to consider pandemics in general.[10]

Most of the major infectious diseases have come from animals. Many of these so-called zoonotic diseases go back to the beginnings of farming circa 12,000 years ago. They reveal the interconnectedness of the social and natural worlds. As Bruno Latour has argued, there is no natural world as such (and also no pristine social world). Nature is part of society and society is embedded in nature. Viruses too are part of the social and natural world. Letting aside the complicated question whether viruses are forms of life, the more relevant consideration is that many viruses enter human populations from animal hosts. Zoonoses jump (often via an intermediator creature) from animals that are natural reservoirs for

---

9 At the time of writing, there is some, albeit inconclusive, evidence of a mutation occurring in SARS-CoV-2 leading to its greater transmissibility. However this does not necessarily mean it will become more dangerous. See https://www.sciencemag.org/news/2020/07/pandemic-virus-slowly-mutating-it-getting-more-dangerous#

10 For these reasons, the relativistic argument of Bernard-Henri Lévy (2020: 26 – 7) that the virus is not a warning from nature is simply wrong. His statement trivialises the argument of Bruno Latour by referring to his position as a claim about a 'message from nature' and comparable to the arguments of Pentecostalists that it is 'a message from God'.

viruses and bacteria to humans who become their new hosts. The classic example is bubonic plague that derived from rats infested with fleas carrying bacteria which enter the human host following a flea bite. Viruses that ceased to be transmitted via a vector (for example smallpox, measles, cholera, polio, or tuberculosis) probably had their origin as a zoonosis at an earlier stage in history. According to Mark Harrison, pandemics normally arise when two strains of virus within fowl come together in a form that can infect humans (Harrison 2004: 189).

The lesson of the history of infectious disease is that everything is connected to everything. Zoonoses can also jump back to animals, as in the reported case of a cat who caught Covid-19 when her owner kissed her. It is now widely agreed that Sars-Cov-2, the specific type of virus that causes the disease Covid-19, derived from bats who infected an intermediator animal, which in turn infected humans in China. HIV is widely regarded as deriving from a virus that had been endemic in chimpanzees, who acquired it from a species of monkey that they hunted, probably as early as the beginning of the twentieth century. HIV took on a new trajectory once it found access to new populations. Many of these zoonoses were contained in their natural habitats or circulated in human populations that were relatively isolated. As a result of global transformations, such limitations no longer apply. Perhaps the really significant factor is worldwide imbalances in ecosystems, which lead to ever-greater 'spillovers' of viruses into human populations. As David Quammen (2013) has shown, a zoonosis is more likely to spillover in a disrupted and fragmented ecosystem than in an integrated one. For this reason, with the cutting down of the rainforests, the growing acidity of the oceans, and the massive expansion in the global industrialization of animal products, it is very likely to be the case that the future will see more, not fewer, pandemics as more and more strains of lethal viruses will be created and released. The propensity for a global spillover is very great for another reason: in view of the huge expansion in the human population, the potential host population available for viruses is now very great, especially if one takes into account the vast and increasing animal stocks that the human population feeds on.

In this light what appeared to be a puzzling anomaly, the HIV virus that caused AIDS and the death of about 35 m people since 1981 when it was first identified, can be viewed in a new way. It was not an exception but a warning of an era of new deadly viruses and the re-emergence of older ones. As Peter Baldwin has shown, the response to AIDS was shaped by the historical experiences with previous infectious diseases. The enduring problem of the modern state was to balance demands for individual autonomy with the community's need for safety (Baldwin 2005). According to Frank Snowden, since 1945 we have lived in an era of ever increasing numbers of diseases, which are not random or accidental (Snowden 2020: x). For Susan Sontag, 'AIDS is one of the dystopian harbingers of the global village, the future which is already here and always before us, which no one knows how to refuse' (2002: 178). These viruses can be seen to be partly a result of globalization and partly a consequence of new imbalances in the relation of human societies to the environment. The last few decades have seen the return of some old infectious diseases, since most of these have never been eradicated. All the major infectious diseases still exist, with the exception of smallpox (and perhaps too polio, which has now finally been eradicated from Africa). Most of these are very old, including the common cold, and have been present since the beginning of human societies. Bubonic plague also still exists and occasionally resurfaces, as it did in Inner Mongolia in 2020, as Bryan Turner points out in his chapter in this volume. It is mostly remembered for the Black Death in fourteenth-century Europe, but between 1896 and 1914 a third wave killed more than 13 m people in India and worldwide as many as 20 million (Snowden 2020: 38 – 9). Diseases such as yellow fever are becoming more prevalent and no longer confined to their traditional locations. Rising temperatures including increased water temperatures can be catalyst for the revival for cholera.

Perhaps more significant is the rise of new infectious diseases.[11] One of the first signs of new viruses was a new avian flu, H5N1 in 1997. Fortunately it died out since it was not highly infectious and many of those who contracted it died before infecting others. According to Mike Davis in *The Monster at Our Door* (2005), it had the potential to mutate into a highly dangerous strain and was a sign of a future viral apocalypse. In 2003 the arrival of SARS, a forerunner of the current coronavirus, which was traced to civets who had become infected from bats, was a further ominous sign of what henceforth became known as Emerging Infectious Diseases or EIDs (see Weir and Mykhalovskiy 2010). Fortunately in this case the symptoms appeared before high infectivity set in. Although only around 800 people died and the outbreak was contained before reaching the level of an epidemic, it sent a chilling signal of further dangers to come. It led to a sadly ignored WHO report, *A World at Risk*, published in 2019[12]. Then there was swine flu H1N1 in 2009, which was highly infectious but not lethal. Ebola, one of the most deadly diseases known to humans, reached an epidemic level in the Democratic Republic of the Congo in 2009, but fortunately was suppressed, though not eliminated.

---

11 See Zimmer (2015) for an account of new viruses. See also Quammen (2013), Waltner-Toews (2020), Washer (2010) and Wolfe (2011). An early account is Garrett (1995).

12 https://apps.who.int/gpmb/assets/annual_report/GPMB_annualreport_2019.pdf?utm_source=mandiner&utm_medium=link&utm_campaign=mandiner_202004

Ebola has been explained as a result of deforestation and land clearance in western and central Africa, since the areas where the outbreaks occurred mapped on to the geography of deforestation. The deadly virus was spread from bats who had moved into urban areas as a result of deforestation (Snowden 2020: 479/80). Circa 11,000 deaths have occurred from Ebola in Africa. MERS in Saudi Arabia 2012 is a further reminder of a virus, in this case a coronavirus, that jumped from camels to humans. West Nile virus between 1999 and 2013 caused over 1500 deaths. Seasonal flu, which currently is the main example of a pandemic, kills about 250,000 people every year. In 1968 a severe pandemic killed 1 million and in 1957, 2 million. Despite the very high annual death toll, societies have fatalistically learnt to live with the common cold, which, perhaps because of its familiarity, does not present the same anxieties as other less common diseases.

The potential for bioterror can also not be excluded. Anthrax is a potentially dangerous source of bio-warfare. Martin Rees in his book *Our Final Century* considers bioterror more serious than nuclear threats (Rees 2003: 47–60). The potential for new viruses to be manufactured and for which there is no possibility of immunization is very great. The impact of even a small bioterror attack has the potential to disrupt social life on a global level. Related to this is the danger emanating from growing risks from laboratory errors and the unpredictable outcomes of high risk experiments. A flu outbreak in the USSR in 1977 was very probably the result of a laboratory strain that escaped. Then, there is the chilling prospect of bio-warfare through the reintroduction of smallpox in populations that now are no longer immunized against what was once one of the most deadly of all diseases. In the twentieth century some 300 million people died from it, roughly one in three of those infected. It is believed smallpox may have killed more people than any other disease in history.

The context to understand the Covid-19 pandemic is this background of new infectious diseases, together with the wider historical experience that we are always between epidemics. To look at the current pandemic in this light is to see it not only as a biological pathology of the body, but also as a social and political reality of contemporary societies. Social and political pathologies are as real as biological ones, but take different forms. Many of the responses to disease have revealed cultural pathologies, such as, for example, stigmatization, scapegoating, mass hysteria and conspiracy theories. Albert Camus' novel *The Plague* may have been a political allegory of the pathology of Nazism and fascism.

The Illusion of Control

It is indeed true that the total number of global fatalities from Covid-19 (at the time of writing in late September 2020, just over 1 million) is relatively low in historical comparison, even within western societies in the past one hundred years. However, the numbers are not insignificant. As widely noted, more people died in the USA from Covid-19 than in the Vietnam war (which claimed more than 58,000 US lives[13]); in the UK 43,000 people died in the German bombing during WW2. But the significance goes beyond the numbers themselves. Since the 1960s Europe and the wider western world was relatively free of epidemic infectious diseases. With the exception of seasonal flu, most dangerous infectious diseases, such as SARS, Avian flu or Ebola, were suppressed or confined within the locations in which they arose. Infectious diseases have largely occurred in the less developed world, where there are over 4 million deaths per year from acute respiratory infections (Harrison 2004: 191). The stark reality is that people die from infectious diseases in the developing world in very large numbers. Malaria, for example, claims more than 2 million lives. The current situation is a significant moment for the western world as it is forced to re-assess its self-understanding as relatively free of infectious diseases. In historical perspective, this period of circa 50 years is relatively short in terms of the history of disease. While the full implications of Covid-19 have yet to be seen, it is evident that it will have a significant negative impact in most western countries. The UK, already reeling from the as yet uncertain outcome of Brexit, will almost certainly face major economic decline as a result of the disastrous management of the Covid-19 crisis (see Horton 2020).

The objective epidemiological reality of Covid-19 is that the source of the disease, the coronavirus Sars-CoV-2, can only be supressed. In the absence of widespread immunisation, elimination is not possible. Even it elimination were possible, eradication will almost certainly not happen. As noted, with the exception of smallpox and polio, eradication is almost impossible once a virus comes into existence. This is especially so if the virus has a capacity to mutate, as appears to be case with the present coronavirus, which is likely to become endemic in human populations. Elimination will require immunization. In the absence of a vaccine, allowing 'herd immunity'[14] to take its natural course would almost certainly entail a very large number of fatalities. This means that suppression is the only viable response. But there are limits to the instruments that can be

---

13 This was of course a fraction of Vietnamese deaths.
14 This is best termed population or community immunity.

used, which mostly revolve around different kinds of lockdown and social distancing on the one hand, and early testing, tracking of contacts and isolation of those affected on the other. Claus Offe's chapter in this volume provides a detailed and rich analysis of the full complexity of the challenges for policy–making arising from the different groups the pandemic has created and from the epistemic consequences of knowledge being essentially based on uncertain assumptions. If a vaccine is finally found, it is very likely it will not be a once in a lifetime shot, but more like the seasonal flu jab with all the uncertainties that go with that. The prospect thus facing the world, including the most technologically advanced societies, is that for the first time almost every country faces the reality of having to live with the Covid-19 virus and with a high level of fatalities and infections. It is worth bearing in mind that it took over forty years for a vaccine for poliomyelitis and measles to be developed and there is, as yet, no vaccine for HIV.

With elimination a long way ahead and eradication almost certainly not possible, suppression is the only possible course of action for states and international organizations. But what lengths can governments go to in order to flatten the curve? How much militarization can democracies tolerate to achieve a collective goal? The medieval and early modern states that first practised quarantine were very different kinds of societies from the complex ones of today, which are not so easily marshalled and have, as Daniel Innerarity shows in this volume, more complex forms of decision-making. Even dictatorships – which appear to be more successful in imposing lockdowns – do not have recourse to summary hanging for those who break the rules, as was often the case in earlier times. It is clear that as a recent volume shows, quarantine, which derives from *quaranta* (forty days) and has deep religious significance, has many meanings in western history (Bashford 2016). Quarantine along with fumigation and disinfection, was once an expression of state power and linked to the surveillance of populations, but was also a mechanism for the purification and disciplining of the political body. There were many debates for and against quarantine in the nineteenth century when there was a fear of rebellion by those quarantined. The famous account of quarantine depicted by Foucault in *Discipline and Punish* in 1975 neglects the alternative history of rebellion (Foucault 1977: 195–200). Many quarantine and policing measures were simply unsuccessful and were abandoned for fear of stirring social discontent (Evans 1992: 166). In fact, disease control, such as sanitary reform, was judged to be more useful for political stability than repressive methods. Quarantine appeared to be a relic of the past until new diseases – SARS in 2003, avian flu in 2009 and Ebola in Africa in 2014 – led to its return. But it was not until March 2020 that it became a new global experience. And for how long? The basic problem of quarantine remains that it based on the detection of symptoms. As many states today experiment with new kinds of quarantine, which require complex digital technology, the old questions return about its viability and effectiveness in the long run.[15]

If the historical experience was that the control of infectious diseases aided the rise of the democratic state – the elimination of cholera during the cold war was explicitly linked to the advancement of democracy – today it would appear to be an indication of the weakness of the state and a potential threat to democracy. Democracy requires time for deliberation, but pandemics and other catastrophes require rapid action that can produce long-term unanticipated consequences (see also Wagner 2020). Political-decision making in democracies, as Daniel Innerarity argues in this volume, is not well designed to deal with pandemics and other emergencies. Emergency governance is a major challenge for democracy, as also noted by both Stephen Turner and Jonathan White in their chapters in this volume. Experts take the place of elected representatives, but very often they fail as much as the politicians. As Roger Koppl writes: "There is always a brisk demand for magical predictions of the unpredictable. Expert failure is likely in the market for impossible ideas even under more or less competitive conditions" (see Koppl 2018; see also Eyal 2010; White 2019). But many experts do not work under such conditions, since they are protected by nefarious governments anxious to hide behind them. Despite the often erratic and incompetent mismanagement of the Covid-19 pandemic and the tendency towards technocracy, the democratic constitutional state, along with international organizations, is still the best equipped to deal with the problems that deadly diseases present. Security is a key function of the state. There is wide recognition today that a broader definition of security is needed than national security. Without a strong state with strong social institutions, vulnerable societies will suffer and social inequalities will worsen (see Horton 2020). Sylvia Walby in her chapter in this volume draws attention to the continued importance of one of the most important legacies of social democracy, namely health care provision for all. Clearly one of the lessons of the present pandemic is that greater foresight will be needed for likely future pandemics.

---

15 In many ways the current situation is a repeat of the cholera epidemic in Hamburg at the end of the nineteenth century (see Evans 2006). All the problems of official statistics and expertise were there for cholera as well. My thanks to Stephen Turner for this observation.

The Shock of the Lockdown

Foucault's path-breaking analysis of a seventeenth-century pandemic in *Discipline and Punish* in 1975 has suddenly become a focus for critical analysis of the current situation, in view of the fact that many countries have been through strict lockdowns following declarations of emergency (Foucault 1977: 195 – 200). Recent contributions by prominent philosophers such as Gorgio Agamben and Slavoj Žižek have sparked debate on some of the political implications of the crisis. While Agamben has highlighted the spectre of a permanent state of exception – the topic of his famous book (Agamben 2005) – and a new authoritarian regime of biopolitical securitization taking shape[16], others such as Žižek (2020) see new political possibilities for a post-pandemic world. While Agamben has surely exaggerated the political dangers and the potential threat to democracy, Žižek may be over-optimistic that a new and more benevolent society might be created. The burden always falls on the poor.[17]

However, there are other perspectives that need to be brought into the picture beyond what are often somewhat exaggerated prognoses and apocalyptical vistas of a permanent state of emergency. Claus Offe in this volume argues that at least in liberal democracies the health crisis remains a health crisis and is not spilling over into a major political crisis in that has not led to major juridical transformations. The middle class, who have the luxury of working at home, do not appear to be worried about democracy in duress. Indeed, some of the most severe lockdowns, as in Spain, were imposed by left-wing governments, while right-wing governments have generally tried to resist the temptations of strict lockdowns. The British government delayed while taking advantage of the opportunity to pass legislation giving excessive powers to government. The Spanish government declared in June 2020 the entry to a 'New Normality'. There is also clearly no uniform political response to the pandemic.

The pandemic raises fundamental philosophical questions concerning the political and ethical responsibility of the state and of the boundary between life and death. As emergency governance becomes the new normal, the implications for democracy and liberty need to be addressed for future emergencies, which might follow from any future, and possibly more severe, pandemic. What is the legitimate moral foundation for extreme and unprecedented measures? To what extent does the right to life have an overriding importance

---

16 https://bookhaven.stanford.edu/2020/03/giorgio-agamben-on-coronavirus-the-enemy-is-not-outside-it-is-within-us/

17 For a further account of the pandemic and political philosophy, see Delanty (2020).

over other human rights?[18] And what kind of life is worth living without dignity? Lockdowns may save some lives, but what about the indirect lives lost? As discussed by Sonja Avlijaš in this volume, the pandemic reveals multiple kinds of inequalities, which intersect in complex ways both within and across societies. It has also been accompanied by an extraordinary digitalization of public space as well as the digital transformation of work and higher education. The significance of the pandemic in hastening the digitalization of contemporary societies is discussed in this volume by Helga Nowotny, who sees Covid-19 as the disease of the digital age in the way cholera was the disease of the industrial age. She makes the important point that big data and AI are now entrenched in contemporary societies. The pandemic has accelerated digitalisation, which will not be reversed.

The historical experience is that major pandemics often led to progressive change. For instance, the 1918 flu led to the creation of national health care systems. The Black Death, which reduced the supply of labour, led to improved conditions for workers, at least in Europe. It is therefore not impossible that out of the current crisis will come some improvements in public policy and a more humanized kind of capitalism than the current precarity that predominates. But such gains took decades if not centuries and pandemics have been unredeemable catastrophes for indigenous populations throughout history. Yet, it is clear that a major pandemic can be a defining moment for many societies, if not for the world. Cholera defined the nineteenth century. AIDS defined a generation. So it is not improbable that the current pandemic may be a defining moment for our time. It may usher in a more social and ecological kind of capitalism and a fundamental transformation in the nature of work and health care; but it may also lead to the undermining of democracy and liberty. The latter has been the focus of right-wing 'anti-lockdown' groups, but – as discussed in this book – there are also opportunities for the radicalization of democracy through the empowering of civil society, as discussed by Donatella della Porta and Albena Azmanova in this volume. Azmanova thus sees the crisis brought about by the pandemic as yet another 'battleground of justice', in this case the fight against massive precarity.

A pandemic virus divides people through self-isolation and lockdowns. Social relations mediated by masks, social distancing and self-isolation is not a basis for progressive social change. Fear of contagion leads to fear of the Other. For now, with the medicalization of nationalism, whether in the search

---

18 See the debate between Jürgen Habermas and Klaus Günther. https://www.zeit.de/2020/20/grundrechte-lebensschutz-freiheit-juergen-habermas-klaus-guenther

for a vaccine or in quarantine, a politics of closure would appear to dominate. All the evidence seems to suggest that the pandemic does not mark the transition to a new era but confirms and solidifies changes that have already occurred, such as the digitalization of work and existing patterns of social reproduction. This is also one of the conclusions of Sonja Avlijaš's chapter. She argues that the pandemic accelerates trends already underway. The pandemic probably does not therefore mark the point of transition to a new era. However, as Syliva Walby also argues in her chapter, there is not just one turning point or a single crisis, but several crises which cascade through intensified conflicts in different domains.

A Metaphor of a Flawed World

As always, disease is seen both as coming from outside the homeland and as a form of stigmatisation, as in the banishment of those inflected with leprosy in medieval times. Since the arrival of syphilis in Europe, probably one of the few infectious diseases that came from the Americas in the wake of the Spanish conquest, disease was seen as coming from the Other and defines the Self as free of disease. Thus, the 1918 flu virus, which probably originated in Kansas was called by the French the 'Spanish flu'. Cholera, which arrived in Europe in the 1830s, epitomised European views of the Orient. Earlier, the Black Death in Europe was used to stigmatise Jews. AIDS, SARS and Ebola were associated with the Other. As Susan Sontag wrote in her influential 1978 essay, *Disease as a Metaphor*, disease is encumbered by the trappings of metaphor. However, she was writing of a time when the causes of diseases were not fully understood (Sontag 2002). Today, we know a lot more about the causes of infectious diseases, which have to come from somewhere and must simply be either a virus or a bacteria as opposed to something mystical from a decadent far-off land. But knowledge does not always bring about enlightenment, as is evident from the spread of post-truth politics, conspiracy theories, and alternative epistemologies, such as the belief widespread in the UK that G5 networks spread the coronavirus. There is also fear. As Sontag pointed out, while cholera killed far fewer people in Europe than smallpox and tuberculosis, it was more feared. This was not entirely due to its association with Asia. Perhaps, it was because smallpox was regarded as normal and was endemic to Europe in the nineteenth century and death did not come with the suddenness that it did with cholera. Similarly, polio, despite its debilitating nature, did not bring about the same degree of horror and fear that cholera did.

In a world when death has become very much invisible – and the belief that longevity is normal – the spectre of large numbers of deaths caused by Covid-19 has produced a certain shock. However, it is doubtful that Covid-19 has produced anything like the sense of horror that accompanied diseases in the recent past. According to Sontag, the most terrifying diseases are those that are dehumanizing and sudden. Covid-19 came with the sudden shock of the new. It remains to be seen if contemporary societies learn to live with it in the way they learnt to live with HIV, which of course by its nature is less infectious than an airborne virus. But the sense of a cultural apocalypse is always present when a major new pandemic arrives regardless of the numbers of infections and fatalities. Ebola had such an effect. Perhaps more relevant is the question of dehumanization and human dignity. In view of the large numbers of Covid-19 deaths in care homes and among vulnerable people this is an important issue that has been ignored by government lockdowns. In this context a relevant question is: exactly who is being protected?

The Covid-19 pandemic reveals a great deal about the nature of contemporary societies. As the chapters in this volume show, epidemiological issues and sociological problems are elucidated in many ways around the themes of power, politics, security, suffering, equality and justice. The pandemic has become a metaphor of a flawed world. But, with Susan Sontag in mind, one must not forget that it is also a disease and one that has had a global scale. So far the reaction to it has been predominantly national and technocratic. One of the challenges for the future will surely be to resist the re-nationalization of politics and to find more cosmopolitical solutions and at the same time to design health care systems suitable for future pandemics that are almost certain to come. This is also with a view to the wider context of the Anthropocene, as discussed by Eva Horn in this volume, since the pandemic plays out against the backdrop of catastrophic climate change. While there is not a direct causal relationship established between disease and climate change, it is highly likely there will be more pandemics leading to endemic diseases. It is an inevitable consequence of increased global connections, population increase and the insatiable desire for destructive forms of consumption, which all unsettle the balance between host and parasite.

References

Agamben, G. (2005) *State of Exception*, Chicago: Chicago University Press.
Aries, P. (1974) *Western Attitudes Towards Death from the Middle Ages to the Present*, Baltimore: John Hopkins University Press.

Aries, P. (1991) *Hour of Our Death*, New York: Random House.

Baldwin, P. (2005) *Disease and Democracy: The Industrial World Faces AIDS*, Berkeley: University of California Press.

Barry, J. (2020) *The Great Influenza: The Story of the Deadliest Pandemic in History*. London: Penguin.

Bashford, A. (ed.) (2016) *Quarantine: Local and Global Histories*, London: Palgrave.

Bashford, A. and Hooker, C. (eds) (2014) *Contagion: Historical and Cultural Studies*, London: Routledge.

Beck, U. (1992. [1986]) *The Risk Society*, London: Sage.

Blackie, P., Cannon, T., Davis, I, and Wisner, B. (1994) *At Risk: Natural Hazards, People's Vulnerability, and Disaster,* London: Routledge.

Davis, M. (2005) *The Monster at our Door: The Global Threat of Avian Flu*, New York: The New Press.

Delanty, G. (2020) Six Political Philosophies in Search of a Virus: Critical Perspectives on the Coronavirus Pandemic, *LEQS* Paper No. 156, May 2020 http://www.lse.ac.uk/european-in stitute/Assets/Documents/LEQS-Discussion-Papers/LEQSPaper156.pdf

Dingwall, R., Hoffman, L. and Staniland, K. (eds) (2013) *Pandemics and Emerging Infectious Diseases: The Sociological Agenda*, Oxford: Wily-Blackwell.

Diamond, J. (1998) *Guns, Germs and Steel*, London: Vintage.

Elliott, A. and Hsu, E. (eds) (2016) *The Consequences of Global Disasters*, London: Routledge.

Esposito, E. (2011 [2002]) *Immunitas: The Protection and Negation of Life*, Cambridge: Polity Press.

Evans, R. (1992) Epidemics and Revolutions: Cholera in the Nineteenth-Century Europe. In: Ranger, T. and Slack, P. (eds). *Epidemics and Ideas: Essays on the Historical Perception of Pestilence*, Cambridge: Cambridge University Press.

Evans, R. (2006) *Death on Hamburg: Society and Politics in the Cholera Years, 1830–1910*, London: Penguin.

Eyal, G. (2010) *The Crisis of Expertise*, Cambridge: Polity Press.

Fassin, D. (2018) *Life*, Cambridge: Polity Press.

Foucault, M. (1977 [1975]) *Discipline and Punish: The Birth of the Prison*, London: Penguin Books.

Garrett, L. (1995) The Coming Plague: Newly Emerging Diseases in a World Out of Control. London: Penguin.

Hays, J. N. (2009) *The Burden of Disease: Epidemics and Human Response in Western History*, New Brunswick, NJ: Rutgers University Press.

Harrison, M. (2004) *Disease and the Modern World*, Cambridge: Polity Press.

Harrison, M. (2014) *Contagion: How Commerce has Spread Disease*, New Haven: Yale University Press.

Horton, R. (2020) *The Covid-19 Catastrophe*, Cambridge: Polity Press.

Honigsbaum, M. (2020) Revised edition. *The Pandemic Century: A History of Global Contagion from the Spanish Flu to Covid-19,* London: WH Allen.

Jones, L. (2018) *The Big Ones: How Natural Disasters have Shaped Us*. London: Icon.

Latour, B. (1993) *We Have Never been Modern*, Cambridge, MASS.: Harvard University Press.

Latour, B. (2017) *Facing Gaia: Eight Lectures on the New Climatic Regime*. Cambridge: Polity Press.

Koppl, R. (2018) *Expert Failure*, Cambridge: Cambridge University Press.

Lévy, B-H. (2020) *The Virus in the Age of Madness*, New Haven: Yale University Press.

McMillen, C. (2016) *Pandemics: A Very Short Introduction*, Oxford: Oxford University Press.

McNeill, W. H. (1998 [1976]) *Plagues and Peoples*, New York: Anchor Books.

Morse, S. (ed.) (1993) *Emerging Viruses*. Oxford: Oxford University Press.

Nancy, J-L. (2015) *After Fukushima: The Equivalence of Catastrophes*, Oxford: Oxford University Press.

Oldstone, M. (2010) *Viruses, Plagues, and History*, Oxford: Oxford University Press.

Opitz, S. (2017) Simulating the World: The digital enactment of pandemics as a mode of global self-observation. *European Journal of Social Theory* 20 (3): 392–416.

Price-Smith, A. (2008) *Contagion and Chaos: Disease, Ecology, and National Security in the Era of Globalization*, Cambridge, MASS.: MIT.

Quammen, D. (2013) *Spillover: Animal Inflections and the Next Human Pandemic*. London: Vintage.

Ranger, T. and Slack, P. (eds.) (1992) *Epidemics and Ideas: Essays on the Historical Perception of Pestilence*, Cambridge: Cambridge University Press.

Rees, M. (2003) *Our Final Century*, London: Arrow Books.

Rosenberg, C. (1989) What is an Epidemic? AIDS in Historical Perspective. *Daedalus* Spring, 144: 1–17.

Snowden, F. (2020) *Epidemics and Society: From the Black Death to the Present*, New Haven: Yale University Press.

Sontag, S. (2002 [1978]) *Illness and a Metaphor and Aids and its Metaphors,* London: Penguin.

Spinney, L. (2018) *Pale Rider: The Spanish Flu of 1918 and How it Changed the World*, London: Vintage.

Tierney, K. (2019) *Disasters: A Sociological Approach.* Cambridge: Polity Press.

Wagner, P. (2020) Knowing How Well to Act in Time, Journal of Bioethical Inquiry.

Wald, P. 2008. *Contagious: Cultures, Carriers, and the Outbreak Narrative.* Durham: Duke University Press.

Waltner-Toews, D. (2020) *On Pandemics: Deadly Disease from Bubonic Plague to Coronavirus*, Vancouver: Greystone.

Washer, P. (2010) *Emerging Infectious Diseases and Society.* London: Palgrave.

Weir, L. and Mykhalovskiy, E. (2010) *Global Public Health Vigilance: Creating a World on Alert*, London: Routledge.

White, J. (2020) Politics of the Last Resort: Governing by Emergency in the EU, Cambridge: Cambridge University Press.

Wolfe, N. (2011) The Viral Storm: The Dawn of a New Pandemic Age, London: Penguin.

Zimmer, C. (2015) 2nd edition. *A Planet of Viruses*, Chicago: University of Chicago Press.

Žižek, S. (2020) *Pandemic! Covid-19 Shakes the World, Cambridge: Polity Press.*

Part 1: **Politics, Experts and the State**

Claus Offe
Corona Pandemic Policy: Exploratory notes on its "epistemic regime"

Every disease, I suppose, allows for categorizing people into groups which are specific to it: those more or less likely to be affected, those currently undergoing medical treatment, those chronically ill, etc. The nature and configuration of these groups is the combined outcome of what epidemiologist, pathologists, medical specialists and public health policy makers know about the incidence and progression of the disease, its treatment, and the assumptions and preferences governing its management. Let me start this think piece by describing the groupings created by the Corona pandemic. This exercise can be compared to a model of three Russian dolls, except that they are not put in a spatial but temporal sequence, or flow chart. Figure 1 (p. 30) tries to illustrate what I mean.

The Virus as a Sorting Mechanism: Six categories of people

(1) The first and by far largest category consists of the vast group of those in a territorially defined resident population who are, at a given point in time, *not* infected by the virus. Yet almost all of its members are, at the beginning of an epidemic, threatened by the disease and thus *infectable* by (because not yet immune to) the Corona virus. At the beginning of an epidemic, this group is, so to speak, the virgin land into which the virus can spread exponentially. The indicator (R-0) by which the initial rate of its reproduction is measured is commonly estimated to be slightly above 3, meaning that every person infected infects on average three others. As the pandemic runs its course, the great majority of the infected who have survived it and are thus immune for a greater or lesser length of time return to the subset of group (1) that, at least for the time being, is no longer infectable.

(2) The second group are the *actually infected*, including those who are not (yet) *known* (to others and even themselves) to be infected, be it because they have not developed any symptoms (which they do in most cases within about five days after infection) or because they were not (yet) diagnosed through testing. The size of this category of the unrecognized/unreported cases is a major unknown – the under-water and invisible part of the iceberg, as it were.

https://doi.org/10.1515/9783110713350-002

There are a number of reasons for this ignorance. First of all, there are people who are currently in the initial asymptomatic period and thus have no reason to seek diagnostic testing. But their number can also be unknown because of limitations of testing capacity. It can also be due to the incapacity or unwillingness of governments and public health agencies to generate a valid picture of the actual situation through large scale testing. The unwillingness can be motivated by the intention to save the direct costs of testing or to avoid a country suffering damages (e. g. losing foreign tourists) as a consequence of rigorous testing and the publication of its results, or to avoid "frightening the public" and "causing panic" (as the American president has put it). Also, governments are aware that additional testing is bound to increase the number of positive findings and that such increases may have all kinds of negative economic and/or political implications they wish to avoid, including the concern that "too many" positives may overburden available treatment facilities or make people anticipate shortages of such facilities. As a consequence of these and other considerations (including the lack of trust in the validity of testing results) there is a systematic underreporting of cases. Schools of epidemiologists differ in their estimates of the size of the category of the latently infected. A widely shared assumption is that, contingent on particular conditions in time and space, the latently and unknowingly infected can number up to ten times of those who have tested positive; but this number can be validated only with the (typically prohibitively costly) iterated testing of large samples.

So the extent to which a population is actually tested depends on testing *strategies* of the authorities of a given political entity. Such strategies derives from what I propose to call an "*epistemic regime*" that imposes, for the reasons just alluded to, limitations on the "desire to know" (and to allow such knowledge to become public) on the part of national and local governments and health-related agencies and professions. The epistemic regime also prescribes more or less inclusive practices of risk-assessment pertaining to particular sub-groups of group (1), such as the elderly, the poor, or health workers. The volume of testing actually taking place also depends on whether the respective population can be persuaded (or coerced or incentivized, e. g. by making tests cost-free to the tested) to actually undergo testing. After all, a "positive" test result involves potentially severe negative consequences (such as having to undergo mandatory isolation) which people confidently trusting in an asymptomatic progression of their infection or a spontaneous healing may be strongly motivated to avoid. There may also be an aversion to having to face bad news or an outright denial of the existence of a pandemic – a belief that would exonerate individuals holding such belief from the inconvenience and ambiguity of undergoing tests. Given all these motivations, even an approximate number of persons arriving in (2) through flow E, the subtotal of people at a particular point in time and territorial space being infected without them (or anyone else) knowing it, seems exceedingly hard to come by. This largely "willful ignorance" shapes national testing strategies to varying extents and thus makes international comparisons and comparative policy evaluations difficult. Moreover, one of the major problems of the Covid-19 disease and its management results from the fact that members of this (presumably) vast group of unreported cases are likely to be infectious and spread the disease to equally unknown others.

(3) The third group consists of the portion of (2) who have *ever* tested positive since the early stages of the pandemic, the cumulative total of whom indicates the overall incidence of cases that have occurred in a given country or region since the arrival of the pandemic. The size of this category, to the extent we can disregard issues of validity and specificity of the testing procedures, and its day-to-day greater or smaller increments (flow F) indicates, after the estimated number of those who have died from the virus (flow D) and those who have recovered (flow C) are subtracted, the overall dynamic of the epidemic, namely the level of its prevalence (number of actual cases) at a given point in time and its rate of change. Yet this assessment of the situation is valid only if the testing strategy of authorities and the compliance of citizens remain constant over time, which is typically not the case. Instead, we see patterns of often hectic policy experimentation, changes in testing practices and vehement contestation of policies. Yet once the increment of currently active cases is zero and its stock declines for a period of time, the epidemic can be declared defeated – provided, that is, the influx of new infections can be prevented, e. g. by sealing borders, which is not a realistic option though for any length of time. What members of group (3) have in common is merely the fact that, at some point in time, they have all tested positive and thus were diagnosed as infected, including those self-diagnosed as infected due to symptoms. This broad category consists of three sub-groups: Those having *recovered* after been tested positive (4), those currently ill (5), and the "case fatalities" who have died with or from the virus (6).

(4) This sub-group of (3) comprises those who have *recovered* from an infection and are now considered immune (with the incidence and durability of such immunity apparently being, for the time being, an unsettled question of epidemiological research). Should immunity turn out to be temporary or if the virus undergoes relevant mutation that undercuts immunity and unless it can be boosted through large scale and iterated vaccination, those in (4) are bound to return to (1) (flow A). Due to the suspected possibility of long term negative health effects, members of (4) need not return to the health status they enjoyed prior to their infection but may suffer chronically from various kinds of physical or mental illness. The notion of "herd immunity" envisages that, once a suffi-

cient number of members of (1) (estimates suggest shares of 40 to up to 70 per cent) have contracted the virus, recover and thus end up in (4) and then return to (1), the pandemic will end as the virus is deprived, as it were, of the fertile ground of never-infected and hence non-immune human organisms that it needs in order to thrive and spread. Such a notion tends to under-emphasize, however, to put it cautiously, the number of years needed to reach this happy outcome as well as the number of fatalities (category (6)) to be expected along the road to herd immunity. Not included here is the (again unknown) number of spontaneous recoveries of those who recover *without* having suffered any, or any severe, symptoms, thus having moved directly, bypassing the stage of manifestation through testing, from (2) to (4) (flow B). Entirely asymptomatic cases are unrecognized and unknown (even to the subject affected); they return to category (1) via flow A where they merge indistinguishably with the immunized portion of the population, the size of which can only be detected by antibody tests. Yet both the duration of immunity and its ability to withstand mutations of the virus seem to be unknowns, both of which stand in the way of the idea to provide people with "immunity certificates" which would exempt them from corona-related hygiene rules

(5) This sub-group consists in the percentage of (3) who request (on their own initiative) and require (according to medical or administrative judgment and contingent upon the capacity of medical and other facilities available to them) some kind of treatment (ranging from physical (self-) isolation to ICU treatment, as long as pharmaceutical remedies are unavailable) and eventually recover (flow C). These are the currently active cases ("prevalence"), which normally make up just a tiny fraction of both (estimates) of (2) and the aggregate numbers of (3). A metaphor is that of a bus line, where the number of those actually riding on a bus is a positive difference between those who have ever stepped on board minus those who have ever left the vehicle at stops (4) or (6).

(6) This last group is the total of those who have died *because of* (or just *with*) the virus (plus, arguably, those who have died from other diseases which they could have survived if the health system had not been overwhelmed by Corona cases or if they had not shied away from seeking timely medical treatment out of fear of getting infected by corona in doctor's offices or hospitals). The validity of data concerning causes of death is contingent upon, among other things such as the administrative capacity of reporting agencies, the capacity for autopsies and the registration of those who have died not medical institutions but at home. Another measure is the size of a spike in the overall mortality statistic that coincides with the virus pandemic, the so-called excess mortality that measures the positive difference between observed and expected deaths during some period of time.

To summarize the argument so far, the presence of a pandemic such as Covid-19 is bound to divide a population into three categories as depicted in Fig. 1. Category (1) is the resident population of a defined space (usually a national territory, federal state or administrative district), the members of which are currently not known to be infected or even (via flow A) known to be immune but to (strongly) varying degrees *at risk* of being infected. Category (2) is the segment of the population that *is*, at a particular point in time, infected and includes those *not recognized* to be infected (be it by themselves or to the health authorities). Such ignorance can be partly attributed to the nature of the *epistemic regime* and testing strategy in place and partly also to features of the virus which makes it exceedingly difficult, due to its *patterns of transmission*, to find out who is actually infected and who isn't. Category (3), subdivided in three sub-groups, comprises all those who *are known* (at least to themselves) to be infected, with the pragmatic consequence of some active convalescence and symptom-suppressing treatment (5). Those with whom such treatment succeeds, fully or partially, end up in group (4) (flow C) and continue, more or less durably, to the immunized subset of group (1) (flow A). The rest ends up, contingent upon the effectiveness of treatment and the (changing) lethality of the disease, in the group of fatalities (6). Needless to state, numerous subgroups within (2) and (3) can be thought of. They would represent groups according to demographic and health-related criteria and thus provide a more complex and informative picture.

This rough flow chart describes how the Corona pandemic generates groups of people with distinctive pandemic-related features as they are observed and reported by the epistemic regime in place. It also demarcates strategic points of policy intervention. Pharmaceutical points of intervention are at the interface between (1) and (2) where infection can be prevented through vaccines. While these are not yet available, huge amounts of fiscal resources as well as entrepreneurial and research efforts have been spent on their development and arrangements for their eventual distribution. Non-pharmacological interventions (NPIs) are all regulations and arrangements that are thought to interrupt transitions from (1), the non-infected, to (2), such as quarantines, lock-downs and hygiene prescriptions. They are intended to flatten the curve of growth of the number of the actually infected in (2). Tracking and tracing measures serve the same purpose of protecting non-infected members of (1) and allow them to stay in that category. The objective is to minimize the volume of flow E. At the interface of (2) and (3) the desired and feasible level of knowledge concerning the actual spread of the virus is generated through diagnostic testing. The transition from (3) to its subset (4) can be favorably influenced through the provision of treatment facilities and their requisite manpower; the same applies to efforts to minimize transitions from

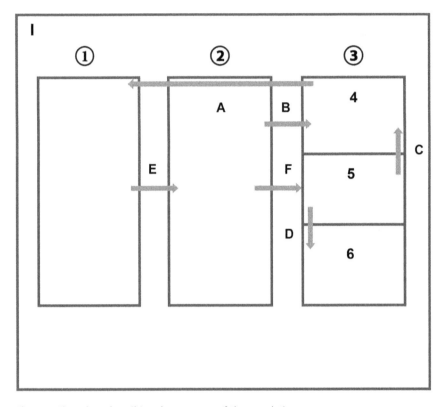

Figure 1: Flow chart describing three groups of the population.

(5) to (6). Capacity building, both for treatment and for testing, has been a priority in many cases. Governments want to avoid shortages and triage situations which can be severely scandalized and held against them with accusations of irresponsible failure to prepare. These are the types of policies that can be adopted as long as neither proven vaccines nor effective therapeutic medications are widely available.

Policy intervention and its epistemic regime

Policies addressing the pandemic follow a complex mix of objectives. These include the following imperatives:

- Slow down the progression of the pandemic so that available treatment facilities do not get overcrowded and triages can be avoided. Yet allow (without necessarily telling the public) for a sufficient level of incidence, provided cases come with just mild symptoms, so that steps towards herd immunity will be generated as a welcome side effect.

- Buy time by flattening the growth curve so that unchecked exponential growth is avoided until the point when a tested vaccine is available and can be widely distributed. In flattening the curve, use policy measures that avoid social and economic disruptions, politically destabilizing mass complaints and conflicts.
- Do everything conducive to the building and maintaining of trust of the public that the ruling network of governments and medical experts somehow know and are capable to execute what the right thing to do is at any given moment.

NPIs can be further subdivided into measures of crisis management that can be implemented by *governments* themselves (such as closing borders, launching income support programs, or building medical and administrative capacity) and measures which need to be implemented by *citizens* and their everyday practices and routines (using masks, keeping physical distance to others etc.). In the latter case, the role of political authorities is limited to that of informing and educating the public, engaging in rhetorical practices of moral suasion, recommending and enforcing preventative health practices, with the individual citizen through her prudent understanding, other-regarding motivation and compliant action remaining the ultimate implementation agent. Mixed cases are more or (mostly) less readily enforceable regulations concerning, for instance, who may leave the house for what kind of purpose how often and for how long.

But the tools of government are extremely limited when it comes to fighting the damages inflicted by the pandemic. Outcomes depend upon not just governments giving the right orders or parliaments passing effective laws and budgets, but on the everyday action of people and their enlightened understanding of what the right thing to do is in order to protect themselves and everyone else consists in. Following the logic, which applies not just nationally but globally, of "nobody is safe unless all of us are safe", the challenge of overcoming the corona pandemic amounts to a familiar problem of collective action: Every beneficiary of a fortunate outcome-to-be-achieved must be brought to fairly *share the burden* which is required to achieve it. But the readiness to do so may itself be undermined by the social and economic impact of the pandemic and the measures taken to control it. Though another game-theoretic approach, the non-cooperative one, would start with the assumption that every person in the non-infected part of the population would devote the maximum effort to her *self*-protection while being interested in the greatest possible number of fellow citizens actually *being* infected so as to shorten the time at which collective immunity is reached and nobody is exposed any more to the risk of infection. Once such immunity is achieved, the non-infected can enjoy living in a virus-free world by having acted as a free rider on the illness of others through which these have contributed to the production of the collective good of herd immunity. Yet as everybody calculates that way, such immunity becomes unlikely to ever be reached.

As the neat sequence of medical pragmatics (*prevention-diagnosis-therapy)* is not (yet) fully applicable in the case of corona and as, on the other side, the consequences of the pandemic are far too severe to allow governments (except for some, but not all authoritarian ones) to adopt a "wait-and- see" attitude of inaction and "benign neglect" or an outright denial of the public health problem caused by the pandemic, authorities have turned to a rich and partly highly imaginative variety of non-pharmacological interventions in order to protect the life and health of citizens while following the agenda just sketched above.

The policy measures adopted in the course of the overall management of the crisis are guided by beliefs and assumption that emerge from an epistemic regime that generates knowledge that ideally would be valid, reliable, objective and thus trustworthy. A well-functioning epistemic regime generates valid and minimally credible definitions of the situation, its prospects as well as responses to its challenges that are demonstrably effective. It also reflexively provides an awareness of current limitations of knowledge, the relevant "unknowns" which need to be addressed by research and development. Moreover, such a regime would be capable to screen out from the stock of beliefs lies, fabrications, cases of wishful thinking, misinformation, putative shortcuts to a solution, magical thinking and all kinds of unfounded conspiracy theories. A well-functioning epistemic regime would also be based upon a system of rules and procedures by which disagreements on facts can be settled through what is recognized as evidence, as well as disagreements on the fairness and legitimacy of collectively binding decisions.

Judging by such demanding standards, the epistemic regime in place must be described as dramatically deficient. Both medical experts and policy makers, to say nothing about individual citizens, find themselves in uncharted territory of frightening uncertainty. Virtually every belief and assumption and prospect it generates is more or less vehemently contested. The same applies to the measures taken to cope with the situation. The unsettled state of the epistemic regime that deals with the corona virus is only partly due to the newness of the virus and the fragmentary nature of scientific knowledge about its origin, spread, impact, and treatment. Nor can it be attributed alone to the multiplicity of stakeholders (i.e. public health agencies, governments on all levels, research organizations, medical professionals, lawyers and courts passing judgments on the need for and proportionality of measures, mass media, "social" media, protest movements) all of whom participate in conflicts over the definition of the situation and appropriate responses. Instead, the generation of widely trusted knowledge that can guide policy intervention is hindered by the massive impact the crisis has on the constellation of *passions* and *interests*.

As to the passions, *fear* is probably the most important. It can be subdivided into primary fear and secondary fear. *Primary* fear refers to the perceived risks for *health and life* caused by the pandemic and its frightening impact on human life. As the virus is widely (though not entirely uncontroversially) understood to be capable to infect any non-immune person at any time and any place in spite of precautionary measures followed, and as it comes with pharmaceutically uncontrollable and individually unpredictable health damages, every person has, although to a different extent, a motive to fear infection. This is so in spite of the fact that the overall probability of being infected by the Corona virus seems to be just marginally greater than it is with the influenza virus. Yet in the case of influenza, there is less reason for fear as we can confidently feel to be to a much greater extent "in control". In the case of influenza we know the season of its outbreak, the age category of people most likely to be affected, the typical trajectory of the illness, and the vaccines, health practices and medicines we can rely on to limit its impact (which nevertheless reaches a number of many thousands of deaths per year, a figure to which we have become "used"). In contrast, in the case of corona, we find ourselves, individually as well as collectively, in a condition of *profound ignorance* and unnerving uncertainty. We cannot know for sure even about our own health status at any point of time, nor about that of people with whom we cannot avoid physical interaction and proximity. Even the validity of test results does not seem to be beyond reasonable doubt. Similarly, we do not know when and where a virus has been transmitted, how to reliably prevent its transmission or heal its health consequences. It kills some and goes virtually unnoticed with others – who knows? Will there be a "second wave"? Are we already in the midst of it? Will our fellow citizens comply with hygiene rules as they are supposed to? We are uncertain about future spread of the virus and the duration of the overall crisis. Finally, we do not know whom to trust with answers offered to all these questions.

Secondary fear refers to the negative *impact of policy measures* (such as a lockdown of large parts of the economy, the educational system and public life in general, the limitation of mobility, people's right to go to work and earn an income, etc.) on the individuals' life chances and their enjoyment of rights and freedoms. Another powerful passion is *suspiciousness* and subsequent *hatred* targeting supposed causal agents. It results from the psychological inclination to follow the faulty logic of "whenever something negative happens to me (and *a fortiori*, to all of us), it must be due to the evil machinations and hostile intentions of some agent" (e. g., agencies controlled by the Chinese government or/and Bill Gates). As this logic is also widely employed by the populist right, there seems to be a "natural" affinity between populism and emotions of suspecting dark forces being held responsible for the corona health crisis. They both advocate *distrust* in science and, in particular, governments, which are both depicted as accomplices to be hated and mere puppets of those fantasized powerful forces behind the scene. Another emotional response to the health crisis (though obviously inconsistent with the ones just mentioned) is outright *denial* of the crisis, its severity and likely duration, leading to the often militant and ostentatious boycott and sabotage of protective measures ordered or taken by governments. The flourishing anti-vax movements we see emerging in many countries are just one case in point.

While the manifestation of these passions and their destructive impact on the epistemic regime has been a growing though still marginal phenomenon of noisy minorities, the same does not apply to distortions of the epistemic regime originating from considerations of *interest*. Economic interests in connection with the pandemic are activated in two ways. First, the spread of the virus involves *direct* negative health effects that damage economic outcomes. People who fall ill and those who desire or are directed to avoid any exposure to sources of infection cannot work for an income. They are forced into a trade-off of life and livelihood. Secondly and much more significantly, there *indirect* negative effects caused by policy measures to contain the further spread of the virus (e. g., a full scale lockdown) have an often devastating and unprecedented impact upon economic growth, employment, fiscal revenues, family and religious life, and many more. In both cases, interests are affected according to highly unequal distributional patterns. Not only are some categories of people in a better position than others to protect themselves and minimize their personal risk of infection (e. g., home office workers *vs.* super market or hospital employees, well-to-do pensioners owning a second home in the country side *vs.* urban dwellers who depend on public transport to get to work). In addition, new kinds of inequality are created by pandemic-related policy measures, such as the closing of schools or the temporary shut-down of the restaurant and tourist industries. Measures to contain the spread of the virus invariably cause at best partially and temporarily compensated losses of income, employment, and many other life chances. There is a clear gradient of social power that enables some types of actors to extract generous compensation from governments while others are left to suffer not just their exposure to health risks but also the hardship of policy measures to contain the pandemic. In combination, these two kinds of inequalities give rise to the by now proverbial "health *vs.*

wealth" or "life *vs.* livelihood" dilemmas. Conflicts over policy and demands for compensations grow the more intense the longer the pandemic and corresponding policy measures last. A situation that at its beginning was largely framed as analogous to a natural disaster is being reframed as being shaped by political decisions. Interrelated with these economic tensions and conflicts are those triggered by *political* interests. Local and national governments, political parties in electoral competition, federal states and entire nations find themselves in an open rivalry over who succeed better at "flattening the curve" of infections and fatalities or, at least, deploys more effective tactics of blame avoidance.

The ambivalence of primary fear of some danger and the secondary fear of measures taken in averting risks that is common in all spheres of social life. Medical doctors face the dilemma every day of striking a balance between prescribing a medication that can heal some health condition while also taking into account its known negative side effects. The experience, professional skills and her professional ethic of responsibility allows the doctor to arrive at this balance; at any rate, she and her professional community of fellow doctors are endowed with the *authority* to decide on such dilemmas, with courts of law only very rarely called upon to review the appropriateness of the decision taken. It is this kind of responsible, trusted and uncontested authority to strike a balance between two kinds of risks that is absent in the case of the corona pandemic. The problem is that nobody knows and is consensually authorized to determine the right balance of measures that can assuage both the fear of damages to life and health and the secondary fear of the vast negative consequences these measures are known to cause for social and economic life.

The goals of saving lives and saving social and economic "normalcy" are incommensurable; there is no metric that allows us to pass an authoritative judgment regarding how much sacrifice of the former is "worth" how much gain of the latter, or *vice versa*. Moreover, as the crisis progresses, the initially clear and shared priority for the former tends to yield to a sense of greater urgency of the latter. After all, or so it is argued, the suspension of normalcy for the sake of saving our health and life can itself be life-threatening. As *nobody* can lay claim to any unequivocal competence and legitimacy to resolve this dilemma, such authority is up for grabs and *everybody* feels entitled to shape outcomes according to particular interests and preferences. It is this condition (plus the giant dimensions of the damages that loom on either side of the "health *vs.* wealth" dilemma) that has demolished the epistemic regime governing public health policy in times of the pandemic. The breakdown of institutional structures that can supply trustworthy knowledge and legitimate guidelines for action creates a vacuum that sucks up all kinds of beliefs and preferences, including heavy doses of plain obscurantism and baseless claims that lack any authority of being demonstrably true or instrumentally rational.

One reason for the perplexities that stand in the way of a widely shared and robust understanding of the nature of the corona crisis and what needs to be done about it can be seen in the fact that there is no other "public bad" (i. e. a "symmetrical opposite of a public good", as a Wikipedia entry puts it) the agreed-upon response to which can serve as a template for corona policy making. An earthquake or tsunami differs from corona in that its impact is sudden, short-lived and localized, never global and infectious and following a pattern of slow motion. It differs from war (in spite of Macron's suggestion "nous somme en guerre") in that there is nobody who has declared war and no enemy who can be defeated and with whom a peace treaty can eventually be concluded – although it is similar to modern interstate warfare in its totalizing impact as it affects and subordinates everybody and all institutional spheres and sectors of the economy. It differs from quasi-epidemic drug addiction (80, 000 deaths from overdoses p. a. in the US) in that there is no substance the production and trafficking of which can be policed; nor are there victims to be blamed. It differs from terrorism because it cannot be fought or deterred by military or other forms of counter-violence. It differs from HIV/AIDS in that with the latter it is exactly and widely known what practices we must refrain from for the sake of staying reliably safe. It differs from air pollution and climate change because it cannot be blamed as an externality of an irrational, exploitative and unsustainable mode of production, consumption, and the human use of natural resources – although the fact of deep inequalities of impact and the overall ill-preparedness of health systems can. And it differs from normal economic crises because it affects (by itself and through lockdown responses) both the demand *and* the supply side of markets, whereas normal crises can mostly be fought by boosting demand through fiscal or monetary intervention. The corona pandemic can at best (and disregarding its global nature and long duration) be compared to what (for instance, in maritime insurance law) is called "acts of God": unforeseeable (as to their time, place and magnitude) events inflicting great damages for which nobody can be blamed and held liable.

Normative considerations

In the early days of the corona crisis, there was a widely shared concern with the fairness and distributive justice of government measures to protect the health of citizens and to compensate them for parts of the losses they have suffered under the impact of lockdowns etc. It was argued that the right to life (and, by implication, the protection from life threatening health conditions) as it is enshrined, for instance, in Article 2 of the German constitution where it is located at the top of the subsequent list of other civil rights to be observed and protected by the state indicates its supreme status, a status that immunizes, as it were, this right from being balanced against other rights with which it may be seen to be in conflict. This supreme and untouchable status might also be claimed for the right to life for the simple logical reason that it is only *living* human beings who are capable of enjoying those other rights, such as property rights or the freedom of opinion and religion. According to this view, the right to life is something like a "meta" right. Against such elevation of the right to life to the status of supremacy, it has been objected by legal experts and ranking politicians that the right to life, as every other civil right, can very well come into tension with other rights and needs to be weighed against them. The issue has been brought up as a warning against age discrimination in the allocation of health care resources. A strict interpretation of the equality of the right to life demands that the elderly, given the typically greater precarity of their health, are entitled to an even *greater* input of resources spent on their behalf than is being spent on younger generations in order to achieve an *equal* life-preserving outcome. The same logic would have to apply to health workers with their greater exposure to risk of infection. The empirics underlying this debate among legal philosophers, however, show that the supremacy claim concerning the right to life is by no means redeemed in actual legal and political practice. If it were, there would not be thousands of refugees drowning in the Mediterranean; nor would the German legislative chamber have refused to pass a transplantation law that does not provide for an opt-out rather than opt-in requirement for potential organ donors. Had it done so, an estimated number of several hundred lives per year could have been saved.

On the other hand, there is the brutal utilitarian argument actually advanced by a German politician. According to him, spending all the resources needed to protect the life of elderly patients whose survival is known to be much more seriously threatened by the virus than the life of younger generations is entirely unjustified as they are going to die soon anyway. This point reminds us that it is not just health policy measures that can discriminate against groups of people – it is the virus *itself* and its epidemiological features that causes a highly stratified risk profile of categories of people as it privileges white over blue collar workers, home office over manufacturing and many services, women over men, users of private cars over those depending on public transport, healthy people over those suffering from obesity and cardiovascular diseases, kids of educated middle class households over their friends lacking adequate resources for home schooling, countryside residents over those living in densely populated metropolitan areas, and, on a global scale, the inhabitants of (most of) the rich countries over the rest of mankind. These massive and deepening inequalities will corrode the solidaristic narrative of "all of us being in the same boat". Some of us, instead, see themselves (to stick with the maritime metaphor) as safely standing on shore observing a sinking boat whose passengers we are called upon to rescue. To the extent we do so, it is not on the basis of *solidarity* but on the much more precarious one of *altruism*.

Normative concerns focusing on discriminatory health practices and the unfairness that consists in the unfair distribution of protective wear, testing materials, respirators etc. across hospitals, regions and countries, the limited readiness of authorities to share these urgently needed resources, and the general state of ill-preparedness of governments stood at the center of normative complaints and political conflict at the *beginning* of the pandemic's trajectory. The accusation used to be that the state, due to its underfunding of the public health system, is not "doing enough" to protect our lives.

Yet after the mass experience of lockdowns and socioeconomic disruptions caused by them, this normative complaint has widely morphed into its opposite. Many thousands of people have adopted a "big brother" narrative and rallied in a number of countries to protest the alleged fact that the state is "doing too much" to control the pandemic, thereby encroaching disproportionally on the freedom of citizens. To be sure, there are very serious infringements of rights involved by pandemic-related policy measures, among them those of property rights, mobility rights, rights of assembly, rights to general education, and religious freedoms. Health policy measures, beginning with the mandatory wearing of masks and the ban on sports events attended by mass audiences, have come under heavy attacks for their "disproportionate" reach. Perhaps there is an analogue at the societal level to what starvation is at the level of the individual body: After their impact has unfolded for a while, restrictions begin to be felt as utterly unbearable. As a consequence, health authorities are being challenged for both the legitimacy and the effectiveness of the regulations they propose and implement: what is deemed *acceptable* at the mass level is not enough as an *effective* strategy to cope with the pandemic, and *vice versa*. This quandary is exacerbated by the competitive pressures for loosening restrictions national states, as well as federal states within nations, are increasingly exposed to. Much of these rivalries follows a "me too" logic: If bookstores are allowed to reopen after a shutdown, why not also barber shops? The level of trust that authorities enjoy concerning whether they know what they are doing and actually do what the best available expertise helps them to know is very unevenly distributed among national and regional governments. It is well possible that trust (a relationship that takes a long time to build and can suddenly collapse) will turn out to be the ultimate strategic variable that determines success and failure of measures to cope with the pandemic. But trust cannot be built in the way a highway can.

Trust in the government's doing the "right thing" has been shown to be strongly correlated with party preferences, and the incitement of distrust is evidently a widely used tactic in democratic party competition.

Given the highly differentiated pattern of both the risks that come with infection and the damages inflicted by policy measures designed to control it, trust is not easy to maintain. After all, what is experienced by privileged parts of the population as, at worst, a mild nuisance means an existential and hopeless catastrophe to others. It would be sociologically naïve to expect all of them to adopt similar attitudes of trust in the authorities and readiness to make sacrifices towards the collective good of defeating the pandemic.

Apart from normative issues of distributive justice as just reviewed, the other normative concern brought up by the pandemic and related health policy measures has to do with the fates of *liberal democracy* und the impact of crisis management. The crisis has helped to make us aware of the fact that democratic procedures are premised on the condition of the *physical co-presence* of citizens and that of the members of their representative bodies, such as legislative assemblies and committees. The power of protest movements depends on the public display of people gathering at agreed-upon times and places in order to jointly express their causes and demands and to ensure each other in the process of their determination and strength. The same applies to court procedures where the physical presence of the parties to a case or the defendants and their attorneys is often prescribed by procedural rules. Stay-at-home rules and the mandatory keeping of physical distance interfere with these modes of communication which are so much richer, due to their informal visual and acoustic signals and perceptions they provide as "noise", compared to communications mediated just by text written on paper, telephone conversation, or digital transmission. Even the democratic act of voting, which traditionally takes place by people visiting a voting locale where they encounter each other, if only for minutes, as the individual bearers of popular sovereignty, is affected by restrictions imposed to prevent infection. Elections have been postponed for the sake of public health. In other cases, citizens have been encouraged to use the nearest mail box for postal voting, which arguably deprives of the voting act of a sense of being an exceptional ritual and trivializes it to being similar to the act of, say, paying your dentist's bill. Also, in the settings of physical co-presence of groups of persons who are identifiable to each other, every utterance is to a degree public, at least non-anonymous, i.e. witnessed by third parties capable to judge and remember what has been said, and by whom. People who are physically assembled in the same place can applaud to what has just been said or express their displeasure, which is nonsensical when in Zoom sessions people sit in their offices and listen to speakers via digital devices.

To be sure, all of this all applies less to the executive branch of government than it does to the judiciary, legislative bodies, and collective actors within civil society. In order to decide swiftly and effectively as the situation demands, governments agencies rely on directives, decrees, executive orders and commands the content of which bypasses the publicity of legislative deliberations. It is conceived behind closed doors. Their operation is not interfered with by rules of distancing, restrictions of mobility and the ensuing communicative isolation. The executive branch comes to prevail over the others and civil society the more the situation can be framed as an emergency. In an emergency, talking is a plain waste of time.

Yet that does not mean that the corona crisis, as has been suggested by a number of authors, has resulted anywhere in a Schmittian "state of exception", a coup, or a take-over of government power by the epidemiologists. While liberal democratic regimes are rightly seen to be endangered by various kinds of challengers and opponents, I fail to see why governments presiding over the corona crisis should be suspected to be one of them. First of all, the unprecedented suspension of basic rights that comes with corona policies, including restrictions on the role of parliaments, is both openly declared and credibly deplored by democratic political leaders, which is not what instigators of a coup are typically inclined to do. Secondly, restrictive measures are explicitly limited, both in their scope and duration, to the perceived requirements of winning control over the pandemic and the damages it causes. Thirdly, the court system, including supreme and constitutional courts, which must make binding decisions on the necessary, effective and proportionate nature of the crisis-related policy measures is compromised in many countries; but I am not aware of any country where an encroachment on judicial independence has been either triggered by or justified with reference to the corona health crisis. One might add that authoritarian regimes typically nurture nationalist inclinations, whereas the very nature of the pandemic calls for supranational cooperation in terms of research, mobility, health-related development aid, and exchange of information. In liberal democracies, it remains a *health* crisis and does not spill over, as overly alarmist commentators have suggested, into anything approaching a *regime* crisis.

There does not seem to be a clear correlation between regime type and success or failure in resolving or mitigating the corona crisis. The harsh modes of intervention that are available to authoritarian regimes (e. g., the Peoples Republic of China) including the suppression of information, the rapid mobilization of huge material and human resources, and a rigid quarantine imposed for weeks on entire cities and regions with many millions of inhabitants has reportedly yielded an astounding success in fighting the epidemic and its impact. But similar success stories can be told of the liberal democracies of South Korea, Taiwan, and New Zealand. Semi-authoritarian regimes of the rightist populist type (Brazil, the US) have been dramatic failures in coping with the pandemic. The study and explanation of the vastly differing achievements of countries and regions, regimes and policies in coping with the crisis will be a gold mine of the fields of political sociology and comparative politics for years to come. For the time being, we are left with speculations such as the gender of top political leaders allegedly making a difference, as New Zealand, Taiwan, Norway, Finland and Germany, all ruled by female prime ministers, have all done remarkably well. Needless to say, much more compelling explanations are called for.

Stephen Turner
The Naked State: What the Breakdown of Normality Reveals

Giorgio Agamben shocked the world by noting that what "the epidemic has caused to appear with clarity is that the state of exception, to which governments have habituated us for some time, has truly become the normal condition." And that "A society that lives in a perennial state of emergency cannot be a free society." He preceded this comment by making the point that the disease had returned people to the state of nature: "Italians are disposed to sacrifice practically everything – the normal conditions of life, social relationships, work, even friendships, affections, and religious and political convictions – to the danger of getting sick. Bare life – and the danger of losing it – is not something that unites people, but blinds and separates them."[1] His critics, for the most part, and in different ways, responded by asking for trust in experts, and implicitly cautioning him and his audience to avoid undermining their authority.

This message, to obey, was repeated over and over in the wider political culture, and especially in the press, which crowed its approval of the measures, mostly in the name of science. The "moderate" columnist for the *New York Times*, David Brooks, was explicit about this message:

> Aside from a few protesters and a depraved president, most of us have understood we need to suspend the old individualistic American creed. In the midst of a complex epidemiological disaster, to be anti-authority is to be ignorant. (Brooks 2020)

The discrepancy between the "complex" character of the "disaster" and the implausibility of any complex matter being resolved by obedience to "authority" was apparently invisible to this writer and to the many commentators like him. But this response is a good opening to large questions about the relation between expertise and authority, and about the role of ordinary people in re-

---

1 Stanford University: The Bookhaven, 17 March, 2020. https://bookhaven.stanford.edu/2020/03/giorgio-agamben-on-coronavirus-the-enemy-is-not-outside-it-is-within-us/ Published "in Italian on the blog *Quodlibet*. The essay was republished on *Medium*, and in an authorized translation by Adam Kotsko, who described it as the important European philosopher's 'indirect response to the controversy surrounding his article about the response to coronavirus in Italy'. It was also included in the *European Journal of Psychoanlysis*, in a round-up of thoughts on 'Coronavirus and Philosophers' (26 February 2020, http://www.journal-psychoanalysis.eu/coronavirus-and-philosophers/), and from there to Facebook."

https://doi.org/10.1515/9783110713350-003

sponse to it. Agamben's point about the normalization of the exception is also apt: suspending the American creed, for Brooks, is not a temporary event. It is a watershed, and the "suspension" is meant to be permanent.

Agamben's language is taken from Carl Schmitt 2014 ([1921]; 2010 [1923]), as are his core ideas about the state. The idea that states of exception are being normalized appears misleadingly hyperbolic: what is being described is merely a set of facts that has become so familiar that we have become accustomed to them and ignore them (Higgs 1987; Scheppele 2010). Only in a state of crisis do they become apparent. And this crisis has brought together and made visible a large number of features of the present political order that have been hidden, though, like the purloined letter, hidden in plain sight. These include the following: the common phenomenon of expert failure (Koppl 2018; Turner 2010), the structure of normal accidents of expertise, the problem of assigning accountability to experts, the variation in national traditions in responding to expertise, the dependence of ordinary governance on usually faceless expert bureaucrats, the tendency of political and historical narrative to conceal the role of experts, the fact of expert disagreement and the means of suppressing and containing it, the predominance in expert-related contexts of ill-formed problem spaces in the crisis that demands the suspension of ordinary life, and that authority, rather than normal legal and political procedure, needs to be obeyed.[2] The expansion of powers is typically in the form of wider discretion by bureaucrats, who respond to a novel situation, one not strictly covered by explicit rules or past practice, but which is viewed under the aspect of necessity – not a formal or declared emergency, but a tacit acceptance that something must be done, after expertise-based "emergency."

What Brooks' comment underlines is that Agamben's appeal to Schmitt was essentially correct: the moderate point of view is that this is a crisis, that it is a crisis that demands the suspension of ordinary life, and that authority, rather than normal legal and political procedure, needs to be obeyed, and that this topic and the use of authority is not to be subject to debate – to debate it is to be ignorant and therefore unworthy of anything but the hand of authority. But it raises another Schmittian question: what is normal? And who decides the situation is not normal or is a "disaster," to use the language of the exception chosen by Brooks? The appeal to science is Brooks' answer: and the easy collapse of the notion of science into the notion of authority calls to mind Schmitt's favorite line from Hobbes: *auctoritas non veritas facit legem*. The appeal to exper-

---

2 All of these are topics of chapters in my *Politics of Expertise* (2014), which contains previously published articles.

tise erases the distinction, and with it the possibility of criticism of authority on the ground of truth: truth and authority are one. Hence to be anti-authority is not merely to be rebellious, or independent, but to be ignorant.

The Normal

Schmitt's account of the state of exception depends on a distinction between the normal situation, in which legal norms apply and make sense, and abnormal situations, in which the suspension of the legal order is necessary to preserve it, or to preserve the state. It is in this moment that we see the naked state—the state in the act of being itself, without the drapery of superficial justifications and minor sanctions that normally suffice to legitimate it. When the police come to quell a riot, we see the naked state: the normal rules are suspended, orders are given and enforced by direct physical violence, and this continues until order is restored. But this suspension of the rules tells us about the normal: that the normal is the absence of riot, but the possibility of riot is nevertheless always present, and not preventable by the mere continued operation of the normal rules. The normal cannot be relied upon to perpetuate itself. Its reliable perpetuation is only possible because of the possibility of the exception. And the exception serves to do what the normal rules normally do, but have failed to do.

In a crisis the normal rules do not suffice, but the central things, that the rules normally do, such as keep order, need to be done in an exceptional way, a way beyond normal rules of enactment, typically by decree or "orders." The exception thus reveals *what* is central, what the conditions of normality are, but also *who* is central, because the execution of the tasks performed under the state of exception has to be done by someone. Schmitt was describing a formal legal institution, Article 48 of the Weimar constitution, which was repeatedly invoked during the Weimar republic, for matters large and small. But he generalized its significance by showing its near or *de facto* universality in legal orders, and its roots in the Roman law of constitutional dictatorship. And we can generalize it further by noting the ways in which normal rules are suspended in a crisis by acquiescence to the expansion of normal bureaucratic discretionary powers. By seeing who acts and how others act in response in a crisis we see what powers that people actually possess, but are latent or unused in normal situations (Bachrach and Baratz 1962, 1975; Debnam 1975).

Agamben's warning that states use crises to expand their power perturbed his audience, which generally favored the benign expansion of state power governed by expert knowledge. The phenomenon is a staple of the specialist literature, which speaks of the ratchet effect of expanded powers (Higgs 1987). The expansion of powers is typically in the form of wider discretion by bureaucrats, who respond to a novel situation, one not strictly covered by explicit rules or past practice which is viewed under the aspect of necessity – not a formal or declared emergency, but a tacit acceptance that something must be done, and done by the agency or official with the resources to do it. In the US, this is often done through a complicated series of indirect administrative means, such as advisory letters, which do not require, or are treated as not requiring, the normal processes for rule-making, which require public input (Turner 2020). These "little exceptions," along with the expansion of discretionary powers they entail, become the normal – which is Agamben's point as well, which he phrases by arguing that the exception has become normalized. This process is not as dramatic as a declaration of emergency, and does not reveal the state naked. But the extent to which the accumulation of little exceptions has altered and expanded the powers of the state can be revealed in moments of crisis.

The C-19 pandemic is such a moment. And what it revealed is the power of experts. We can think of the relation between expertise, the state, and the public as a three-legged stool, or a triangle. In this crisis, the relations were clear: governments relied on experts; the experts had legitimacy apart from their formal roles and independent of the legitimacy of the state or its representative institutions; the public accepted, or declined to accept, state authority because of their acceptance or rejection of the experts, but the experts depended on the state for its patronage and to some extent on their recognition as experts.

In normal circumstances, this three-legged stool, of state, public, and experts, is stable and invisible. The public feels secure in the idea that the discretionary powers of the state, and more generally the policies, are being carried out in accordance with expert knowledge and reflect expertise. The experts are faceless and unknown to the public. Their disagreements and the precarious nature of their expertise are not known. The relationship is one of trust. The state, Hegel-like, pretends to represent the interests of the whole people.

The *hidden* relations between these three legs are best understood as relations of non-decision: the public doesn't revolt against the state; the experts do not denounce the state; the state does not defund the experts or restrict them; the public does not disbelieve the experts, the state, or the mass media; the experts do not directly deny what the public knows; the state does not directly assault the public or deny its competence to judge it. In a crisis, the stool becomes unstable. Each leg had its own de-stabilizing tendencies, which became apparent only in crises. Part of the stability of the expert leg was owed to the hiddenness of expertise. The "public" is a myth that gets represented to itself and the state by the media. The state, with its labyrinthine complexity, is barely intelligible, except when it acts. And its acts are themselves often inscrutable, by design. Expertise is by definition a mystery to those who do not possess it.

The Three Legs

Experts

What is normal for experts in a pandemic? Pandemics and epidemics are relatively frequent occurrences, and there are normal procedures for dealing with them. In the US, responsibility devolved to the CDC, the Centers for Disease Control and Prevention (Bennington 2014: 12). The processes developed as a result of several bad experiences, but the H1N1 flu response of 2009 was generally regarded as a success. It featured good interorganizational relations with different parts of the US government and the WHO, and acceptance and approval by the public.

What worked in this earlier case was a system in which a key team integrated the ideas of a large number of contributors – there were over 200 within agency comments on a preliminary report (Bennington 2014: 186) – in the agency itself to address as many aspects of the situation as could be contained in a reasonably short and clear set of messages. This was an act of social construction: the team made up the message out of disparate material, selecting for relevance and importance, with an eye to influencing behavior in order to reduce the impact of the disease. This was not "science" in the raw sense – research results fresh from the lab or field, or the product of a long process of sorting out these results through peer-review and scientific competition – but a carefully refined consensus message produced through bureaucratic methods.

The agency is well funded – over $4 billion annually. It does not have a monopoly on research in this area, but its presence is overwhelming. The production of advisories and policies during a pandemic uses medical science – medical being an important qualifier – but is a product of multiple bureaucratic and value judgments, and founded to a significant degree on guesswork based on past experience. Medical knowledge is short of scientific knowledge in the normally understood sense: it needs to be adapted to individual circumstances to be applied, and is almost always short of full understanding of a complex biological process. In the case of so-called "observational epidemiology," matters are even more difficult: this is essentially standard social science causal modelling and statistics, with the usual problems of confounding and multiple causes. The field has been in crisis for decades (Grimes and Schulz 2012).

To speak of these public statements as "the science" is thus wildly inaccurate. They are boundary objects, carefully constructed for public consumption, but also to synthesize a great deal of knowledge, judgment, guesswork, and uncertainties that are hard to estimate. And they are purposive: they are written to change behavior, and also to protect the agency in the event of failure. Preserving trust is an important value. Disagreement is aired privately, and dealt with; bureaucratic infighting is always in the background, and some voices get a larger say than others. Nevertheless, the process is, in normal circumstances, effective at crowding out other expert voices, or accommodating them. So there is not, if the system works, significant expert dissent.

But the realities of patronage lie behind these organizational niceties. A court case after the Katrina disaster gives some indication of the power of the state to coerce consensus. An obscure engineering researcher at Louisiana State University criticized the Army Corps of Engineers, which was responsible for the levee that failed and flooded much of the city of New Orleans, for its errors. The university, apparently encouraged by its own professors, had the researcher fired. The case went to court and eventually was settled without a trial with a payment to the researcher.[3] The issue, however, was important: it was believed that the criticisms would affect the relationship between the university and the federal government, on which it depended for research grants, even though the Army Corps was not itself a source of funds. The situation with the CDC is precisely parallel. The main source of funds in the area of infectious disease was the National Institute of Allergy and Infectious disease (NIAID) which received $5.89 billion in the 2020 budget. The total NIH budget is over $40 billion. These funds are a matter of scientific life or death for researchers in this area.

NIAID did not have responsibility for pandemics – but it did have responsibility for funding the vast research apparatus of academic medicine on these diseases. This in itself raises fundamental questions about science policy: was the money spent on the wrong topics? But for our purposes the issue is latent power. The unusual feature of this pandemic was that the CDC was sidelined early, and a new body, The White House Coronavirus Task Force, operated under the Department of State, was established on January 29, 2020.[4] On February 26, 2020, Vice President Mike Pence was named to chair the task force. Deborah Birx was named the response coordinator. Anthony Fauci, the head of the NIAID, and De-

---

3 Mark Schleifstein, 2013, LSU Spent Nearly $1 Million on Legal Fight over Firing of Coastal Researcher Ivor van Heerden. *The Times-Picayune*, 3 April. https://www.nola.com/news/environ ment/article_6851241d-1c3b-5b5e-ac50-b4db0ddcf0b0.html
4 Statement from the Press Secretary Regarding the President's Coronavirus Task Force, 29 January 2020. https://www.whitehouse.gov/briefings-statements/statement-press-secretary-regard ing-presidents-coronavirus-task-force/

borah Birx, became the key representatives of "science" in the public pro-nouncements of the national government and stood beside Trump and spoke with and after him on the crisis as it unfolded.

This was a departure from the normal. And it was a result of a breakdown in the normal processes themselves. The CDC and Anthony Fauci had failed to rec-ognize the severity of the virus, in large part for reasons intrinsic to the problem of detection, the limitations of the scientific knowledge available, and the need to make judgements about it. Not for nothing did one of the founders of public health medicine declare that it was part science, part art. These issues have been discussed extensively elsewhere, and as this is written continue to unfold. From the point of view of the problem of normalcy, however, one issue is crucial. The CDC asserted exclusive power over the provision of detection kits at the begin-ning of the crisis, and developed kits which turned out to be faulty as a result of contamination in manufacturing. The kits were found to be faulty by another powerful agency, the Food and Drug Administration. This embarrassing failure led to the loss of control of the CDC over the process, and to an open expression of distrust of the work of the agency by Deborah Birx.

With this failure the possibility of public dispute between experts opened up, and, in contrast to past pandemics, and as a result of different policy choices by other countries, the façade of unified expert agreement – that there was such a thing as "the science" that could be simply obeyed – was ripped off. Diverse expert opinions were aired. Different policies were adopted, both in different countries and in different states in the US, where public health, under a federal system, is primarily a responsibility of states. Private foundations entered the fray, with their own programs and research agendas (Morcillo 2020). Recommen-dations, such as for masking, were given and withdrawn, and given again. And most visibly, projections were made and failed to be fulfilled. These included the most politically volatile ones, which revolved around the availability of ventila-tors, which were thought at the early stages of the crisis to be crucial for care, but which turned out to be sufficient and not uniformly helpful as it became clear that the disease was not simply a respiratory problem.

But there were more departures from the normal. The pandemic demanded immediate answers – not something that the science system normally delivers, and this was especially true for the medical science system. Science has, and is, an elaborate system of social control, which operates with multiple redundant mechanisms, all designed to produce conformity in results. The peer review sys-tem for grants is one; it is closely connected with the status hierarchy, which is another, along with the degree system, the certification and licensing system, and several other bureaucratic systems, including Institutional Research Boards which approve research and privacy protocols for human subjects, and most powerful of all, drug approval agencies, which normally demand years of testing and an encyclopedia length application for approvals. The system of publication itself of course depends on peer-review and is often slow.

All of these systems were challenged in the crisis. Preprints and unreviewed papers appeared, and clinicians and outsiders to the medical research hierarchy were able to present research results without the usual barriers. Issues immediately arose. Retractions became common, and important figures, such as John Iaoniddes, the medical statistician, who promoted certain pieces of research and warned against taking seriously much of the research that was being presented, were savaged in the elite press (Heer 2020) for taking funding from "right-wing" sources. This was a sign of system failure: the dirty linen of science was exposed to public view, along with the opinions and claims of many different scientists. The effort to suppress views that were unwelcome, of course, also became visible, rather than being hidden in confidential referees' reports.

The "science" became nakedly political when two studies appeared in major journals, *The Lancet* and the *New England Journal of Medicine*, that had already editorialized against Trump. The articles supported the contention that the familiar and notably safe anti-malarial drug Trump had touted was in fact both unsafe and useless. They had immediate effect: research into it was halted and public statements were made by official agencies. In a short time, however, the articles, which had been rushed into print without the usual slow review and without availability of the data, which were proprietary and kept secret, in one case, had to be embarrassingly retracted. As some of the commentators on these retractions noted, while these retractions were presented as exceptions, this too was a case which merely revealed what was normal: retractions, shoddy research, and the use of research to advance interests were all commonplace in science (Marcus and Oransky 2020).

The expert leg failed. What it needed was to keep the façade: to hide or prevent behind the scenes disagreements, which are normal both in science and bureaucracies, from becoming public and therefore an object of political side-taking. What happened instead was that the choice of policies drove the choice of experts: governors who imposed draconian lock-downs appealed to the experts with the most dire predictions, and when these predictions failed, to the experts who predicted a second wave. The governors who opted to reopen their state appealed to the experts who rejected the predictions, who typically did so on the basis that there was insufficient high-quality evidence to support the interpretation of the disease that they depended on. The differences between states also reflected the severity of the outbreak and their localization. At this point, two-thirds of the deaths have occurred in a geographically small portion of the country, most heavily in New York City and environs, and in a few urban centers. In the rest of the country a large proportion of the deaths have been in nursing homes.

The expert resolution to the issues raised by the pandemic, if there ever is one, is far in the future. Even the basic mechanisms of mortality are not understood. The crucial problem of transmission is still poorly understood and debated. Whether infection confers immunity in the future is not sure. The answer to the question of whether lockdowns will prevent an increase in infections, is unknown. The effects of the vaccine are unknown. Yet these are the questions that policy depends on. So at this stage, with the future of the pandemic still unknown, there is no expert resolution. In real time, this was a case of expert failure. And this meant that the expert leg of the stool could not bear the weight and it shifted to the other two legs. The illusion of apoliticality was nevertheless destroyed. The experts chose sides, and the public and politicians chose experts that fit their preferences. The failures of prediction and inconsistencies in the claims made by experts and politicians were instantly recorded and monitored on the web.

The State

The use of emergency powers in response to riots or insurrections, is the state in its pure form: using violence to defend itself. This was Schmitt's model, and it can be seen today in the many uses of emergency powers that litter the globe. The absolutist states of early modern Europe operated, in effect, using these powers all the time: they recognized no limits on the sovereign's power. Schmitt modelled his general account of these powers on the Roman institution of temporary dictatorship, in which the temporary character of the powers was regulated *de jure*, to one year. But there is a similar *de facto* limit on emergency powers that is especially relevant to nominally democratic states: they cannot go on too long or seem too ineffective without producing enough non-co-operation to delegitimate the state or leader employing them. Dictatorships can succeed, and people acquiesce in them. But if they do not, they will be temporary, and replaced by other political options, such as revolution or invasion.

In the case of pandemics the same principles apply, but because the pretext for the state of emergency is expert claims, the experts become entangled with the legitimacy of the rulers assuming dictatorial powers themselves. This strengthens the rulers, but binds the experts to them. Experts become part of the legitimation of the powers, but also become subject to de-legitimation if they fail to produce the results that justified the state of emergency.

One of the striking features of this crisis is the resemblance between it and the cholera epidemics of the nineteenth century, and with the differences between national state traditions in responding to it. States responded to this crisis in much the same way as they had before: bureaucratic traditions are astonishingly robust and long lived. In Britain, the task was given to a single great man, who headed the statistics office, and was challenged, unsuccessfully, by an outsider of lower social rank, until, as the result of a crucial experiment, even he had to admit to being wrong; interestingly enough on the relative importance of water and air as a means of transmission. The Germans worked on a bureaucracy led stakeholders model, and listened to the experts they wanted to listen to. The Americans, with their federal system, had state and local governments with bodies which were pressured by voluntary organizations, in the case of New York a body of physicians, and established best practices which were copied by other jurisdictions. The history was littered with reports of committees and councils (G. F. Pyle 1969). The fact that a commission was created for C-19 was another use of this political method. The current oddity of the Swedish response also ran true to form: the bureaucracy, legally insulated from ministerial interference, made its own decisions by consulting the experts of its choosing.

Each of these solutions to the problem of assimilating expert knowledge had their own problems, and critics. But they also illustrate the gap between good science and successful policy. In London, adherence to the miasmatic theory of transmission prevented the improvement of the water system, though it did occur but for other reasons. In the US, the policy, sanitary reform, worked despite being wedded to the miasmatic theory. In Hamburg, scene of the most horrific and last great European outbreak of the disease in 1892, the best science was available, but the city leaders chose the wrong expert, and rejected the national leader on the subject.

States, to a greater or lesser degree, generated internal conflicts. This was especially true in the United States, where doctrines of the separation of powers and limited government were foundational for the political system, and in which the federal government had, under the constitution, only a short list of "enumerated powers," with "police" powers in the hands of the states alone. These divisions of powers were made even more complicated by the creation of independent agencies with their own rules for public participation, one of which, the Food and Drug Administration, played a large role in the C-19 crisis, first by rejecting the test kits of the CDC, then stopping research projects, and regulating testing.

In normal circumstances, conflicts between units of the state are rare, but only because practices and judicial doctrines have developed to avoid them. A fundamental political feature of modern states, also noted by Schmitt, is that they combine within themselves conflicting constitutional principles. Sometimes this is by design, as with the doctrine of separation of powers and the creation of independent agencies in the US; in Europe more often a result of historical continuities in which parliamentary institutions were imposed alongside a monarchical bureaucratic and advisory system which was never abolished, or in Britain, where the monarchical, aristocratic, and parliamentary system have a formal role and relation, but the civil service has continuity, self-selection, and thus considerable *de facto* autonomy. One even has odd cases, such as Iran, in which rule by jurists is the fundamental principle, but there are nevertheless parliamentary institutions and an executive with a president. Quangos, quasi-nongovernmental organizations, are among the many hybrid innovations that have replaced privy councils and similar bodies.

In the normal situation, these do not conflict: they are designed to have separate domains. In a crisis, they are prone to conflict, and the point of emergency declarations is to override them, if they do not function. Expertise, and rule by experts, is its own constitutional principle, one which the people who say "listen to the science" are embracing. But expert rule has its own institutional forms, of committees and commissions, or independent agencies, which are, by design, separate from democratic accountability and influence. And it also has its own claims to legitimacy and public support.

The US lacks a constitutional emergency power, a problem that concerned some important political thinkers in the past. States, however, have "police" powers that by custom include emergency powers. But emergency decrees are reviewable by courts, can be nullified by legislators, and can be held to violate the federal constitution. The major conflicts so far have been in the courts, and there have been multiple cases. Most of them involve the reasonableness of emergency decrees. They indicate how problematic normal legal standards of equivalence, reasonableness, and so forth are in the face of expert claims, and therefore how difficult it is to draw legal limits on the state or its agencies. The simplest conflicts involve rights which are absolute, on paper, but subject to interpretation and "balancing" in the courts, and in which the courts are likely to "defer" to the supposed expertise of the executive branch, usually of a state government, but also to federal agencies, where there are a plethora of doctrines which courts appeal to in order to limit their responsibility for enforcing constitutional rights (Turner 2020).

These patterns embody Agamben's concept of normalizing the exception, for each of these cases creates an exception to the plain text of the law, and from what people expect of the legal order. And there is a crucial background to this. The great triumph of continental liberalism was the *Rechsstaat*, the state of laws, not men, superseding the *Obrigkeitstaat*, the magistrate state, in which judges acted according their sense of right, or less creditable motives. Schmitt regarded the *Rechtsstaat*, with its pretension to neutrality and rule following, to be a fraud: there was no such thing as neutrality, and rule-following still depended on the arbitrary interpretations of judges. Discretionary power for Schmitt was visible throughout the legal and bureaucratic system, and especially at the top, where the power to decide to suspend the law – to declare a state of exception—was located.

In the common law world, ruled by precedent, and with courts which can appeal to non-democratically created judicial doctrines that articulate precedent in congealed form, the self-limitation of the courts amounts to the normalization of discretionary power. Normalizing this power amounts to hiding it in plain sight: deferring to agencies and executives citing experts, and refusing to object to it on the grounds of judicial doctrines designed to keep the courts free of conflicts with other parts of the state. In the Civil Code world, courts, especially constitutional courts, have this role, and are more open in principle to being used by ordinary citizens. In practice, however, they run into difficulties in cases involving expert knowledge. A recent German constitutional court decision against the money creating powers of the European Central Bank, for example, failed to grasp the relevant economic principles. But these are exceptions. Normally courts avoid this kind of conflict.

Parliamentary systems, in their own way, normally suppress conflicts with the bureaucracy: party discipline limits the topics the party addresses, so the public is allowed to express itself only on this small menu. In Sweden, the elected ministers are forbidden to interfere in the work of the bureaucracies. In much of the rest of Europe, this is the *de facto* situation. In the pandemic, this discipline breaks down: the bureaucracies are scrutinized for their actions; parties cannot control the menu of topics allowed to be public concerns, and the press cannot ignore the crisis. The public comes into its own. But the public itself is exposed as something less than it was taken to be.

The Public

What is the public? In normal times, it is represented by the media. What the public thinks, feels, wants, emotes about, is recreated into an image. The image is created by elites, who tend to remake the public in its own image. But the history of Western thought from Plato forward is replete with dualisms about the public; the good public is the one which acquiesces. The bad public is the one which does not. The good public accepts the myth of the metals. The bad public, the mob, follows demagogues, silver tongued orators, and today "rejects science." Jürgen Habermas spent much of his career attacking the actual public in favor of an ideal public. But he made his peace with a certain picture of public discourse, which we can treat as a representation of the normal: the important public discussions are undertaken in the high-class press, by worthy discussants; the people gain access to this higher order of public thought through the press; they can then choose between the worthies (Habermas 2006). Social media, such as Facebook and Twitter, and blogs circulated through these media, as well as open comments sections on mainstream digital news media, have undermined this model, and the response has treated this "wild" form of public exchange as the embodiment of the bad public, which needs to be controlled and the content it produces and consumes policed.

The old normal and the new digital mob coexisted for a time. But in the crisis they diverged. The old form, of elite discourse played out as a drama for the public, failed, because the opinions of experts were so divergent, changed so often, they could not be gravely endorsed by people like Brooks for the masses to consume. By a familiar process of interest-detection, the public seized on the political motivations of the experts, the policy makers, and the pundits. Much of this resembled conspiracy theorizing. The *bien pensants* were horrified by this commentary. For them it proved that the unrestricted flow of actual public engagement spread falsehoods, and did not lead, as the theatre of elite discussion did, to consensus. It becomes a Gladiatorial arena, as some social science commentators put it (Costa and Murphy 2020).

This, however, was the actual public, which was now able to express itself, focus on the facts that it understood best or could understand best, and make inferences from these facts, without deferring to correct opinions paraded before them. The inferences were not flattering to the major sources of information, which exposed themselves as partisan and wrong on many matters that could be readily assessed through a variety of sources. The vast explosion of cases that was supposed to follow the students' spring break was never mentioned again. When protests broke out over the death of George Floyd, the advice to avoid large crowds and the restrictions on gathering not only disappeared, but the people most adamant that public events and churches should be shut down for months suddenly approved of the protests and encouraged participation. These inconsistencies exposed the partisanship of the "expertise" on offer. The information the public worked with was not the best. But neither was the information held by the experts, or the state. And it was the only domain in which self-interest and agenda-driven policies could be openly debated for what they were.

The End Game

One of the many internet commentators invoked the ghost of Karl Popper in the course of the discussion, and asked what had happened to "falsifiability," which for Popper had marked the line between science and non-science. It did not go away. The pandemic controversy evolved into two sides. Each side made a large epistemic bet on the outcome. The exponents of shutting down insisted that the worst was yet to come, that nothing should be allowed to happen until there was a vaccine, and that the most stringent state measures should remain in force indefinitely. For them it was important that many people, especially the people they disliked, who had resisted the measures, should suffer. The price of what they regarded as science denial should be death. It was an embarrassment to them that in the US after three months of crisis, two-thirds of the deaths were in the communities controlled by their kind of leader, who had imposed their kind of policy. Having others die would confirm the correctness of their opinions. They eagerly relayed any information suggesting that there was a "spike" in the number of cases in places that had re-opened to normal business and life. Having poor and Black people die would confirm their moral evaluations of the politicians who resisted the measures. It would show that they valued profits over people. The proponents of re-opening had their own bet: that the effects would not be severe, and that the effects of shutting down, not only on people's financial well-being but on their health, were likely to be worse than the results of re-opening.

Agambem's question remains. Is the pandemic the exceptional event, after which a new normal will emerge? Or is it the normalization of the exception, the making permanent of a state of affairs in which the state expands its powers of surveillance and control, and extends its substitution of the legitimation of the expert for democratic legitimacy? Is it the result of a long process of expansion and substitution which was merely revealed by the pandemic? Tocqueville, in his *Ancien Regime*, treated the French Revolution in this way: as a visible episode in the centuries-long workings of the secret force of equality. But it reveals more. The illusion of the liberal democratic order, in which state policy emerged from reasoned discussion and in which experts merely stated truths was stripped away. The yawning gap between the messiness of conflicting experiments and lab notebooks and a coherent, accountable policy that balanced interests in the face of a wicked problem was revealed. Brooks' collapse of expertise into authority erased the illusion of the non-politicality of expertise. The demonization of the public by the trope of science vs. anti-science dispelled the illusion of a public that participated in its own governance vanished. And the eagerness of politicians to use emergency powers despite the confusion showed how much latent power was already there.

References

Bachrach, P. and M. S. Baratz (1962) Two Faces of Power. *The American Political Science Review* 56 (4): 947–952.

Bachrach, P. and M. S. Baratz (1975) Power and Its Two Faces Revisited: A Reply to Jeffrey Debnam. *The American Political Science Review* 69 (3): 900–904.

Bennington, B. (2014) Crisis Communication: Sense-Making and Decision-Making by the CDC under Conditions of Uncertainty and Ambiguity during the 2009–2010 H1N1 Pandemic. PhD Dissertation, University of South Florida, 20 June, 2014.

Brooks, D. (2020) The First Invasion of America: And the Cultural Earthquake It's Unleashing. New York Times Opinion, 21 May. https://www.nytimes.com/2020/05/21/opinion/us-coronavirus-history.html

A version of this article appears in print on Jan. 10, 2020, Section A, Page 27 of the New York edition with the headline: Trump Has Made Us All Stupid.

Costa, C. and M. Murphy (2020) The Future of Public Intellectualism Lies in Reforming the Digital Public Sphere. *Blogs LSE*, 9 January. https://blogs.lse.ac.uk/impactofsocialsciences/2020/01/09/the-future-of-public-intellectualism-lies-in-reforming-the-digital-public-sphere/?fbclid=IwAR3hMnlsHkszbM014X4jq4W4 g7k987kTWPr6QV3NCbuCb-tQYDb7Lt_3ohY

Debnam, G. (1975) Nondecisions and Power: The Two Faces of Bachrach and Baratz. *The American Political Science Review* 69 (3): 889–899.

Grimes, D. A. and K. F. Schulz (2012) False Alarms and Pseudo-Epidemics: The Limitations of Observational Epidemiology. *Obstetrics & Gynecology* 120 (4): 920–927.

Habermas, J. (2006) Political Communication in Media Society: Does Democracy Still Enjoy an Epistemic Dimension? The Impact of Normative Theory on Empirical Research. *Communication Theory* 16: 411–426.

Heer, J. (2020) How Stanford Lost Its Soul. *The Nation*, 20 May, 2020. https://www.thenation.com/article/society/stanford-lost-soul-coronavirus/

Higgs, R. (2012 [1987]) *Crisis and Leviathan: Critical Episodes in the Growth of American Government.* Oxford: Oxford University Press.

Koppl, R. (2018) *Expert Failure*, Cambridge: Cambridge University Press.

Laiz, M. Á. (2020) New Viruses, Old Foundations. COVID-19, Global Health, and the Bill and Melinda Gates Foundation. *Order beyond Borders*, 28 May. https://ordersbeyondborders.blog.wzb.eu/2020/05/28/new-viruses-old-foundations-covid-19-global-health-and-the-bill-and-melinda-gates-foundation/

Marcus, M. and I. Oransky (2020) Just How Historic Is the Latest Covid-19 Science Meltdown? *Wired*. 9 June. https://www.wired.com/story/just-how-historic-is-the-latest-covid-19-science-meltdown/

Pyle, G. F. (1969) The Diffusion of Cholera in the United States in the Nineteenth Century. *Geographical Analysis* 1 (1): 59–75. https://doi.org/10.1111/j.1538–4632.1969.tb00605.x

Scheppele, K. L. (2010) Exceptions That Prove The Rule: Embedding Emergency Government In Everyday Constitutional Life. In: J. K. Tulis (ed.) *The Limits of Constitutional Democracy*, Princeton: Princeton University Press, 124–154.

Schmitt, C. ([1921] 2014) *Dictatorship*, trans. M. Hielzl and G. Ward. Cambridge: Polity Press.

Schmitt, C. ([1923] 2010) *Political Theology: Four Chapters on the Concept of Sovereignty*, ed. and trans. G. Schwab, The Chicago: University of Chicago Press.

Turner, S. (2003) *Liberal Democracy 3.0: Civil Society in an Age of Experts*, London: Sage Publications.

Turner, S. (2010) Normal Accidents of Expertise. *Minerva* 48: 239–258. DOI:10.1007/s11024–010–9153-z http://www.springerlink.com/content/jt755540u5294274/

Turner, S. (2014) *The Politics of Expertise*, New York: Routledge.

Turner, S. (2020) Democracy, Liberalism, and Discretion: The Political Puzzle of the Administrative State. In: D. F. Hardwick and L. Marsh (eds.) *Reclaiming Liberalism*, London: Palgrave.

Jan Zielonka
Who Should be in Charge of Pandemics? Scientists or Politicians?

Liberals have long complained that populist politicians ignore scientists and science.[1] However, since the outbreak of the pandemic it seems that our lives are in the hands of scientists rather than politicians. On April 10th the Italian weekly *L'Espresso* ran the headline: "The seven most powerful people in Italy: today scientists (alone) are at the helm."[2] When the coronavirus exploded, the British government established a Scientific Advisory Group for Emergencies, also known as SAGE, to address the emerging crisis. Even President Trump has made frequent references to experts and "scientific" evidence when promoting new medical "wonders" for combatting Covid, or trying to convince the American public of his "superior" way of handling the crisis.

Should we rejoice that Trump, Kaczyński or Johnson seem to be following science and perhaps are no longer fully in charge? This chapter will argue that there is no simple answer to this question. Economists, too, are offering suggestions on tackling the economic impact of the pandemic – albeit suggesting different solutions than medical doctors – but both groups are working on the basis of patchy evidence. Some of them have murky relations with either governments or firms, or even both. And in a democracy we want to know that those in charge are elected and accountable. This is the case with politicians, however imperfect – but not with their scientific advisors.

Are Doctors always Right?

We tend to assume that during a pandemic, medical doctors are in a better position than politicians to decide which course of action is correct. This may be so in some cases, but there are some difficult questions about the role of medical expertise which ought to be addressed.

First, medical specialists do not represent a unified front because there are different ways of combating Covid-19. Differences emerge from diverse specialisa-

---

1 Part of this chapter appeared in *OpenDemocracy:* https://www.opendemocracy.net/en/can-europe-make-it/who-should-be-charge-doctors-or-politicians/
2 https://espresso.repubblica.it/inchieste/2020/04/10/news/i-sette-scienziati-che-comandano-in-italia-1.347039

https://doi.org/10.1515/9783110713350-004

tions – clinical doctors have a different perspective than those specialised in health administration, for instance. Even doctors from the same specialisation embrace competing theories and empirical data. Since data regarding Covid-19 are still scarce, these theories often resemble speculations. The "Herd Immunity" theory is the most notable example. So how do we know which doctors are right and which are wrong? And who should make this judgment?

Second, combatting Covid-19 involves a difficult balancing act between economic and medical factors. Doctors are seldom specialists in economics, and someone needs to weigh the merits of various factors when making the decision on how to combat the virus. In many countries, not only factories, but also schools, museums, stadiums, theatres and restaurants were closed for extended periods of time at the peak of the virus. In some countries, these establishments remain closed to this day. Fields as diverse as services, sport, education and culture are being affected by medical decisions. Moreover, making "rational" calculations (such as weighing up the economic, cultural and social impact of the pandemic) is difficult when dealing with ethical issues, and tackling Covid-19 is literally a matter of life and death. Although deaths are caused directly by the virus, they may also be indirectly caused by the "medicine" against the virus, which leads to economic or social hardship.

Third, medical specialists are not immune to corporate and political pressures. Many scientific advisors to governments are appointed along party lines. Others have intimate relationships with big pharma, insurance companies and the healthcare industry. All of these links represent ties to the corporate interests of the medical profession.

Asking these questions is not intended to discredit the merit of medical professionals' advice. Such advice is of course indispensable during a global pandemic. Rather, addressing these questions highlights the danger of drawing a simplistic dichotomy between competent, unbiased doctors and incompetent, partisan politicians. The extent to which this dichotomy reflects reality varies from place to place, and from person to person. I understand why many Americans prefer Dr Fauci over President Trump to lead the campaign against the virus. However, perhaps this points to pathologies of the US political system and does not necessarily apply to other countries.

Things are even more complicated when medics are appointed as ministers of health, which is a frequent practice in some countries. Where is the loyalty of such a minister located? Within his party/government or within his medical profession? Is a cardiologist a competent person to lead the fight against a viral pandemic? (Poland's minister of health till August 2020 was a cardiologist, for instance.) Is it better to have a medic as a minister of health than an economist or professional politician? There are no simple answers to these questions, and the empirical record of health ministers varies from place to place.

Competing Expertise

We usually understand that politicians are partisan and those from different parties tend to have conflicting views on most matters. It is often less appreciated that scientists are also partisan because they represent different scientific branches, theoretical schools and methodological preferences. Moreover, and quite understandably, scientists seek attention, recognition and funding. From the early days of the pandemic, economists and medics have been competing to be the bearers of bad news. The latter warned us about the dangers of Covid-19, especially if left to spread unchecked. For instance, Dr Marc Lipsitch (of Harvard) predicted early on that some 40 to 70 percent of people around the world would be infected by Covid-19.[3] Meanwhile the Institute for Health Metrics and Evaluation estimated up to 175,000 deaths in the United States related to the pandemic.[4] (This figure has sadly been already reached by the summer of 2020.) In the absence of adequate medicines to tackle the disease, doctors recommended measures which would effectively bring economies to a standstill, with no defined exit strategy.

Economists warned us not only about the financial costs of the measures recommended by doctors, but also the social and human ones. For instance, the UK Office for Budget Responsibility envisaged the UK economy shrinking by as much as 35 per cent, and two million more people unemployed.[5] Joseph Stiglitz, a Nobel prize economist, predicted that unemployment in the United States could hit 30 percent in 2020. Unemployment and hardship will in turn have a "negative effect on human capital,"[6] Barry Eichengreen (of Berkeley) argued: "it can lead do demoralization, depression, and other psychological trau-

---

3 https://www.theatlantic.com/health/archive/2020/02/covid-vaccine/607000/

4 http://www.healthdata.org/

5 In August 2020 the Office for National Statistics said that the GDP in the UK has actually fell in the second quarter by 20.4% compared with the previous three months – the biggest quarterly decline since comparable records began in 1955. See https://www.theguardian.com/business/2020/aug/12/uk-economy-covid-19-plunges-into-deepest-slump-in-history

6 https://www.theguardian.com/business/2020/apr/22/top-economist-us-coronavirus-response-like-third-world-country-joseph-stiglitz-donald-trump

mas, lowering affected individuals' productivity and attractiveness to employers."[7]

To be fair, some doctors and economists refused to join the gloom campaign, and tried to act as cheerleaders for the depressed public. On the day when the global death toll surpassed 100,000 (April 10, 2020), an Oxford Professor of Vaccinology, Sarah Gilbert, made headlines by saying that she is "80 per cent confident" that a vaccine could be developed by her team and ready for application by September the same year.[8] A few days earlier, a Professor of Economics from the University College London, Mariana Mazzucato, declared confidently "we now have an opportunity to use this crisis as a way to understand how to do capitalism differently.... [and] to bring a stakeholder approach to the centre of capitalism."[9]

Whether they put a positive or negative spin on their predictions, economists and doctors have been talking about a fast-moving and under-researched topic. This leaves a huge space for different interpretations (if not abuse) of their presented arguments and data. And this space is where politics of various types enter the game.

Great Confusion

Politicians who introduced universal lockdowns have been presenting statistics showing how many lives have been saved by their "prudent" measures. Politicians arguing against universal lockdowns or in favour of lifting restrictions have been offering statistics showing how many jobs (and perhaps lives) have been saved by their "sensible" approach to the virus. Since the virus has affected diverse regions, professions, genders and age groups differently, the public has been left guessing on what the true "best" approach is to combat Covid-19. Some politicians themselves have been unable to stick to one clear course of action; some who initially favoured lockdowns started to argue for greater freedoms

---

7 https://thebftonline.com/11/06/2020/barry-eichengreens-thoughts-rage-against-the-pan
demic/

8 https://www.bloomberg.com/news/articles/2020‑04‑11/coronavirus-vaccine-could-be-ready-
in-six-months-times. By the end of August, England's chief medical officer, Professor Chris Whitty, said that there was a "reasonable chance" there could be vaccines for the virus before the
winter of 2021–2022. Source: https://www.theguardian.com/world/2020/aug/22/whitty-says-it-
would-be-foolish-to-count-on-having-covid-jab-by-winter.

9 https://www.theguardian.com/commentisfree/2020/mar/18/the-covid-19-crisis-is-a-chance-to-
do-capitalism-differently

even though the number of victims claimed by Covid was rising rather than de-
clining. Poland in the summer of 2020 is one such example.

Scientific institutes, for their part, have been frequently revising their statistical estimates as well as models of gathering data. There is not necessarily anything sinister about this, because new medical data is arriving constantly, often
suggesting different interpretations. It is common practice for scientific and medical research to go through rounds of testing, revision and peer review and yet
more revision before results are publicised. However, it was difficult for citizens
to judge whether the announcements about new ways of counting Covid deaths,
for instance, were driven by medical or political considerations.[10] The result of
all this uncertainty has been the rise of conspiracy theories, ideological brink-
manship, and economic egocentricity.

As soon as April 2020, thousands of Americans took to the streets in several
states to protest against the Covid-19 lockdowns and stay-at-home orders issued
by their governors. Some of the people protesting were politically motivated and
rallied behind President Trump's campaign against governors from the Democratic Party. Other protesters were mobilized by the conspiracy theory site Info-
Wars that attacked Dr Anthony Fauci, the top public health expert on the White
House coronavirus taskforce. And there was also a group of protesters who prin-
cipally stood for their freedom and economic rights – even if the exercise of these
rights would curb the rights of their fellow citizens to health and safety. (According to a Pew Foundation Center survey published at the time, two thirds of Americans feared that state governments would lift restrictions on public activity too
quickly.[11] One third of the respondents worried that they would not do so quickly
enough.) In France, lockdown tensions also erupted around the same time, manifested in several nights of violence and vandalism in the suburbs of Paris, Tou-
louse, Strasbourg, Lyon and Bordeaux. Protests against the Covid-19 lockdowns
have only intensified with time, despite the rising numbers of victims. In the
spring of 2020 a small anti-lockdown protest took place in Berlin. In the summer,
a similar protest saw roughly 17,000 people gather under the slogan: "Day of

---

10 See e. g. Coronavirus: England death count review reduces UK toll by 5,000. Source: https://
www.bbc.com/news/health-53722711
11 https://www.huffpost.com/entry/coronavirus-country-reopen-pew_-
n_5e993099c5b63639081c1ddf?guccounter=1&guce_referrer=aHR0cHM6Ly93d3cuYmlu-
Zy5jb20v&guce_referrer_sig=AQAAAE38z72dERvEUNCgWXGC6EnGIfCWVspsBehOuO-
FIUfsjmlPqljruAIYnW7mGHaaZcDqgiksvfqt29aApfGKvd6WBBnAp_UuBnn4O_DyeC18aWEt-
Bo4ksklUHd7oOYT4lGYqLil6YlqF52j_y2se7bqtLHGq4JUbQ7CAlm6yzfaQD

Freedom – The End of the Pandemic". According to CNN, some protesters could be heard yelling, "We are the second wave."[12]

Confusing scientific evidence has given premium to ethical considerations, valuing preserving lives about all else. But even these considerations lack straightforward conclusions. The answer to these ethical dilemmas often depends on the questions being asked. Can human lives, even those of non-productive people, be sacrificed on the altar of mammon for the sake of the wider economy? Can we make the younger generation pay the huge price of prolonged lockdowns? Do poor people have the luxury of choosing between health security and employment security? Are the lives vulnerable to the virus more important than those at risk from the isolation, hunger, mental illness and spiralling domestic violence brought about by lockdown?

Are We All in the Same Boat?

The threat posed by the virus seems universal, but the capacities to address health and economic challenges vary greatly from place to place. Discrepancies in wealth and governance are especially striking between developed and developing regions, with Africa representing the greatest preoccupation. The Executive Director of the World Food Programme has predicted that Covid-19 will cause multiple famines of "biblical proportions."[13] In relatively wealthy Europe, the pandemic has most severely stricken two heavily indebted countries, Italy and Spain. In both these states, choosing the dates to close and reopen factories involved extremely difficult compromises between medical and economic considerations. As always, the power of organized interests matters in taking decisions. In Lombardy, the *Confindustria* (Italy's key business association) exerted considerable pressure on the regional and central governments to keep factories open despite the evolving epidemic, and only when trade unions organized a series of strikes were these factories closed.

The power of money has been particularly on display in the world of professional sport. The European Football Champions League matches between Atalanta (Bergamo) and Valencia, as well as between Liverpool and Atletico Madrid, were played in packed-out stadiums at a time when the virus was already widespread. When it was established that these matches contributed significantly to the explosion of infections, a video featuring a Spanish nurse asking the million-

---

12 https://edition.cnn.com/2020/08/01/world/berlin-germany-covid-19-protest-intl/index.html
13 https://edition.cnn.com/2020/04/22/africa/coronavirus-famine-un-warning-intl/index.html

aire-players to do her underpaid hospital work circulated widely on social media. The multi-billion-euro football industry has also been pressuring governments to allow matches to resume early, against medical advice.

Ideology has also played its part in the ongoing dispute. Neoliberals have always been suspicious of state intervention in private business. Yet as the virus has brought economies to a standstill, states have begun to intervene to help both employers and their employees to survive. The scale and duration of this state intervention has been a matter of hot debate, however. In an interview with Poland's daily *Rzeczpospolita*, the father of Eastern European post-communism neoliberal reforms, Leszek Balcerowicz, argued against "printing money" and distributing it in a way that "leads to abuse."[14] In his view, Poland's government used the crisis to extend the state's control over the economy and in particular the financial sector. The economy will soon bounce back, he argued, and hence there is no justification for state intervention, protectionism and the breaking of financial discipline.

Some "deeply concerned" economic commentators have gone even further and demanded the suspension of labour rights and environmental standards to help struggling enterprises. Whether such moves would equally benefit employees and shareholders is a matter of debate, of course. This brings us to another crucial point, namely the uneven distribution of benefits granted by governments in response to Covid-19. As governments throw huge money "out of a helicopter," it is important to examine who is benefiting from this policy most. The above-cited Professor Balcerowicz has argued that clients of the ruling party will be the key beneficiaries of unprecedented aid packages, while others have argued that big business will benefit most, regardless of political affiliation. The UN Special Rapporteur on extreme poverty and human rights, Philip Alston, has been particularly blunt:

> "The policies of many states reflect a social Darwinism philosophy that prioritises the economic interests of the wealthiest, while doing little for those who are hard at work providing essential services or unable to support themselves."[15]

The question has also been raised: who will settle the unprecedented bill? Will governments try to balance their budgets by raising taxes for the rich and by clamping down on tax avoidance schemes? Or will ordinary citizens be asked

14 https://www.rp.pl/Gospodarka/304139986-RZECZoBIZNESIE-Leszek-Balcerowicz-Ratunek-nie-moze-prowadzic-do-katastrofy-gospodarki.html
15 https://www.theguardian.com/politics/2020/apr/26/uk-coronavirus-response-utterly-hypocritical-says-un-poverty-expert

to shoulder most of the cost of the pandemic via value-added-tax (VAT) on their consumption, for instance?

The issue of international solidarity is also being hotly debated. Should the debts of poor countries be cancelled? Should the Eurozone introduce the mutualisation of debts? Should aid to the most stricken countries be linked to strict economic and political conditionality? And will the imposed conditions enhance or damage already fragile healthcare systems in poor countries?

The Dangers of Technopopulism

The coronavirus initially froze political battles and amplified the role of medical expertise. Yet with the passage of time, political battles resurfaced, and medical arguments were pushed aside. This has naturally sparked protests among the medical profession. For instance, in August 2020 a group of independent British medics openly distanced themselves from the UK government's decisions on contact tracing, reopening schools, restaurants and pubs, and relaxing social distancing.[16] The group was right in pointing to the political manipulation of the alleged scientific evidence. However, one can argue that there is the danger of converting serious political, economic and even cultural problems into medical ones. Policies to combat the pandemic have numerous implications, not just medical ones. These policies re-order our personal and professional lives; they challenge our interests and values, and produce losers and winners. The process of representing and mediating these different interests and values has practically been suspended, and we are in the hands of governments making speedy decisions with historical implications.

The hope that politicians and experts will engage with each other and in the end produce fair, non-partisan outcomes may prove naïve. The key protagonists on both sides are part of the state machine and bound by common interests. The group of medical experts working for governments includes not only physicians, but also a plethora of administrators in charge of the health infrastructure, purchasing medicines and medical equipment, negotiating with doctors, patients and insurers, and assessing the implications of health-related environmental, demographic or technological developments. These civil servants, administrators and experts are often self-interested, prejudiced, and as political as any other professional group close to power. Politicians are dependent on these experts

---

16 https://www.clickorlando.com/news/world/2020/08/12/uk-scientists-openly-question-gov ernments-pandemic-response/

to find a way out of the current crisis. They also need these experts to legitimise all the adopted policies and their huge costs.

The danger is that instead of advancing a common good, politicians and experts may form an informal network operating in a mode of "dirty togetherness" by exchanging favours, propagating expedient statistics, and silencing inconvenient truths.[17] Since there is no clear end to the current crisis and the stakes involved are huge, leaders may even face the temptation to rule by decree for a prolonged period of time with little transparency, public deliberation or accountability. This evokes the ghost of technopopulism.

In a forthcoming book on technopopulism, Chris Bickerton of Cambridge and Carlo Invernizzi-Accetti of New York argue that that technopopulists advance an "unmediated", monolithic conception of the common good, framed as the 'popular will', but which is essentially technocrats' "specific conception of political 'truth'". Bickerton and Invernizzi-Accetti's study of France, Italy and Spain – pre-Covid-19 – already demonstrates closed fusions of populists and experts leading to different local versions of technopopulism. Emmanuel Macron's *La République En Marche* was established by a tight-knit group of policy experts to challenge the "remote and self-serving" political establishment. French voters were invited to support an enlightened and effective leader capable of "achieving results" irrespective of ideological biases and parliamentary squabbles. The Spanish anti-establishment movement *Podemos*, which is part of the current coalition government, is called the "*partido de profesores*" and offers radical, but fairly pragmatic, if not technocratic solutions to Spain's political problems. The Italian Five Star Movement which used to campaign against vaccinations and other scientific "truths" is now part of a coalition government led by "Professor" Conte, acting in a highly responsible manner to combat the pandemic.

One would be tempted to believe that experts have a soothing and enlightening effect on populist politicians, but Bickerton and Invernizzi-Accetti argue that this is not necessarily the case. Instead we witness the politicisation of expertise. Technopopulists come forward with alternative scientific "truths" with little effort to establish a scientific, let alone political consensus. In their view "technopopulism increases the conflictuality of democratic competition, while at the same time depriving it of substance." Technopopulism also "exacerbates the separation of society from politics, while compensating for it with an increased use of the repressive apparatus of the state."

---

17 The term "dirty togetherness" was coined by Adam Podgórecki. See Podgórecki (1987). See also Wedel (2003).

These processes can now be observed in some countries of Central and Eastern Europe such as Hungary or Poland where populist politicians are utilizing anti-virus emergency measures to augment their powers beyond constitutional constraints. However, even in old democracies the "war" against Covid-19 is giving a platform to technopopulist manipulation. In the crisis caused by the virus, parliaments can hardly work normally, and citizens prioritise action over deliberation. In effect, we may erode democracy without strengthening healthcare systems. This could be one of the unwanted side effects caused by Covid-19.

The Battle for Truth

Covid-19 has arrived in Western democracies in the period of intense political conflict and chaos. "Populist" politicians question liberal policies and values; they are accused of twisting facts, manipulating statistical data, and lying. They are being blamed for playing on voters' prejudices, sentiments, and emotions while ignoring evident truths and facts. Facts are not only abused; the authority of facts themselves is also being questioned. It is often asserted that we live in the era of "post-truth."[18]

The pandemic has not stopped politicians from abusing facts and questioning science. President Trump's daily briefings provided the most vivid manifestation for this. Yet most of us assumed that the pandemic would vindicate science and bring the era of post-truth to its end. Unfortunately, there are few signs that this is indeed happening. In some sections of the public there is a growing realization that ignoring early warnings from doctors and entertaining illusions that Covid-19 is just another flu lead to thousands of otherwise avoidable deaths. Grave implications of ignoring or under-playing economic costs of the pandemic and the uneven distribution of the related burdens seem also apparent to many. That said, conspiracy theories are also more in vogue than ever. This has something to do with the roots of post-truth that the pandemic could hardly eradicate.

Post-truth is defined by the Oxford Dictionaries as "relating to or denoting circumstances in which objective facts are less influential in shaping public opinion than appeals to emotion and personal belief".[19] Several diverse factors are usually seen as responsible for post-truth, and they are usually associated with the Internet revolution: the availability of statistical data, complexity of

---

18 I spelled out this argument in Jan Zielonka (2018), especially pp. 25 – 29.
19 https://www.oxforddictionaries.com/press/news/2016/12/11/WOTY-16

human transactions, plurality of opinions, and sophistication of communication channels. So far, the pandemic has not eradicated any of these factors. Emotions played a very important part in people's responses to the pandemics. The pandemic generated a fury of new data, different ways of interpreting these data, and novel means of communication between experts and the public. This has obviously generated some confusion. Moreover, post-truth has much to do with the nature of science itself – a nature which has not been altered by the pandemic, but in my view, reinforced.

Scientists usually cherish pluralism, free speech and free choice, while refusing any simple truths and dogma. The best science, in their view, emerges from questioning the established truths and orthodoxies. Of course, scientists believe that the quest for truth(s) should be informed by empirical data. No wonder that we have seen a proliferation of institutions gathering statistical data, leading to what William Davies called the rise of the "facts industry."[20] In "media-saturated societies," success of this industry largely depends on the ability to "sell" its "scientific" results directly to the masses with the help of smartphones and laptops.[21] The problem is that on Facebook, Twitter, or WhatsApp everybody can be a provider of facts and truths, but being truly competitive requires sophisticated marketing skills, extensive PR, and effective spin. Each provider of new "evidence" has to distinguish her/his truths from those provided by others. More often than not it pays to be outrageous rather than just objective or "truthful". We now have sites generating "fake" news and those trying to counter them with truths, so called fact-checking sites. Most of these adversarial sites claim to rely on "scientific" evidence. "Consumers" of many competing, and often contrasting facts and truths are increasingly confused, distrustful, and biased. They tend to form like-minded clusters; they trust only facts that support their personal views or feelings. Technology reinforces that kind of partisanship. Facebook's algorithms are designed to crowd individuals' newsfeeds with content similar to material they previously "liked" or shared. Thanks to this "filter bubble", those who believe that Covid-19 is just another flu are most likely to follow people with similar views on the social media. As a result, they probably think that their views are popular and legitimate.

In his review of a book on the history of magic, John Gray suggested that magic and science are not at odds but inextricably linked. [22] This seems partic-

---

20 http://www.nytimes.com/2016/08/24/opinion/campaign-stops/the-age-of-post-truth-politics. html?_r=0. See also, Davies, William (2016), *The Happiness Industry: How the Government and Big Business Sold Us Well-being.* (Verso)
21 https://www.johnkeane.net/media-decadence-and-democracy/ See also, Keane (2013).
22 https://www.newstatesman.com/culture/books/2020/08/realism-magic

ularly cogent in the era of post-truth. The pandemic exposed numerous flaws of the science "industry", competing for attention, funds and access to power. Science requires ever more data, and competing interpretations of this data, yet the greatest asset of science is turning out to be its greatest liability. If there is no one single truth, how do we know which scientific truths are to be trusted? How can we distinguish scientists from magicians? Are truths with better spin and PR not more likely to prevail? Will those with greater connections and funds try to impose their own truths on all of us?

Conclusions: Why Politics Matter

It is far from my intention to suggest that science is worthless, and scientists are greedy and incompetent. My intention is to show that science is not about absolute truths, and always works with incomplete data. This particularly concerns such fields as economics where it is often hard to distinguish theories from ideologies. However, natural sciences are also subject to revisions and contrasting interpretations as manifested by such famous figures as Copernicus or Einstein. Scientists, as all humans, have virtues as well as flaws and it is wrong to entertain any sweeping generalisations about their propensity to do good or evil. The last comment also concerns politicians, of course.

Three general observations can be drawn from this chapter. First, the marriage of science and politics is not only confined to crises. All well-functioning states ought to have their respective health and economic policies informed by science. Politics intervenes in healthcare, for instance, to make citizens' wellbeing less dependent on chance, fate or money. Political interventions in the healthcare system are believed to make it more rational and scientific; they are supposed to optimize the use of the newest technologies, collective financial resources, and administrative capacities. For example, hard choices have to be made between the use of extremely expensive devices which will save the few, and more traditional ones which will benefit the many. At times, the medical profession has resisted political interventions in its work, but more often than not, doctors have joined politicians in expanding state intervention in medical affairs. This is because state intervention has often implied more resources for healthcare and increased political influence for doctors.

The problem is that political interventions are seldom non-partisan, and do not always lead to the greater professionalisation of the healthcare system. Right-wingers often argue that personal health is chiefly a private rather than a public matter. They also tend to insist that the market rather than state is better suited to govern healthcare. Left-wingers believe that health policies are a matter for the public and not for individuals to decide. For them, an important aim of the healthcare system is equality, and this aim can hardly be secured by the private market alone. The poor, migrants, refugees, and disabled are affected by the current pandemics more than other groups and they are seldom able to access the private health care system; sometimes even the public one.

Moreover, the professionalisation of the healthcare system has often depended more on local, country-specific capacities than ideological preferences. In fact, many right-wing governments have embraced a public health system, while many left-wing governments have overseen the growth of private hospitals and cuts to public ones. The bargaining power of the medical profession and health industry also plays a role here, as do societal trends such as demographics and aging populations.

Although private and public investments in health and healthcare are now enormous across the entire Western world, there is no unified solution to deal with them. After World War II, the financing and organisation of healthcare shifted from the private toward the public sector. However, this trend was halted or even reversed in some cases with the arrival of the neo-liberal revolution. In Western countries we have also witnessed the tendency to respect the authority of the scientific and medical professions, and to keep healthcare insulated from excessive political control. And yet, since the late 1960s the technical authority of doctors has repeatedly been challenged not only by those demanding more "democratic" health care, but also by those unhappy with the soaring health budgets of their respective governments.

The second observation concerns a difficult balance between economic and medical considerations. It is hard to strike this balance in a period of relative tranquillity, but in crises, the pressure of competing claims can prove unbearable for governments. This is evident in responses to the Covid-19 pandemic. Keeping economies locked down for one or two years was found impossible, yet lifting restrictions could not but cause further illness and death. As the mayor of Bergamo put it dramatically on La7 TV: "We have to choose: do we want to die from the virus or from hunger?"[23] (The northern Italian city of Bergamo was stricken by the virus more than most other places and this has brought its sizeable economic sector to virtual bankruptcy.)

The dichotomy sketched by the Italian mayor was overly dramatic, we may argue. Economic and health considerations are not mutually exclusive. A quick glance at the body of work in the field of developmental economics is

---

23 https://www.la7.it/piazzapulita/video/gori-bergamo-stiamo-navigando-al-buio-23-04-2020-321219

enough to see that growth and productivity depend on public health, education, working conditions, and even levels of equality. The opposite is also true: it is hard to have a sound healthcare system with a bankrupt economy. However, in the heat of the public debate caused by Covid-19, these nuances and interdependencies have been lost. Tough decisions have had to be made under the pressure of time and rapidly-evolving events. The contrast between economic and health security has been artificially blown out of proportion. Decisions on whether to reopen factories, stadiums, schools, theatres and restaurants have had to be made quickly on the basis of conflicting arguments and patchy evidence. Politicians have had no option but to step in and make these difficult decisions. They may have been poorly prepared for this task, but they could no longer hide behind scientists – either economic or medical ones.

The third observation concerns democratic processes. In the initial stage of the pandemic, governments could adopt stringent policies with tacit public acquiescence. This permissive public consensus did not last long, however. The risks and burdens were enormous, and they have been distributed unevenly. Successive governmental decisions have involved difficult trade-offs, which have had to be explained, justified and hopefully backed by the public, or at least large part of it. Working out a much-needed social contract has proved difficult for politicians without a loyal electoral base and ready-made strategies. No wonder some of them have failed to resist the temptation to rule autocratically by trial and error. The problem with this autocratic approach is that each serious error could lead to misery and rebellion. Politics can only enjoy lasting legitimacy when it is done "by the people," and not just "for the people." The former requires a serious dialogue between the rulers and the ruled. It also requires difficult bi-partisan compromises and the intelligent balancing of medical and economic necessities. In countries where national leaders are admired by only half of voters, and hated by another half, it is difficult to strike compromises and perform sensible balancing acts. Unfortunately, this situation was the case in most democracies at the time Covid-19 began to "bite."

Solutions for dealing with this danger are not particularly innovative. We should unmask myths of national unity and challenge claims that there are no alternatives to the policies of our "enlightened" leaders. Democratic politics is about managing conflicts of interests and values because pandemics or other calamities affect diverse groups of people differently, and these people cherish different values. None of the calamities we are experiencing argue against transparency and accountability. Without observing these principles, rulers will always try to escape responsibility for their behaviour and spread convenient lies, however "scientific."

Scientists have always played an important role in formulating, communicating and legitimizing policies. However, I have tried to argue that they should not replace politicians in doing their job. This is not only because scientists are insufficiently accountable, but also because we do not want to have an overly politicised science. The job of scientists is to confront us with some hard truths and present possible options for handling crises. In democracy, it is ultimately for the citizens to make their choices. Politicians can facilitate a democratic decision-making process, but obviously, this is not always the case for reasons beyond the focus of this chapter.

References

Bickerton, C. J. and Invernizzi-Accetti, C. (2021) *Technopopulism. The New Logic of Democratic Politics* Oxford University Press.

Davies, William (2016), *The Happiness Industry: How the Government and Big Business Sold Us Well-being.* (Verso)

Keane, John (2013) *Democracy and Media Decadence*, Cambridge: Cambridge University Press.

Adam, P. (1987) Polish Society: A Sociological Analysis, *Praxis International*, 7 (1).

Wedel, J. E. (2003) Dirty Togetherness: Institutional Nomads, Networks, and the State-Private Interface in Central and Eastern Europe and the Former Soviet Union, *Polish Sociological Review*, 142: 139–159.

Zielonka, J. (2019) *Counter-Revolution. Liberal Europe in Retreat.* Oxford: Oxford University Press.

Jonathan White
Emergency Europe after Covid-19

Europe entered the 2020s like it entered the 2010s, with authorities engaged in the politics of emergency. 'Extraordinary times require extraordinary action', declared ECB head Christine Lagarde in March 2020 when announcing a new purchasing policy.[1] It was time for a 'unique response to a unique situation', said German Chancellor Merkel when outlining a new European fund.[2] Like national lockdowns and border closures, such measures were announced as exceptional and temporary, though the duration of their application was often unclear. For an unspecified period of time, authorities found themselves governing in unscripted ways to fend off far-reaching threats. While similar patterns unfolded across much of the world, in Europe they followed a decade of emergency politics increasingly distinctive in form, centred on the structures of the European Union.

Emergency rule is an old idea. In one form or another, it has been enacted and theorised from the Roman Republic to the modern state. Thinkers as diverse as Machiavelli, Rousseau, Marx and Schmitt have approached it as a foundational political question, exploring how cities, republics and states might enact it. Many still build on their insights (Honig 2009; Lazar 2009; Manin 2008; Agamben 2005; Lemke 2018). But more recently emergency government has become cross-border in range, acquiring novel dynamics in the process. In Europe especially, the story of the 2010s, from the Euro crisis to migration politics, was the rise of a distinctively *transnational* politics of emergency. Whereas emergency rule has tended to be conceived as concentrating power in the hands of a unitary sovereign, here one saw the interplay of national governments with supranational agents of various kinds, working through the EU and around it. Decisions involved those spread across multiple institutions and territories, without a clear hierarchical relation. This was emergency rule without a defined sovereign, informally co-produced by the many.

While the handling of Covid-19 differs in ways from Europe's emergency politics of the preceding decade, the new template of exceptionalism shines through. This chapter revisits the study of 'Emergency Europe' (White 2015a, 2015b, 2019) in the light of recent developments, drawing out the characteristi-

---

1 The PEPP: https://twitter.com/Lagarde/status/1240414918966480896
2 https://www.theguardian.com/world/2020/jun/26/for-europe-survive-economy-needs-survive-angela-merkel-interview-in-full

https://doi.org/10.1515/9783110713350-005

cally transnational forms of exceptionalism on display. It charts the transition over the course of the crisis from domestic exceptionalism to cross-border emergency politics, as governments started coordinating and building new collective arrangements, and as supranational authorities expanded their powers. It shows how these developments gave rise to some familiar democratic challenges to do with the concentration and informalisation of power, here involving a plurality of executive agents (cf. Scheuerman 2017). Additionally the chapter explores how these manoeuvres can engender a characteristic response, a form of *anti-emergency* politics that denounces this template while resembling it. Whether EU representatives should be granted more powers to act in an emergency is one of the questions examined in conclusion.

Rather than just adaptation to the force of necessity – 'crisis management', as it tends to be termed – the politics of this period reflects a distinct governing logic, beyond the specifics of any one crisis (Calhoun 2004; Head 2015; White 2019; Kreuder-Sonnen 2019). Far-reaching measures in extreme situations are employed to keep existing power relations broadly intact. EU representatives have moved fast in the name of recovery, but with innovations tending to reinforce a highly imperfect pre-Covid order and give actors more discretion to defend it in future. While crisis moments also present opportunities for more radical change, established authorities seem unlikely to lead this. For all the innovations and the talk of new beginnings, their actions are generally restorative in focus: more drastic change awaits its agents.

Transnational Emergency Politics: Origins and Forms

Unlike many recent crises, that of Covid-19 did not begin in the economic sphere. For many years prior, Europe's leaders had been invoking disease metaphors to describe the business of government – contagion on the markets, exposure to risk – but this time the language was literal. For all the apparent naturalness of its origins in disease, there is nothing more exogenous about the Corona story. Things become crises only in their encounter with human institutions and value-systems. But the relation between political and economic power has been distinctive in this instance. Whereas in the Euro crisis, financial markets, banks and major corporations lined up to support emergency interventions broadly in their favour, with Covid-19 one is reminded that (fractions of) these interests can be rather less enthusiastic towards emergency measures and keen to hasten their end. How far there is really a trade-off between disease control and corporate interests is doubtful, both in the sense that early lockdowns may be ultimately less disruptive, also given the market opportunities presented by a health crisis[3]. But emergency rule in the age of Covid-19 was not driven in the first instance by economics.

The EU governs crises as crises of markets, money or the movement of people, or it does not govern them at all. Founded on a core set of purposes to do with economic interdependence, it is best able to act when these goals are in question (Isiksel 2016; White 2019). With Covid-19 framed early from a public-health perspective, it took time for the EU apparatus to be involved. The handling of Covid-19 looked initially like an aggregate of national responses. Governments closed borders, sought to re-nationalise their economies, and adopted urgent measures of their own devising. This was emergency rule in the image of the sovereign state; the order for lockdowns was not going to come from Brussels. Yet in a variety of ways this has been the *transnational* politics of emergency, in its origins, conduct and likely legacy.

Emergency modes of rule, though often associated with dramatic displays of power, tend to arise from some form of weakness. Both in their rhetoric and context, they are a politics of last resort. In the Euro crisis of the early 2010s, that was the weakness of executive agents before the financial markets; in the migration politics of 2015/6, it was their weakness before far-Right movements turning mass publics against them. In the Corona-crisis, it has first and foremost been about the weakness of state capacity – underfunded, part-privatised and under-prepared health systems, and administrations where the voices of neoliberal economists still carry loudest. Generally speaking, the weaker the institutions and those in charge, the more extreme the response to hard times. Weak leaders find themselves pressed to do radical things to keep order. They are also pressed to do symbolic things – e.g. closing national borders, thereby suspending in Europe the Schengen regime – which, experts tell us,[4] add little in security terms but convey the impression of activity.

Could an emergency response to Covid-19 have been averted? The question is always central to the normative evaluation of such measures (Sorell 2013, p.5). Given the threat of a global pandemic was foreseeable and foreseen – it was 'SARS2', not something wholly unprecedented[5] – one may assume the weakness of state capacity could have been addressed. Countries going into the pandemic with relatively robust public services – e.g. South Korea, Japan, Germany – were

---

3 https://jacobinmag.com/2020/05/neoliberals-response-pandemic-crisis
4 https://www.dw.com/en/will-more-mobility-in-europe-increase-coronavirus-spread/av-53624159
5 https://www.versobooks.com/blogs/4608-on-the-epidemic-situation

able to avoid the most extreme lockdown measures in spring 2020, while those with weaker systems – in central Europe and the Balkans – were amongst those to close down early. That countries varied in their response underlines that this was not just 'crisis management', understood as functionally-determined adaptation, but an emergency *politics* in which different courses of action were available. Were they, though, equally available to all? In a global system of financial capitalism, combined with regional constraints like those of the eurozone, it is easier for some countries than others to prepare for extreme circumstances. It is easier for some to borrow and invest, raise taxes, and avoid loans whose conditions require austerity budgets. The capacity for preparation is unevenly distributed. While recourse to emergency rule is always at some level a choice, it is guided by structural factors beyond the sovereignty of individual states.

Once some countries started to introduce emergency measures, the pressure increased on others to do likewise. In public discourse, the disease threat and the response were assessed comparatively from the beginning, with daily charts showing how countries fared against peers, also locating them in time (Italy as 'two weeks ahead' of Spain, etc.).[6] A mix of upward and downward transnational comparisons was central to the narrative in each country, a way to find orientation in the face of the unknown. Perhaps this accounts for some early decisions to pursue lockdowns, as governments sought to avoid falling out of step or cajoled their neighbours to stay aligned.[7] As the Swedish government learned, to do things differently is to announce your agency and attract critical assessment; to chart the same path as neighbours is to minimise the responsibility burden. The same dynamics of comparison explain the difficulties in discontinuing emergency measures: peer countries offer counterfactuals for the choices made, and each government has reason not to seem lax. Even in the most 'nationalised' phase of the pandemic, the cross-border frame was central.

As the economic dimensions of the crisis became more pronounced, executive activity in Europe became overtly transnational. From mid-March 2020, a series of initiatives, from ECB activism (PSPP, PEPP, its extension in early June) to new cross-national arrangements for loans and grants (the Recovery and Resilience Facility), were promoted to contend with threats to the eurozone both direct (speculation) and indirect (macro-economic divergence). With some notable variations, these measures extend the governing template seen in Europe's emergency politics of the 2010s. Actions at odds with how the EU is ex-

---

6 https://www.ft.com/content/a26fbf7e-48f8-11ea-aeb3-955839e06441
7 https://www.independent.co.uk/news/uk/politics/coronavirus-france-travel-ban-british-boris-johnson-cases-a9408221.html#gsc.tab=0

pected to work are pursued in the name of exceptional circumstances, nominally for a temporary period but with potentially lasting effects, in a way that supports existing socio-economic relations and foregrounds executive power. These actions go beyond merely domestic forms of exceptionalism, and beyond unilateral departures from EU norms, to include exceptional measures by supranational authorities and state governments acting in concert.

Transnational executive power was not channelled on this occasion through new 'de novo' bodies (Bickerton, Hodson & Puetter 2015). There has been no Troika equivalent, nor the country-specific targeting it enabled. The core EU institutions have been more prominent than at times in the 2010s. Possibly this is a lesson learned, or simply a quirk – setting up new bodies under lockdown is hard. Arguably it is also an effect of the pandemic being treated as hitting all states equally. Though its uneven course has been shaped by past policies – including a decade of Troika-mandated austerity in the European South – there has been a preference amongst EU authorities for treating this as a 'universal' shock for which blame should not be apportioned.[8] Once questions of culpability and moral hazard are removed, it becomes easier to govern through a general framework.

What remained constant though was the embrace of unscripted modes of rule. Existing forums offered plenty of scope for working around the norms of the core institutions. With the failure of the European Council to reach agreement on a common economic response in late March 2020, this task was transferred to the 'Eurogroup', the name given to informal gatherings of Eurozone finance ministers.[9] As in the Euro crisis, its uncodified character meant discretion could be exercised with fewer constraints and burdens of publicity. One can detect from the Eurogroup press release of 9th April the range of issues discussed in this way, from the SURE loan system to the conception of the Recovery Fund.[10] In addition to the Eurogroup, the European Stability Mechanism was another shadowy entity to enjoy second wind.[11] There was little need, it seems, to create new para-institutional formations, since those inherited from previous rounds of emergency politics could still play the role required.

---

8 https://www.ecb.europa.eu/press/blog/date/2020/html/ecb.blog200319~11f421e25e.en.html

9 https://www.consilium.europa.eu/media/43076/26-vc-euco-statement-en.pdf

10 https://www.consilium.europa.eu/en/press/press-releases/2020/04/09/report-on-the-compre hensive-economic-policy-response-to-the-covid-19-pandemic/

11 https://www.esm.europa.eu/content/europe-response-corona-crisis

Hour of the Pluralised Executive

The use of unconventional arrangements in the name of emergency is one way executive power builds pre-eminence over other institutions and the wider public. This pattern has been pronounced at the state level during Covid-19, most clearly where governments have used open-ended emergency decrees (Hungary), also in the challenges posed by parliamentary suspensions and limits on gathering. But the use of informal contexts in transnational politics gives ample further scope for the ascendancy of the executive, here understood not as a unitary institution but the precarious coordination achieved by the elites of several.

Especially in a system without a sovereign centre, emergency rule encourages the concentration of power in the hands of individuals and their networks. Leaders retreat into inner circles and strengthen their ties *across* institutions at the expense of those within. It was said of Commission President Von der Leyen in this period that she 'surrounded herself with two or three people and is not listening to other people.'[12] The observation echoes things said of ECB head Draghi at the height of the Euro crisis – that he ran affairs through a 'kitchen cabinet' of loyalists.[13] Presidentialisation may be a secular trend, but it is in periods of emergency that it is accelerated and most easily rationalised. Fast-moving conditions offer a warrant for cutting out chains of delegation and reclaiming power in informal networks. The diffusion of power across many institutions – what Alexander Hamilton once called the 'plurality of the executive' (Hamilton et al, 1787 / 2008, no. 70) – creates an elaborate system inviting centralisation and de-institutionalisation in times of stress.

The concentration of executive power is paired with a recalibration of the kind of authority invoked. The technocratic principle has always been central to EU affairs, and never more so than when urgent problem-solving is the order of the day. Decisions improvised swiftly by leaders will typically be hard to legitimise by appeal to a democratic mandate: presenting them as responsive to expertise is logical, if only sometimes sincere. But the technocratic principle has to be rethought in the emergency context. Discretion comes to be emphasised over rules. 'COVID-19 represents a new form of economic shock that cannot

---

12 https://www.ft.com/content/775c4db2-4e3d-426f-b937-243f0673cc14?segmentID=09cf3415-e461-2c4a-a8cc-80acc4846679; the *FT* piece here quotes an EU official; more generally it talks of her 'over-reliance on a small group of trusted advisers – some of whom came with her from Berlin – to lead a 32,000-strong bureaucracy.'

13 https://www.reuters.com/article/us-ecb-draghi-insight/draghi-leaves-lagarde-to-heal-rift-at-european-central-bank-idUSKBN1X80HC

be tackled using the textbooks of the past,' Lagarde observed in April 2020.[14] Officials recast themselves as practical, flexible, and independent-minded – possessors of the deeper insight that lies in knowing when to set aside yesterday's formulas. Eurozone policy rules were re-described as 'self-imposed limits,' revisable to preserve deeper goals of stability.[15] With Lagarde echoing Draghi's willingness to invoke 'broad discretion', this was technocracy as know-how, as a feel for the situation. Importantly, as discretion comes to the fore, the notion that technocrats are enacting defined, delegated tasks becomes hard to maintain. What expertise demands in an unfamiliar situation is inherently difficult to determine: it can be recruited to rationalise any number of actions, ranging from the more scientifically-informed to the less so. The boundary between technocracy and politics becomes more blurred, and the power of individuals more elastic.

Of course, discretionary power need not be arbitrary or self-serving, and one may grant that policy-makers act for the public interest as they see it. Theirs is, let us assume, a good-faith effort in a difficult situation. But even the best motivations are deployed to serve some ends rather than others. Emergency discretion leaves citizens few opportunities to clarify and contest the decisions made and why: it requires them to take authorities on trust. This holds especially in a transnational context where the constraints on executive power are traditionally weak. Even where executive dominance is not openly abused, it is an unwelcome condition nonetheless.

Emergency logic is slippery not just because much hangs on the discretion of those in power, but because they acquire a licence to be vague in how they plan to use it. When governing is approached as responding to necessity, decision-makers acquire great flexibility, for who can know what necessity will demand. Such a rationale allows the maintenance of a policy indefinitely or with serial extensions, while also preparing the possibility of its termination at whatever point normality is said to be restored, when 'recovery' is complete. This gives measures an ambiguous status. Emergency logic can be used to render potentially desirable moves temporary – e. g. the suspension of state aid rules that restrict public spending,[16] and new fiscal policies intended to support workers, business and states[17] – on the understanding they are suited only to exceptional times. It can also be used to render some questionable measures permanent – e. g. those

---

14 https://www.ecb.europa.eu/press/blog/date/2020/html/ecb.blog200409~3aa2815720.en. html

15 https://www.ecb.europa.eu/press/pr/date/2020/html/ecb.pr200318_1~3949d6f266.en.html

16 https://www.bbc.com/news/world-europe-52058742

17 https://www.ecb.europa.eu/press/pressconf/2020/html/ecb.is200604~b479b8cfff.en.html

built into the ESM that were first trialled as standalone, temporary arrangements – on the understanding they prevent a relapse. Emergency measures are aimed at solving specific problems: how they relate to general principles is always unclear. They can be withdrawn just as suddenly as they were introduced, and if necessity demands it then reintroduced again. Structurally, this can easily become a rationale for minimising democratic controls, including the influence of parliaments.

These patterns were evident in the Recovery and Resilience Facility agreed by the European Council in July 2020. Despite its supposed temporary status,[18] this has been widely interpreted as a new and promising departure in EU politics – the point at which principles of collective borrowing and common debt are introduced. That this fund may have a lasting legacy is very possible, but it may well be more mixed in character. A different way to read these developments is as ones that leave the basic, widely-criticised policy regime of the pre-Covid order intact, indeed create new resources for reinforcing it. Each country hoping to receive grants must draw up a 'recovery and resilience plan' detailing how it intends to reform its economy, to be scrutinised by the Commission and Council,[19] while an emergency brake (Art. 19) allows any national government to suspend the process should it have concerns about delivery of the reform agenda. The positive story is that there is now potentially a new tap of money flowing from which weaker states may draw. But access to it is conditional on commitment to the agenda of existing policy,[20] and the possibility of turning the tap off, even temporarily, becomes a significant way to enforce this agenda. Whereas the Troika enforced its demands directly as conditions for loans, here the mechanism is anticipatory compliance. Clinched in the name of emergency response, the arrangement amounts to a new means by which a pluralised set of executive agents – governments individually and collectively, alongside supranational authorities – can pressurise those that might chart a different course.

Executive discretion, the concentration of power, and innovations that bestow more options for the same in future – these are effects of emergency politics that run contrary to what is often considered the EU's character as a community of law and impersonal administration (Joerges and Kreuder-Sonnen 2017). If the making of modern authority was a project of regularising the exercise of power, transnational orders have often been seen as an extension of that project, even

---

18 See Art. 4 of the Council Conclusions: https://www.consilium.europa.eu/media/45109/210720-euco-final-conclusions-en.pdf
19 Art. 18.
20 I.e. that anchored by the 'European Semester', as emphasised by Economy Commissioner Gentiloni: https://ec.europa.eu/commission/presscorner/detail/en/speech_20_960.

an effort to preserve it against currents that threaten it. The EU has been cast as thoroughly modern in its attachment to rules and procedures, sometimes to the point of excess. In the age of Covid-19, just as in the crisis politics of the previous decade, one sees a different face emerge in which informality and discretion are key. Even where decisions are taken by those with an electoral mandate, these bear little relation to the reasons for which they were elected, and are pursued in ways that make them hard to contest.

Though undoubtedly more visible today, emergency politics has a place in the longer history of European integration. Some key features of its architecture were born first as a temporary fix. Consider the emergence of the European Council itself in the mid-1970s, a reconfiguration and informalisation of executive power aimed at protecting the core commitments of European integration. Jean Monnet, himself an advocate, cast it as a 'Provisional European Government' that could secure and consolidate integration under crisis conditions – the oil shock of autumn 1973, the international banking crisis of summer of 1974, and a wider economic recession. Rather than a permanent institution, he proposed an interim arrangement that would strengthen the leadership of Europe's executives. The EC's existing structures 'do not meet the need to move quickly and to decide.'[21] Decision-making had become 'too bureaucratic'. The creation of the European Council was an effort to escape procedural constraints and concentrate authority in leaders. From today's perspective, it is tempting to see its formation as part of the logical development of the EU's procedures (it would eventually be incorporated into the Union framework with the Lisbon Treaty). But at the point of its introduction it was extoled as an ad hoc arrangement, one of uncertain duration ('provisional'), and rationalised by appeal to circumstances jeopardising the achievements of European integration. It was an extension of executive discretion, sealed in a context of urgency.

Recent events are thus the continuation and radicalisation of an existing template. While the social and economic implications of Covid-19 are quite different from those of previous crises, the political response they give rise to is familiar. And it is a template in which some observers find positive appeal. There are those for whom executive activism is part of a welcome story to be told of crisis management and political consolidation. The rise of the unbound executive is admired as the rise of an agent that can get things done, more capably than legislatures and lower-tier bureaucracies. The EU's transformations over the 2010s

---

21 Cit. in Pascal Fontaine (1979), 'Jean Monnet's role in the birth of the European Council', available at: https://www.cvce.eu/content/publication/2006/12/7/ad29595e-0b0a-49b7-ae65-c41c54344a41/publishable_en.pdf

have been endorsed as its coming of age – an 'emancipation of the executive' that augments its capacity and global standing (van Middelaar 2019, pp.175–6).

Yet in the EU, not only is executive power weakly constrained by a democratic process, but the executive forms emerging remain closely tied to defined policy goals, however emancipated from law or procedure they may be. The discretion displayed tends largely to reinforce the existing socio-economic order, with all its attendant inequalities. Existing debt structures are for the most part preserved, and innovations are intended to make them viable. If one is confident of the representative or technocratic capacity of institutions, improvised decisions from within a small circle of elites may be tolerable, but it is harder to defend if policy-making is predisposed to serve certain ends. Moreover, if decision-makers rely on an atmosphere of emergency to get things done, they promote an idea of rule as essentially reactive. The business of governing becomes about responding to demands – something that can influence how authority is met by the wider public.

Anti-Emergency Politics

Detached as executive power may become in these circumstances, it does not go undisturbed. Emergency rule can nourish anti-system politics. Executive exceptionalism fosters a counter-politics in its mirror image, one that builds on themes of collusion, necessity, and the right to disobedience *in extremis*. It is sometimes suggested the Covid-19 crisis has marginalised Europe's right-wing 'populists', depriving them of key messages on migration and welfare. That may be so in the short term, but it is worth observing certain tendencies that play in their favour. Here the links to the EU are currently less pronounced, given the public-health focus and the centrality of states to the most dramatic emergency measures, but it remains vulnerable nonetheless.

One aspect relates to informality. Far-right parties generally define themselves less by opposition to a socio-economic structure than by opposition to national and supranational elites, positioned as figureheads of a corrupted class. The concentration of power and use of unofficial channels in emergency times offers rich material for such accounts. It also cultivates the public desire they feed off to find agents responsible for the management of the crisis. In a context of centralised authorities taking extraordinary measures, there is a natural desire to know who is calling the shots – indeed, to know that someone *is* calling the shots, that even in extreme circumstances there are people in charge. Unmasking the face of power is a task that the EU's critics may be only too happy to take on, and not always to provide reliable answers.

A second aspect relates to how emergency politics is conducted as a politics of necessity, reactive to events as they arise. Authorities adopt far-reaching measures not so much on the grounds that they are intrinsically desirable as that they help ward off a threat (the spread of disease, economic breakdown, etc.). While emergency rule entails frenetic decision-making, its decisions are rationalised as unchosen and unavoidable in substance and timing – a variation of the 'TINA' logic (Seville 2017). It is characterised by heightened executive activity – what one may call *doing* – coupled with heightened disavowals of *agency*, i.e. the capacity to choose freely between options. It is against this reactive mode of governing that many contemporary political groups claiming the mantle of insurgency define themselves. They seek to offer, however dubiously, the promise of agency (White 2019, ch. 6).

An aversion to necessity and 'doing' is one way to understand the slow, dismissive reactions to the Corona-crisis of governments led by such figures as Johnson, Trump or Bolsonaro. They showed clear unwillingness to be forced into an emergency response by the World Health Organization (WHO). Partly one may assume this was materially motivated – a desire to keep economies running and to retain the support of those most invested in them – but it also seems to reflect a political outlook. This entails hostility to technocratic authorities determining for a population what counts as a threat and what actions are needed to counter it. At the personal level, it is expressed in individual reluctance to be told what to do, even outright denial of the threat. At the macro level, it is expressed in politicians and movements taking issue with a governing style they consider acquiescent. 'I want' has apparently been Johnson's verbal expression of choice in this period, in direct contrast to the preference of more centrist politicians for 'we need'.[22] To such leaders, embracing a merely reactive mode of politics would be a capitulation, an expression of weakness, fear, or lack of ambition. There is a democratic impulse here, but taken to a contrarian extreme, emerging as a form of voluntarism. Even where governments led by such figures have ended up imposing lockdowns and other emergency measures, those at the top have sought to convey that they were personally reluctant or opposed.[23]

This is also a way to understand anti-lockdown protests. Opposition to 'tyrannical lockdown'[24] in the name of freedom has been a theme of protests in many countries across Europe and beyond, ones with which far-Right parties

---

22 http://www.sussex.ac.uk/broadcast/read/52112#.XtEk5 m7lIz4
23 https://edition.cnn.com/2020/03/23/uk/uk-coronavirus-lockdown-analysis-gbr-intl/index.html
24 https://www.independent.co.uk/news/uk/home-news/coronavirus-lockdown-protests-uk-london-hyde-park-5 g-conspiracy-theories-a9518506.html

have tended to align themselves (e. g. the German AFD[25]). These are not just the efforts of individuals to avoid the constraints imposed on them, but movements intended to dispute the governing response as a whole – on their own terms a form of 'resistance' (*Widerstand2020*) seeking the 'end of the emergency regime'.[26] They emerge from, but go beyond, the reasonable arguments to be had about which emergency measures are justified and for how long. They are the basis of a more general libertarian outlook ('*Anders denken ist kein Fehler, sondern Freiheit!*'), but one whose themes of strength and will give a bridge to fascist thought. The hostile reaction in Britain to the introduction of compulsory mask-wearing in shops was another expression of this attitude.[27] To reject the mask is not just to reject an inconvenience but a perceived emblem of acquiescence, 'mass panic' and emergency rule.[28]

Just as the Euro crisis provided opportunities for parties to emerge denouncing a politics of necessity and no-alternative – Brexit expressed this outlook – so Covid-19 has presented favourable conditions for those who likewise define themselves by their non-conformity. Indeed, when migration is not quite the rallying concern of before, and the role of protecting the nation's security can be claimed by almost any government fighting the pandemic, it is by developing a brand of *anti-emergency* politics that voices on the far Right can seek to maintain their relevance. When all politics is at least nominally about protecting 'the people', so-called populists have to reinvent themselves as champions of something else – of volition in contrast to necessity.

There are historical analogies for these currents. The emergence of libertarian ideas has often been associated with opposition to state-building efforts in response to emergency situations. Royal absolutism in seventeenth-century England and eighteenth-century France was typically pursued in the context of war or civil war and rationalised in terms of the provision of security, and it spawned counter-movements like the Levellers or the American revolutionaries who defined themselves by their opposition to expansions of prerogative. Negative liberty as an ideal emerged in these settings (Bailyn 1992). In the twentieth century, Roosevelt's New Deal – promoted in response to the economic state of emergen-

---

25 https://www.euractiv.com/section/coronavirus/news/anti-lockdown-protests-in-germany-in filtrated-by-far-right-extremists/; https://www.politico.eu/article/german-coronavirus-deniers-protest-test-angela-merkel-government/

26 https://www.deutschlandfunk.de/covid-19-wie-widerstand-2020-die-corona-krise-in-frage.1939.de.html?drn:news_id=1137796

27 https://www.telegraph.co.uk/opinion/2020/07/12/face-masks-should-not-made-compulsory/

28 https://www.deutschlandfunk.de/covid-19-wie-widerstand-2020-die-corona-krise-in-frage.1939.de.html?drn:news_id=1137796

cy presented by the Great Depression – likewise encountered a libertarian critique. There can be a rational aspect to such critiques, corresponding to how crisis situations can be exploited by elites. But it is an attitude that easily becomes negativistic – an instinctive hostility to whatever is instituted in the name of necessity. In this sense it can be no less reactive than the emergency politics it denounces.

An obvious concern is that this voluntarist outlook is difficult to sate. Insofar as populists in power find themselves implementing the policies they had previously opposed, they create the conditions for second-wave movements more trenchant in their critique. For the left, the appropriate lesson cannot be to dismiss this outlook outright, but to try and harness it to a substantive programme. A progressive politics needs policies its adherents can defend on principled grounds rather than as responses to necessity; it needs its own promise of agency, more credible than that of the right. For the EU meanwhile, the lesson is cautionary. For as long as the emergency measures in focus are public-health ones, the EU may spared much of the critical attention – so far, the WHO is the main transnational entity to have been drawn into critique and conspiratorial thinking. But this is unlikely to remain true as the social and economic consequences of the pandemic start to loom larger than the disease itself.

Beyond Emergency Europe?

What then of the EU's future? There has been much optimism in this period about the prospect of a major advance in its functionality and legitimacy. The creation of new structures of emergency financing have been widely heralded as ways to alleviate the inequalities accentuated by the crisis, also to address disillusionment with the EU's initial response. There is the sense once more that the EU prospers in a crisis, indeed that this time especially it has risen to the occasion. After the abortive efforts of the early 2000s, the missed opportunities of the 2010s, and with the new opportunities afforded by Brexit, is the EU being forged anew in the shadow of Covid-19?

Given the uncertainty concerning how far into the pandemic we are, it is clearly too soon to know. But as a long-term observation, if one accepts the preceding remarks about *anti-emergency* politics, the EU's prospects would seem to depend on distancing it from this governing mode. Shifts in policy would be part of this, away from a socio-economic model that weakens political authority and leaves it resorting to emergency interventions in times of difficulty. But it would also be about changing the way decisions get made and justified. If supranational executive power is associated mainly with actions in the service of necessity, the merits of particular policies will count for only so much. Here the current discourse is unpromising. One hears a lot about building 'resilience' and 'crisis preparedness',[29] but the concepts reproduce a reactive model of governing based on adapting to emergencies-to-come.

Giving the EU enhanced emergency powers to deal with future challenges clearly has an intuitive ring. Many may feel the lesson of recent events is that supranational and intergovernmental institutions need the capacity to act more decisively in exceptional moments (for a cautious defence after the Euro crisis: Tucker 2018). Such powers would presumably enable a quicker, more predictable response. But there are reasons to be wary, partly given the problems of accelerated decision-making generally (Scheuerman 2004), but also given the nature of the EU today. Since, as we have observed, EU authority is closely tied to predefined goals – notably the stability of the Eurozone and the single market – the discretion displayed by officials in crisis politics tends to be aligned with these things. Understandable as this may be given their mandate, it is not a desirable basis for expanded powers. Bolting these onto the EU in its present guise would simply entrench its existing priorities, given such powers would be deployed in their service. Value disagreements would be marginalised further, just when they need to be recognised. What counts as an emergency depends on what parts of the status quo one wants to preserve: these issues need to be contested. Until a democratisation of the process by which EU priorities are set and enacted, stronger emergency powers would most likely just lock in the existing settlement.

A more fundamental refoundation – an EU *constitutional moment* – would seem an important prelude to any bolstering of its crisis capacities. For all the talk in summer 2020 of a 'Hamiltonian moment'[30] that sees economic resources pooled at a European level, such a step does little to address the political questions key to the EU's future – the contestability of the policies it is committed to, and the structure of its decision-making. On the latter, it is Hamilton the constitutional thinker who is the more relevant guide. For him, the key challenge in a federation was to simplify institutional arrangements so as to constrain executive power without neutering its capacity to act. '[T]he plurality of the executive tends to deprive the people of the two greatest securities they can have for the faithful exercise of any delegated power, *first*, the restraints of public opinion, which lose their efficacy, as well on account of the division of the censure attendant on bad measures among a number as on account of the uncertainty on whom

---

29 https://ec.europa.eu/commission/presscorner/detail/en/ip_20_940

30 https://www.zeit.de/2020/22/olaf-scholz-europaeische-union-reform-vereinigte-staaten

it ought to fall; and, *second*, the opportunity of discovering with facility and clearness the misconduct of the persons they trust, in order either to their removal from office or to the actual punishment in cases which admit of it' (Hamilton et al, 1787/2008). Important was to create orderly hierarchies of authority so that power was not claimed chaotically and opaquely in times of crisis.

Such arguments seem all the more pertinent transnationally, given the range of executive agents spanning the national and supranational spheres. Even if, as modern democrats, we may be more sceptical than Hamilton towards placing executive power in the hands of the few, there would seem great merit in institutional simplification and codification. A more integrated transnational executive embedded in institutions of transnational democracy has much to recommend it. It would be less prone to informality and the ad hoc concentration of power. It would be better equipped to change its economic priorities in line with changing circumstances and public opinion, inviting a more organised contestation of the direction of policy. Less dependence on state-based legitimacy claims would mean less reliance on convoluted and opaque negotiations. To the extent that a transnational executive still lapsed into arbitrary or unresponsive methods, it would be a more visible target of critique. As Hamilton argued, the attribution of responsibility would be improved.

It would be too pessimistic to exclude genuine reform as an outcome of the present, but clearly these are difficult outcomes to achieve. Even the smallest first step – tying for instance the composition of the Commission more closely to European-Parliamentary elections (Lacey 2017, pp.221–3) – currently seems a challenging prospect, and one for which there is little support. There is a basic transition problem to contend with. On the one hand, crisis moments are when the need for change can seem strongest. They represent opportunities for constitutional overhaul, since there is typically greater will to innovate. On the other hand, it is exactly in such moments that new initiatives should be viewed with caution. Actions taken in extreme situations carry something like an 'original sin'. Measures are chosen for their effectiveness against the problems of the moment, which will often mean excluding procedural constraints as things that might derail them or retard their success. They are advanced by executive power at the moment when it is most detached from democratic controls. Moreover, when emergency measures are advanced on a transnational scale, they are especially hard for publics to scrutinise in real time, and hard to reverse afterwards given the many actors involved. Here the challenges of exceptionalism are writ large.

If the EU is to be meaningfully remade, it is more likely to be by those at the political margins than those who held power as the crisis erupted. The EU's latest round of emergency politics should not be mistaken for a constitutional advance, but perhaps it will foster the agency that can press for one. One thing states of emergency reveal is the malleability of the political order. Even temporary measures and suspensions show that things could be different, that arrangements are not set in stone. Just as it can spark reactionary mobilisations, might the present situation spark a left-wing internationalism? No movement of stature has so far emerged, but the conditions are not wholly unsuited. We do not know where in the story we are; the 2020s are only beginning.

Conclusion

Faced with the remarkable events set off by Covid-19, it is tempting to emphasise the uniqueness of the situation. As Adam Tooze put it in summer 2020, 'my impulse isn't to tell you that we've seen all this before; it's to say we ain't seen nothing yet.'[31] History as a chain of extraordinary occurrences, each singular and resistant to comparison – 'one unbelievable, intellectually indigestible shock after another', in his words – is one way to picture the recent past, and perhaps the perspective most alert to what is new in each crisis episode. Europe's unfolding experiences can plausibly be told in these terms, giving March 2020 the status of a watershed.

But equally there are important continuities in the logic and practice of rule from the 2010s through to the present. While the challenges faced have been markedly different, some key tendencies in governance and its critique have consolidated. A transnational form of emergency politics has taken shape in Europe, combining some of the familiar patterns and problems of domestic exceptionalism with others distinctive to this setting. To be sure, the social effects of COVID-19 threaten to dwarf those of the preceding years, occurring as they do against the backdrop of an existing crisis of western capitalism. Big change is surely coming. But in the way that it has been governed so far, this crisis resembles much that has recently gone before, while much done in its name aims to bolster the pre-crisis order. How far that will be possible remains to be seen.

---

31 https://nymag.com/intelligencer/2020/08/adam-tooze-how-will-the-covid-19-pandemic-change-world-history.html

References

Agamben, G. (2005) *State of Exception,* Chicago: University of Chicago Press.

Bailyn, B. (1992) *The Ideological Origins of the American Revolution,* Cambridge Mass: University of Harvard Press.

Bickerton, C., Hodson, D. and Puetter, U. (2015) The New Inter-governmentalism: European Integration in the Post-Maastricht Era, *Journal of Common Market Studies* 53 (4): 703–722.

Calhoun, C. (2004) A World of Emergencies: Fear, Intervention and the Limits of Cosmopolitan Order, *Canadian Review of Sociology* 41 (4): 373–95.

Hamilton, A., Madison, J. and Jay, J. (2008 [1887]) *The Federalist Papers,* Oxford: Oxford University Press.

Head, M. (2015) *Emergency Powers in Theory and Practice: the long shadow of Carl Schmitt,* London: Routledge.

Honig, B. (2009) *Emergency Politics: Paradox, Law, Democracy,* Princeton: Princeton University Press.

Isiksel, T. (2016) *Europe's Functional Constitution: A Theory of Constitutionalism Beyond the State,* Oxford: Oxford University Press.

Joerges, C. and Kreuder-Sonnen, C. (2017) European Studies and the European Crisis: Legal and Political Science between Critique and Complacency, *European Law Journal* 23 (1–2): 118–139.

Kreuder-Sonnen, C. (2019), *Emergency Powers of International Organisations,* Oxford: Oxford University Press.

Lacey, J. (2017) *Centripetal Democracy: Democratic Legitimacy and Political Identity in Belgium, Switzerland and the European Union,* Oxford: Oxford University Press.

Lazar, N. C. (2009) *States of Emergency in Liberal Democracies,* Cambridge: Cambridge University Press.

Lemke, M. (2018) What does state of exception mean? A definitional and analytical approach, *Zeitschrift für Politikwissenschaft* 3.

Manin, B. (2008) The Emergency Paradigm and the New Terrorism: What if the end of terrorism was not in sight?. In: Baume & Fontana (eds.), *Les usages de la séparation des pouvoirs* Paris: Houdiard.

Posner, E. A. and Vermeule, A. (2011) *The Executive Unbound: After the Madisonian Republic,* Oxford: Oxford University Press.

Scheuerman, B. (2004) *Liberal Democracy and the Social Acceleration of Time.* Baltimore: Johns Hopkins University Press.

Scheuerman, B. 2017), 'Die Globalisierung von Carl Schmitt?', *KJ Kritische Justiz* 50, pp.30–37.

Schmitt, C. (2013 [1921]) *Dictatorship,* Cambridge: Polity Press.

Seville, A. 2017. *"There is No Alternative": Politik zwischen Demokratie und Sachzwang.* Frankfurt am Main: Campus.

Sorell, T. (2013) *Emergencies and Politics: A Sober Hobbesian Approach,* Cambridge: Cambridge University Press..

Tucker, P. (2018) *Unelected Power: the Quest for Legitimacy in Central Canking and the Regulatory State,* Princeton: Princeton University Press.

van Middelaar, L. (2019) *Alarums and Excursions: Improvising politics on the European stage,* Newcastle: Agenda.

White, J. (2019) *Politics of Last Resort: Governing by Emergency in the European Union,* Oxford: Oxford University Press.

White, J. (2015a) Emergency Europe *Political Studies* 63(2): 300 – 18.

White, J. (2015b), Authority after Emergency Rule, *Modern Law Review* 78 (4): 585 – 610.

Daniel Innerarity
Political Decision-Making in a Pandemic

"If we winter this one out,
we can summer anywhere"

(Seamus Heaney)

Crises are moments that put many things into question – especially our decision-making procedures. These decisions can be examined in a chronological order, from the decisions that governments have to take in order to be prepared for a crisis before it takes place, to the decisions that are taken during the crisis and to those that are taken as a result of it. I pose four questions raised by critical situations: The first question is whether we were prepared for the crisis, that is, how it is decided when there is, so to speak, nothing left to decide. When crises erupt, their outcome is largely conditioned by the ways in which our democratic societies anticipate them and prepare for them. The second question is whether populist systems (or, if you prefer, the populist features of many governments) offer an appropriate decision-making structure to deal with a crisis such as the current health crisis. Third, I examine the drama that inevitably characterizes political decisions taken in the midst of a crisis that affects different parts of society unequally. And fourth, I explore the debates that we must hold on globalization which, from this point of view, are going to require that we review the level of governance that is most appropriate for each kind of risk.

Governing Crises

The 2008 financial crisis tested our systems for preventing and managing these types of situations. The Congressional Committee in the USA, which is investigating the origins of the crisis and the bailout of the banks, has revealed that almost everything that could have failed did fail. Political actors continue to protest about the slightest irritant, but the political system as a whole is incapable of identifying, foreseeing or governing crises such as the economic-financial crisis, the euro crisis, Brexit and other dynamics of European disintegration, the immigration crisis, or the tensions created by the intergenerational redistribution of a pension system that is difficult to sustain in its current form.

It is impossible to govern well if politicians do not keep their eyes open, scanning the horizon for latent or incipient problems. Among the clear shortcomings of any political system are: the short-sightedness of its programmes;

https://doi.org/10.1515/9783110713350-006

its tendency to address symptoms rather than confront causes; its dependence on current voters at the expense of future generations; the inability of both representatives and those represented to deal with underlying problems; the irresistible siren call of simplifications, whether technocratic or populist. As a society, we are not especially well prepared for anticipatory governance, and the continuous parade of daily emergencies distracts us from long-term challenges. Crises are rarely predicted, and once they have taken place, we do not generally agree on how to interpret them or what we should learn from them.

Democracies need strategic management for future crises. We know that there will be crises stemming from climate change, financial capitalism, immigration, the energy supply, the aging of the population, wars and conflicts, pandemics, the sustainability of pensions. The only thing left to be determined is when and how these crises will happen and the responses that are most appropriate to counter them. A more strategic process would allow us to identify tendencies and anticipate solutions, in other words, to act before it is too late.

Improving strategic coherence in a system that is subject to the fluctuations of urgent short-term crises requires, in the first place, more and better information about the long-term impacts of our current political decisions and their alternatives, instruments that allow us to weigh the risks that we are confronting or creating, and a holistic or systemic approach. Only in this way will politics manage to move beyond a focus on repair to a focus on configuration.

In dynamic systems, we must introduce the future into our planning processes so we are not caught unawares by emerging problems that we haven't made any provisions for. When anticipating the circumstances that could be unleashed, it is not enough to rely on best practices – which are always the best practices of the past – or to rely on accumulated experience. Strategic management requires an exercise of the imagination regarding future conflicts and crises. Since we have no reason to assume that the next crisis will be similar to previous ones, extrapolation from past experiences is not sufficient.

Whether we are dealing with global financial crises, ecological disasters or problems of sustainability, politics always arrives too late, when recovery efforts are more expensive than preventive measures would have been. Governments are often not able to cope when the dynamics of unwanted events have already begun to accelerate, their ability to detect and respond to emerging events is reduced, and regulatory measures have become obsolete or less effective. Governments are then limited to managing crises after they emerge instead of focusing on the events that precipitated them. These are not challenges that are resolved with the creation of a 'crisis cabinet' which is constituted when the crisis has already taken place and which only serves to remediate part of its consequences; they are resolved by improving the ability of governments to think and act strategically in a world that is changing in a radical fashion. What is needed is the ability to change before the necessity for change becomes desperately obvious (Hamel and Välikangas 2003: 53).

Acting before, during and after crises is difficult because many crises do not stem from simple causalities but from complex realities. Changes take place quickly and in a multifaceted fashion. They require many interactions between diverse areas of governance, without respecting bureaucratic and jurisdictional delimitations. It is not possible to establish a moratorium and resolve each of the challenges piecemeal. Seemingly stable solutions can turn into new problems that must be resolved. All of this challenges the adaptive capabilities of our systems of government which stem from the very beginning of modern democracies, the nation state and the industrial revolution. These systems are vertical, hierarchical, segmented and mechanical.

We must prepare to govern a world in which crises appear regularly, where we live with greater instability than we have expected. We need a political system that is capable of understanding the interactions and phenomena of crises; that can tackle novelty and change, a political system able to reinvent itself on a continuous basis – that is not static and atemporal, but alive and continuously evolving. Ultimately, we need a new way of doing politics that is more receptive to the different approaches that will need to be adopted in a society that is increasingly unpredictable, and which understands these requirements as opportunities to be more democratic.

And in order to do that, we must expand the modes of government (classically reduced to hierarchy and command) to include others that are more suited to complex societies (cooperation, participation, deliberation...) and combine them with procedures for rapid learning and strategic ability. We are not simply facing the decision to change policies, much less the need for administrative reform. We are confronting the choice to reconsider and transform politics or to continue with a system designed for a world that is no more.

If we have not been able to anticipate recent crises, have we at least been able to learn from them? Everything seems to indicate that we have not learned from the financial crisis to configure a stable global financial system with appropriate institutions and regulations. We can ask similar questions about equally crucial issues in other areas, such as the reform of public administrations or the movement toward other productive models: Are we engaging in the necessary reflections and corresponding reform processes?

If we are not capable of taking advantage of crises like the current one(s) to carry out necessary reforms, the future of our forms of government does not hold great promise. To those who always prefer to wait for better times, we must tell them that the calm, when it returns, usually brings more problems.

Virus versus Populism

When it comes to people, the ones who are most affected by the coronavirus crisis are the most vulnerable among us but, from an ideological point of view, what will be most affected is populism. There are three things that populist leaders hate whose value is increased by this type of crisis: expert knowledge, institutions and the global community.

Let us begin with the first one: expert knowledge. In times of crisis, there tends to be a re-appreciation of expert knowledge. This occurred in 2008–2009 when the decisions of the US Federal Reserve and the European Central Bank were vitally important, even though some of their recommendations were unpopular. It is also true that the experts made mistakes, such as the lack of foresight or their obsession with austerity during the economic crisis. But, in general, expert knowledge is more highly valued at times of concern and uncertainty in which disinformation flows so easily on the social networks.

Let us consider how that necessity contrasts with the scorn that Trump has for science and how he disregarded the warnings that his advisors were offering. He even said that Covid was just a simple flu and that it could help the US economy, while at the same time he reduced the budget of the office dedicated to pandemics at the National Security Council. Or let us recall Pablo Casado, the ring-wing Spanish opposition leader of the Popular Party, who accused President Pedro Sánchez of "hiding behind the science" to fight against a pandemic, as if it would have been better to leave it in the hands of a fortune-teller or a couple of astrologers.

I do not mean to imply that we must trust everything the experts say, but simply that their opinion must be taken into special consideration. Not even the specialists are all in agreement and there is leeway when it comes to political decision-making. There have been a variety of strategies, each one supported by its corresponding experts, such as the British and Dutch strategy of controlled contagion versus the European and Asian strategy of confinement. Furthermore, democracy is not a government of experts, but a popular and representative government which must articulate a variety of voices, institutions and values, one of which is knowledge – especially important in the midst of a crisis like this one. In any case, one of the lessons that we should take from this situation is that we need to exit it with a more intelligent and less ideological style of government.

The second aspect that gains importance during a moment of crisis is institutional logic. This is not a moment for great leaders who lead their people vertically, but for organization, protocols and strategies, when social services and a quality public sector are particularly valued. All of this goes hand in hand with collective intelligence, both when it comes to the medical response as well as to the organizational and political responses. Of course, presidential communications are very important, but much more decisive is our collective capacity to govern crises, both in anticipating them and managing them. We are facing an unprecedented crisis that was very difficult to anticipate, but we are dealing with a political system that is under-prepared when it comes to strategic capacity, excessively competitive, obsessed by the short term, opportunistic and unwilling to learn. The key value of institutions is trust, but we are suffering a crisis of confidence in our institutions that we have not managed to overcome.

Institutional logic requires loyalty and confidence (among the different levels of government, between the government and the opposition, between the people and the political system), which are attributes that we have in short supply. In the end, all the political actors think that this is a great opportunity to attain things that would be unattainable without a large-scale catastrophe: governments try to consolidate their hold on power, there is recentralization, political oppositions try to take power, and so on. The subconscious of political systems believes that normal institutional life does not allow for change, it benefits those who are in power and alternations in power are always due to catastrophes that have been used successfully: the economic crisis and maybe this virus could represent an opportunity to get power. Opportunistic behaviour is a clear sign of institutional weakness.

The third factor that become significant during crises is the global community. This crisis has struck at a time of anti-globalism (Brexit, Trump, trade wars, protectionism, unilateralism, a disunited Europe), a situation that is very similar to the 1930s.

However, although the crisis seemed, at the beginning, to reinforce our tendency to focus on our own self-interest, closing ourselves off along national lines, we subsequently opened up to a more cooperative response, once we rediscovered our shared destinies and the fact that no one is fully isolated and safe. We need to contain the expansion of the virus on a global level, not only within our own borders, because viruses are barely neutralized with strategies of delimitation or confinement, which only slightly manage to curb their expansion. Measures involving closing things down are only superficial, the real way to escape this situation is cooperation: cooperation in science, in politics, in the economy. There is no solution with a single chain of command or with self-interest pursued at the expense of other people's interest. Ulrich Beck (1992) warned about this after the catastrophe in Chernobyl: even though the first impulse may be protectionist, shared risks are the main uniting force in a world in which we are all equally threatened.

The Drama of Deciding

It is said that a priest came to see Thoreau on his death bed to offer him the solace of religion and evoke the other world, the afterlife. Thoreau, with a slight smile, responded: "Just one world at a time, please". Beyond the religious issue, a worrisome question often arises in life: to how many worlds do we belong? How many things do we have to keep track of at any given time? How do we reconcile all the possible perspectives of reality? We all have to keep too many plates spinning at once.

Critical moments bring us face to face with this diversity of perspectives in a tragic fashion. Those who have had to take the most important decisions to handle the coronavirus crisis could not allow themselves the luxury of occupying one single world. Instead, they had to balance various worlds with divergent values and interests: the vital need for public health but also for economic performance, the need for schooling, the importance of culture precisely at these moments. I imagine myself in their shoes, deciding in favour of some objective they consider a priority, knowing that their decision could cause serious harm to another objective. The triage carried out by doctors was preceded by the no less tragic triage carried out by politicians. Should we prioritize health over the economy? Is the right to protest more important than the still uncertain risks of contagion? Is home confinement a good decision when we know that it seriously harms schooling?

Sociologists use the term 'functional differentiation' for the process through which, as civilization advances, where there was previously a "total social fact", as Marcel Mauss (1966: 76–77) put it, there are now distinct spheres or social subsystems, each with their own logic: the economy, culture, health, law, education. Society is an incompatible set of perspectives. From the economic point of view, the world is a problem of scarcity; from the political point of view, it is something to be configured collectively. What is plausible for a consumer is different when it is observed by a voter or artist. These spheres are not harmonically integrated, and they give rise to many problems of compatibility and even to open conflicts. The most shocking case is what is happening with the environment, which improved with the economic slowdown. Another curious case: the reduction in air traffic is decreasing the amount of atmospheric data that is necessary to make forecasts which help us understand the extent of the pandemic. What is going well for some people can be devastating from other vantage points. On top of that, a plurality of perspectives also exists within each sphere; not all epidemiologists see things the same way, and this is also the case with those who work in the health care industry. Psychologists and paediatricians have some objections to all the attention currently focused on the epidemiological perspective when it comes to confronting the crisis.

Politics is precisely the attempt to articulate that diversity of perspectives. Bourdieu defined the state as "a point of view of points of view" (2012: 53) and declared that this privileged observation was no longer possible because of the difficulty of determining the common good when it comes to the entire society. The political system no longer enjoys many resources; its knowledge and authority are very limited, so it is reduced to creating confidence rather than sovereign power. Societies have to act as if they were united while knowing that they are not. There is no way to impose a single dominant criterion about what should be done. Crises open a parenthesis; they momentarily silence that diversity and provide a unified authority and unusual obedience, but they are no more than brief interruptions of the habitual discord among different perspectives of reality.

The fact that there are diverse perspectives about a single issue does not release us from the obligation to get right what is most important in every case. It allows us to realize the drama involved in decisions within environments of complexity, which is especially the case with a crisis. The demand for accountability must always keep these tensions in mind, and those who make decisions must improve decision-making procedures. Complexity is not an excuse, but a demand. Unlike Thoreau, who spent much of his life in a cabin in the woods, we have both the good fortune and the misfortune of living in various worlds at the same time.

Where and What is Decided? Alternative Globalizations

One of the unusual questions that the involuntary social experiment of the pandemic presents is whether we are entering into a period of de-globalization or whether globalization will continue as before. There is in this question some unreality, since it seems to assume that globalization is a process that can be detained and that we originally made an express determination to put it into motion. Human beings did not gather together and vote on whether to enter the Iron Age or to abandon the Renaissance. Why has this question, which seems to grant us a sovereignty we do not possess, arisen now? Probably because we are allowing ourselves to be carried away by the seduction of having a lot of control over reality since we just did something that seems to resemble deciding to stop the world: we carried out the confinement and put a halt to a large part of the economy. This was not the same as the recessions or economic crises we have *suffered*, with which we have plenty of experience, but was a halting of our habitual mobility and a hibernation of the economy that came from *decisions* we made. While we were forced to do so by a health threat, we made the decision voluntarily. The radicalism of the measures adopted to combat the pandemic may fool us with the mirage that we are capable of controlling everything, even something very close to bringing the world to a halt.

The flip side of believing there are sovereign actors is the idea that there must be guilty parties whose ineptitude or evil explains everything. We love to seek guilty parties responsible for crises, and we should moderate that impulse if what we want is to make good diagnoses (that will, without a doubt, include identifying elements of irresponsibility). Globalization is now presented to us as the wild card for all explanations. The fact that the coronavirus has expanded globally makes us think that it has something to do with globalization, but de-globalizing ourselves is not simple, nor is it clear what that might entail. In the first place, the virus does not seem to have spread primarily through business, but through tourism. Should we prohibit pilgrimages to Mecca or tourism in Florence? The idea that the virus is now sending us the bill for haphazard globalization is a half-truth. There were plagues back in the fourteenth century, and growing interdependence also has very positive aspects when it comes to fighting off these pandemics (such as scientific cooperation, the nimbleness of information or the communication of successful experiences). If the virus came from China and has had such devastating effects, it was not because of excessive globalization but because they globalized the virus but nationalized the information. We must diagnose the type of political constellation the coronavirus comes from and what interactions it obeys. Contending that it is a virus of globalization would be a simplification that does not correspond to the fact that we live in a more complex world, in which there are dimensions of our existence that have been highly globalized, others that have been less so and even some that have experienced a reduction of globalization. The heart of the question is that we should balance the risks by pooling the information, technologies and institutions that we need to confront them. The goal is a balanced globalization, which is something we can achieve, rather than de-globalization, which is completely unrealistic.

As a consequence of the shock of the pandemic, the overarching questions have returned to the political agenda, even with, I would argue, a touch of grandiloquence, as if the future of the world were in our hands in a way that does not correspond to our limitations. There is a debate between those we could call the contractionists and those we could call the expansionists; between some who argue that this crisis makes the case for deglobalization and others who sustain that we must bolster globalization and give it the appropriate political structures.

The management of the crisis has, at first, followed a contractionist logic: the closing of borders, reserving our resources for national citizens, orders for confinement, a greater demand for protectionism toward governments, the interruption of global supply and mobility chains. At the same time, once we overcame the instinctive first reaction in favour of retreating, there were events that implied greater opening: the configuration of more unified global public opinions when discussing similar matters, advances in digitalization, telework and on-line education, demands for intervention from the European Union, a desperate race to discover a vaccine through international scientific cooperation, and a comparison of the strategies taken by different countries that situated us in a framework of best practices or global benchmarking.

The fact that both positions seem to be right, depending on the examples that are employed and the perspective from which things are observed, tells us a great deal about the nature of globalization: it is inevitable, it is our destiny, but it is also ambivalent and even contradictory, with movements that are contradictory, even if the final result is an increase in interconnection. Talking about globalization means also mentioning its opposite, it is like the shadow that accompanies us. There are times when, in order to allow globalists to be right again, we must move backwards in a way that might be interpreted as agreeing with those who are in favour of stopping progress. All we need is a quick glance at the history of globalization to verify that it has always oscillated between expansion and contraction.

There is a case in the current debate that is invoked as an example of the success of de-globalization. The economic slowdown has had immediate beneficial effects on the quality of the air, rivers and seas – for the obvious reasons of closed industries and decreased mobility. It is true that the orders for confinement, the hibernation of many economic activities and the decrease in international business because of the pandemic have resulted in a reduction in pollution and greenhouse gas emissions, but it would be a mistake to think that this contraction reduces the risks of climate change beyond the immediate horizon. The emissions will return once activity returns, and if the pandemic provokes a serious economic crisis, a lot of money and political attention will be withdrawn from the fight against the climate crisis. The situation could even be aggravated because the attention being paid to the immediate dangers of the pandemic would distract us from the more latent and long-term threats to the climate. We should also consider that businesses might be less able to invest in the transition toward sustainable projects: lower prices for crude oil will make electric cars more expensive (as is suggested by Tesla's falling stock prices); supply chains for certain renewable energies, that are very dependent on production in China, could be interrupted; the generalized fear about health and financial risks will receive all our attention, while concerns about climate change will move to the back burner. In any case, the fact that the climate is improving during the pandemic because people are dying and less work is taking place does not seem to be the best way to resolve the problems of the climate crisis. We should find solutions that allow us to juggle all the goods that are in play (life, the economy, the planet), beyond the sacrificial promise that, by slowing the world, the problems associated with movement will necessarily be fixed.

My conclusion to this debate is that globalization is not going to come to an end because we decide it should or because governments make that decree. However, there are a series of decisions we can make that will encourage or slow globalization. This will be like repairing a ship while out at sea. We cannot employ a large parenthesis or an intentional interruption of history, so we find ourselves forced to reflect while we are in movement. A quarantine is an elimination of contacts for a specific period of time, but the concept of 'de-globalization' points toward discontinuing relationships we have established, or at least changing the way they been configured, since we have been talking about this phenomenon. We would have to distinguish between the relationships we should limit, those that should be modified and the ones that it does not seem reasonable to give up.

This collective reflection will not make us think about using an emergency brake to stop the world but it will allow us to consider resizing it. The big debate focuses on resizing the decision-making environments based on the nature of the risks that threaten us. We must redefine the appropriate tiers of management and production: local, national, international, supranational, transnational, global. The primary thing that this health crisis has revealed is the fragility of open globalization, both when it comes to the mobility that led to the spread of the pandemic as well as certain difficulties when we needed to stock up on masks or respirators and we verified our enormous dependence on the supply of basic goods and services (items whose production we had delocalized and which did not seem to have a special value added or more relevance for security than sophisticated military equipment). Our first reaction is to place more value on regional markets, interrupt global supply chains, return to classic protectionism and the local scale; but we have also begun again to value the cosmopolitanism of the scientific community, the strengthening of global public opinion and the advantages of digitalization precisely because we do not want these things to stop. Nervous globalization must be followed by sustainable 'glocalization'.

The coronavirus is not going to bring a halt to globalization (if that idea even makes any sense). The question is to determine what the best type of organization is to rebalance a world that was already showing many imbalances the pandemic has merely highlighted. Even if it were possible, the return to closed worlds would not help provide the global world with better governance; instead, this would leave it without the influence of institutions and actors that can balance its uncontrolled dynamic. We will need to distinguish beneficial or inevitable interdependence from the types of dependence that entail serious threats to security. Instead of oscillating between discipline and disorder, retreat and acceleration, what this globalization needs is more and better regulation. Before and after the pandemic, it continues to be true that the public good demands global institutions, global cooperation and global solutions.

References

Beck, U. (1992) [1986] *The Risk Society*, London: Sage.

Bourdieu, P. (2012) *Sur l'État. Cours au Collège de France 1989–1992*, Paris: Seuil.

Hamel, G. and Välikangas, L. (2003) The Quest for Resilience, *Harvard Business Review*, 81, 52–63.

Innerarity, D. (2012) *The Future and its Enemies. In Defense of Political Hope*, Stanford: Stanford University Press.

Luhmann, N. (1970) *Soziologische Aufklärung 1. Aufsätze zur Theorie sozialer Systeme*, Opladen: Westdeutscher Verlag.

Mauss, M. (1966) [1954] *The Gift: Forms and Functions of Exchange in Archaic Societies*, London: Cohen & West.

Rosanvallon, P. (2020) *Le siècle du populism*, Paris: Seuil.

Volkmer, M. and Werner, K. (2020) *Die Corona-Gesellschaft. Analysen zur Lage und Perspektiven für die Zukunft*, Bielefeld: transcript.

Willke, H. and Willke, G. (2012) *Political Governance of Capitalism. A Reassessment Beyond the Global Crisis*, Northampton: Edward Elgar Publishing.

Part 2: **Globalization, History and the Future**

Helga Nowotny

In AI We Trust: How the COVID-19 Pandemic Pushes us Deeper into Digitalization

Only a few months ago the world still seemed to be in its normal state of an orderly mess. Abruptly, a new virus brought to an end much of what had been previously taken for granted. The COVID-19 pandemic that followed laid bare the
fragility of health care systems, itself the result of systematic disinvestment
into public health, and the inaptitude, if not outright incompetence, of many
governments. It brought the vast already existing inequalities and fissures in society to the fore. It reinforced old anxieties while generating new ones. In countries with an already weak democratic order the confusion is deliberately used to
instill fear and to expand authoritarian rule. Overall, trends that were already
under way are accelerating while the long-term consequences remain unknown.

The message forcefully brought home by the SARS-CoV-2 virus was that we
are not as much in control as we thought. As shown by the long list of previous
epidemics and pandemics in the history of humanity new viruses are extremely
common. Exacerbated by climate change and the still increasing population
pressure on the natural environment animals living in the wild are pushed closer
to human habitats. The transfer of viruses from animals to humans, zoonoses, is
therefore likely to persist in the future. Epidemiologists have warned repeatedly
that such occurrences will happen, it is only not known when and where. Yet, the
overall state of unpreparedness is obvious. In his scathing criticism of the global
response to the COVID-19 pandemic, Carlo Caduff argues that what makes this
pandemic unprecedented is not the crisis but the response to it. His focus is
on the results of the extreme fallouts that cause unprecedented distress and
enormous harm, especially in the Global South which houses the most vulnerable parts of the world. He maintains that the response to the pandemic has been
driven by a fantasy of control that overestimates and overreacts, leading to the
changes that are happening today and that we will have to grapple with for
years to come (Caduff 2020).

There is another major change happening today that will transform the
world further in unexpected ways: it is the fact that the SARS-CoV-2 virus pushes
us further along the path of digitalization and datafication. Many of the other
changes that can be observed during the pandemic, or yet to follow, are directly
or indirectly connected to the ongoing digital transformation of contemporary
societies and the functioning of their economies. The digital transformation al-

https://doi.org/10.1515/9783110713350-007

ters our relationships to each other and to ourselves. It is a systemic and a paradigmatic change. Ultimately, it is about the newly evolving relationship between humans and the digital machines we have created. Humans have embarked on a co-evolutionary path with their digital machines – with the outcome unknown.

Such a larger picture of a rapidly moving and dynamic transformation must be kept in mind when examining in a critical perspective the many ongoing socio-economic and structural changes, but also the more subtle ones that involve an altered understanding of the world. It is as though the COVID-19 crisis offers one of those rare historical moments when parts of the familiar past vanish before one's eye while at the same time one discovers that the future has already arrived, at least partially. It is a digital future that makes a confounding, yet dazzling appearance. Confounding, because only parts of it are visible in the form of digital gadgets and technologies with which we are familiar and which already shape our daily lives. We have come to rely on predictive algorithms in our consumer habits that tell us what we will buy next and which health risks lie ahead of us. Predictive algorithms are already deployed to assist decision-making in a variety of areas like finance and logistics, but also in the judiciary, insurance or police.

Yet, we also sense that a much larger part is hidden from view. The invisible part of the digital future exists somewhere in the labs of the large corporations that have assumed the task to develop and sell us our digital future. It is hiding in the dark web in which hackers, criminals and the secret services move with ease and confidence. But the digital future in the making displays itself also in a dazzling appearance when we can glimpse some of its enormous possibilities that may catapult humanity into a new phase of its existence – or mark the end of it. Seeing the past and the future at the same time is both scary and fascinating.

These are fleeting moments far from dominating the day-to-day experience during the COVID-19 crisis or afterwards. Of course, all epidemics and pandemics share certain characteristics, but they are also different. Historian Frank Snowden characterizes each of them as individual, each with its own personality. Not every virus can afflict every society because each society has particular vulnerabilities dependent on the kind of society it is (Snowden 2019). Seen in such a historical perspective the COVID-19 pandemic appears as the disease that reveals the vulnerabilities that come with a tightly interconnected global world, but it is also linked to the enormous and unregulated pressure exerted on the natural environment. It originated from an encounter between an hitherto unknown virus carried by horse-shoe bats in caves in China, or perhaps even earlier, in Myanmar, Vietnam and Laos. With the help of a still missing link it jumped to infect humans at the wildlife market in Wuhan. The inadequate response of unprepared societies around the world resulted in the current predicament. Just as the SARS-CoV-2 virus binds with its characteristic spike to the ACE2 receptor of human cells, it seems that the response of societies around the world is binding to the processes of digitalization and datafication. It will leave a trail of suffering and despair in its wake, including the possible collapse of countries and social groups that lack resilience. But it also accelerates a major societal transformation.

Despite obvious similarities with previous epidemics and pandemics what distinguishes the COVID-19 pandemic is not only the generally advanced state of biomedical knowledge and the unprecedented high level of health care, highly unevenly distributed as it is. Rather, it is the unique interconnection between disease, response and Artificial Intelligence in its various manifestations in digital technologies and infrastructures. Whether through testing and diagnosis or through modeling the number of Intensive Care Units needed, through justification of data-based policy measures or the hope of an ultra-fast development of a vaccine and therapeutics – the response is directly or indirectly related to AI and digitalization, and to the digital infrastructures and technologies that enable its efficient deployment. So is communication, including deliberate misinformation and the dissemination of fake news. It is as though we are witnessing a 'fast-forward' movie, an acceleration of the digital transformation that has been in the making for some time. Now, intended and unintended consequences run their course in multiple directions, with highly uncertain outcomes.

Therefore, it is not only the high visibility that mathematical disease modeling has attained or the role that data play in legitimizing the policy measures taken to attempt to contain the pandemic that create awareness of the role played by digital technologies. Science received an enormous boost through AI that enabled the unprecedented speed with which the genomes of the virus were sequenced and their mutations traced around the world almost in time. None of this would have been conceivable in previous pandemics. Nor does this period in history lack its moment of irony. No sophisticated algorithm was needed to predict the eruption of the pandemic. Well-honed epidemiological observations and good old statistical tools were sufficient to warn ahead of time, even if they went unheeded.

Instead, it was the seemingly mundane but crucial experience that everybody went through in the lockdown period to combat the spread of the pandemic took effect. Suddenly, we were deprived of our social contacts and anxiously waiting for news from family and friends. At this very moment digital technologies emerged as the new lifeline. Not only did they provide comfort and reassurance as a way out from isolation. They became essential for maintaining the functional backbones of a social reality that no longer reassembled the previous normality that was rapidly disappearing. Social closeness was replaced by a measured physical distance and digital technologies became the pivot for rearranging social relationships on the micro-level of daily lives as much as on the societal macro-level.

'Social distancing' is a misnomer as it prescribes the physical distance to be kept in public and private spaces. What actually happened was that physical distance was turned into virtual closeness and social closeness into physical distance that becomes virtual. This rearrangement of social relationships is likely to spill over when measuring physical space will sink into our minds. Our brains will learn to juggle, triangulate, extend or shrink a new topology of intimacy. The mobility patterns we are used to become subject to a reassessment what distance means in physical as well as in social terms. Everyone who spent hours in front of their computer screens in virtual meetings realizes how exhausting it can be not to be physically in the same room. Our brain is constantly searching for the cues it normally receives in face-to-face communication. It suffers from the dearth of stimuli and cues which are reduced or eliminated from the two-dimensional image on a screen. The brain desperately attempts to compensate the under-stimulation it receives in virtual communication. Just as overstimulation may lead to exhaustion, under-stimulation may result in zoom-fatigue.

Therefore, we cannot permit ourselves to go completely digital. Humans rely on the interpretation of many signals that are transmitted consciously and unconsciously. Our tacit knowledge of others and of situations allows us to interpret what is being said or remains unsaid. We interpret body language, a smile and the raise of an eyebrow. We can read in others whether they are bored or feign interest and, like many animals, we are clever in deceiving others. Machines are getting better and better in imitating communication between humans, but the pandemic is also teaching us what we value most. Our deep-seated ambivalence vis-à-vis digital technologies, oscillating between trust and distrust, will be with us for some time.

From Office to Home: The Digitalization of Work

Many other changes immediately took effect, generating new patterns of interaction with the digital machinery that seemed to have been lying in wait. From now on digital technologies quickly take center stage. They seem indispensable. Working from home gives a foretaste of the organization of work in the future, at least for those whose digital skills and tasks are already an integral part of the ongoing automation of work reaching the professions and the middle classes. It quickly turns out that juggling work while having to take care of children at home involves new levels of multitasking with multiple overlapping chunks of time. Digital time conflicts with social time, yet can no longer be separated from it. Especially for women having to switch continuously between digital tasks and social tasks is one of the most arduous and unfair effects brought about. Although the early closure of schools was a policy measure that proved to be highly effective as it forced parents to stay at home, a disproportionate burden fell on women. It also led to a quick deepening of the digital divide, adding to the enormous hurdles that must be overcome if children from already disadvantaged backgrounds are to be enabled to catch up.

Shifting work from office to home implies far more than making sure that high power WLAN and broadband connections are available or that the kids need their own home-space and digital infrastructural support. Will this give employers the opportunity to upload more of the operational organization on their employees, initiating a kind of 'uberization' of office work? How to prevent that women will have to bear the brunt disproportionally also in the future? Meanwhile, architects have seized the moment and are in the process of re-designing the interior space of housing in ways to make work from home feasible under more adequate conditions. Urban planners are re-thinking the design of urban neighborhoods. Again, this includes more than introducing 5G connections and bicycle lanes, but also what to do with shopping malls that rapidly become empty as consumer habits shift on-line. Doctors who had to improvise to keep their studios open are considering expanding their services to on-line consultation. Digital infrastructures that were largely invisible permeate many organizations that struggle to accommodate them. A huge restructuration is under way, implicating social relationships and hierarchies of power, creating new interdependencies and the formation of assemblages that consist of digital objects interlinked in different ways with users and owners.

The push towards digitalization by moving work from office to home and by transferring teaching from face-to-face to digital and hybrid forms demonstrates how closely technology is entangled with the social context in which it is embedded. It is at these interfaces where a further blurring between public and private occurs and the on-line part of human existence increasingly mixes with the off-line part. When schools and universities were closed a scrambling set in for replacing the teacher-student interaction in the classroom or lecture hall with tablets, laptops and all the digital content that had to be newly designed and uploaded. Many governments had pushed for digitalization since some time with political rhetoric ahead of pragmatic implementation. Now it just happened – with sobering results. Soon after the lock-down started empirical social science research was quick to analyze these and related changes as they happened on the ground. What emerges from these studies is a broad and scaled-up picture of the deepening of many existing inequalities and vulnerabilities. They show not only the lack of preparedness on the part of public institutions, but point to the long-term dismal effects if preventive action is not taken (Prainsack, Kittel, Kritzinger, and Boomgaarden 2020).

The problems thus revealed and the urgent questions they raise call for responses that are not yet in sight. The entire education system is challenged by how well it is prepared to offer digital education for all and whether it is able to prepare the children for a future that will be very different from the one imagined until now. Universities will have to reconsider questions equally crucial for their future. What kind of students do they want to teach when it is obvious that digital teaching models, including blended learning, are not restricted to educate only 18-year olds? Will universities be able to reach out to society in completely new ways? It also turns out that the lock-down and restart were managed well where feed-back loops were in place, including negative feedbacks. They are indispensable for mutual learning processes that will benefit us only if the learning process is collective and inclusive, going beyond the merely technological operations.

Those who are responsible for introducing an AI, for instance in the form of Machine Learning algorithms, that are designed to predict and render decision-making more efficient in policy contexts such as unemployment offices, policing, criminal justice or economic policy, are usually not aware of the unintended consequences the digital policy tool will produce. Most researchers in AI who spend their days working on what for them are beautiful and useful systems have difficulty in even conceiving that their products might produce or deepen existing inequalities. Yet, technologies cannot be separated from their social context to which they are linked through modes of co-production. What is at stake is a question that had been kept in the background far too long: how to re-form a society that will be shaped by digitalization but needs to gain the capability also to shape digitalization. This includes answers to questions like how to educate the next generation; restructure a healthcare system that optimizes technological interventions with the need for care that only humans can provide; how to safeguard democratic values and institutions. In short, it calls for a digital humanism (Werthner et al. 2019).

The future will not be shaped at our will. It obliges us to engage anew with the uncertainty it brings, especially when we crave certainty and want to feel safe. It requires a larger, more systemic view and to take context into account. The crisis challenges us to reflect on a future that suddenly appears as open and uncertain again, while we have less confidence in approaching it (Nowotny 2015). The innovation hype with its exclusive focus on hi-tech products is somewhat receding to the background when investors want to play it safe. Meanwhile, millions of people struggle to make their living after the economic basis of their existence collapsed. The pandemic has shown that nature can confront the hubris of political leaders who deny the existence of a reality they cannot control. But the push towards digitalization triggered by the pandemic is also an invitation to resist that we become the passive adjuncts of a technology that follows its own dynamics. It alerts us to the process of co-evolution between humans and digital machines and sharpens awareness how every interaction with digital technologies affects us in our definition of what makes us human, but also opens a range of new and exciting possibilities that may answer it in novel ways.

The Rise – and Limitations – of Datafication

For science and especially for the bio-medical sciences having recourse to AI and the most recent digital instruments and technologies proves to be a great asset. It means access to masses of data and sophisticated algorithms as well as to computational power that allows to sequence the genome of the virus and subsequent mutations in record time with researchers sharing samples around the world and repurposing equipment in their lab in order to provide added test facilities. The COVID-19 High Performance Consortium, a public-private initiative that includes IBM, Google, Amazon, NASA and other member organizations brings together researchers working in bioinformatics, epidemiology, molecular models and simulations for screening outputs. It enables them to aggregate the computing capability from the world's fastest and most advanced supercomputers and to reduce 1 billion possible molecules to less than a few thousands with the help of DeepLearning methods. A significant part of the research is directed towards faster diagnosis, the search for new compounds for therapeutic treatment and, of course, vaccines. The fit between AI, computing power and rapid advances in knowledge about the virus, seems a perfect match. At the same time, scientists have to acknowledge humbly how much is still unknown.

The beginning of the pandemic saw a return of trust in science combined with the expectation that a vaccine could soon be developed and therapeutic cures are in the pipeline. But as science proceeded speedily, boosted by data and computational power, a nasty 'vaccine nationalism' appeared with some governments trying to buy at all cost sufficient supplies. This was one of several regrettable returns to a narrow-minded illusion that nations could close borders to keep the virus out. The interface between science, politics and the public is in trouble again. Conspiracy theories are flourishing, together with anti-vax and extreme political movements. It is as though the pandemic had created a void in liberal democracies in which opposing strands are competing, one trying to resurrect a past that never was and the other to move rapidly forward towards a future where Big Data will save us.

The response to the COVID-19 pandemic brings a vastly increased role for data, also called datafication. Data are often, but wrongly seen as a fixed, context-independent body of evidence that can be deployed in modeling predicted outcomes. The discourse on Big Data comes with the expectation that more is better and that an increase in the volume of available data will yield more and better knowledge. Such views obscure a critical, but necessary understanding how data come to serve as evidence and under which conditions. It is therefore urgent to focus on the actual practices and the techniques, infrastructures, instruments and institutions that are involved in the processes of mobilizing data so that they can actually serve as evidence. This includes data collection, aggregation, cleaning, dissemination, publication, visualization and ordering – necessary steps that have to include knowledge about the possibilities and constraints of interpreting data (Leonelli and Tempini, 2020).

During the COVID-19 pandemic the pressure was enormous to proceed as quickly as possible with whatever data were available in order to feed them into the simulation models that data scientists, epidemiologists, mathematicians and others were engaged when making forecasts. The aim was to predict the various trajectories the pandemic could take, plotting the rise, fall or flattening of curves and what would it mean for different population groups or for the health care infrastructure and available equipment and supplies. The range to be covered by forecasting modeling is vast. Soon regional, national and international comparisons were included as well as attempts to measure the effectiveness of the policy measures taken in different countries at different points in time. Yet, despite the important and visible role given to data throughout the COVID-19 pandemic, no quick quantitative data fix emerged.

The importance of access to the right kind of data in the quality needed is one of the important lessons to be learned from the pandemic so far, a reminder of the old adage 'garbage in – garbage out'. Whenever data are poorly classified they cannot be rendered comparable. It also became obvious that the collection of data and their measurement is often arbitrary, as these processes are divided among different administrative entities operating at different levels. Such problems are not new for statisticians and epidemiologists, but given the time pressure under which modelling and predictive outcomes had to be produced, their impacts have far-reaching consequences. Especially in the early phases of the pandemic, the lack of data led to projections of the number of infected people that were unreliable. The reasons varied: first, a lack of data in the early stage of disease spreading, second, the fact that saturation effects and turning points become evident only with later data points, and third, changes in behavior, which have a massive impact on the spreading dynamics and its outcome[1]

The COVID-19 crisis thus offers a unique field of experimentation for simulation models and algorithm-based predictions and the underlying socio-technological processes. It acts as a testbed for Big Data and AI predictions – and quickly shows their limitations. Expectations from the public and politicians alike are focused on getting clear-cut answers which turns out to be impossible. Initially at least, politicians and the public left the stage to scientists and experts whose modelling activities tried to show that depending on the data input and underlying assumptions predictions could differ. Although the experts were wary to underline that their predictions depended in the data available and insisted that predictions are conveyed in probabilities, the craving for certainty in what otherwise is a sea of uncertainty remains overwhelming.

Trust and Distrust in AI

Trust in AI and Big data sits uneasily with distrust that can flare up anytime. This was the case during the COVID-19 pandemic when digital tracing apps became a major concern for privacy. The technology allows for tracing all contacts, their distance from the user and the duration of interaction. When 2,5 billion people world-wide find themselves under a lock-down with an unknown fraction of them being infected without showing symptoms, it seems reasonable to deploy digital technology to monitor and trace hotspots and alert and test people in order to intervene immediately. Despite this laudable goal the adoption rate has been disappointingly low. From the beginning developers were acutely aware that privacy issues could hinder the adoption rate needed for the app to be effective. Although in Europe remarkable progress that has been achieved, including the cooperation of two of the world's largest digital companies, tracing apps have not met the ambitious goals they were developed for. The fear persists that the data can be passed on to the authorities despite assurances that they would be deleted after a certain period and that emergency measures would not be prolonged.

At the core of citizens' attitudes and responsiveness to new digital technologies are concerns about safeguarding privacy rights that should guard them from undue surveillance by the state beyond the emergency. It is largely about

---

1 Personal communication. See also Helbing, D. 2020, <https://www.youtube.com.watch?v= kKpwyL xh-E>.

trust or distrust of their governments. Despite assurances that the tracing apps developed in several European countries have incorporated safety standards approved by privacy advocacy groups and meet European Commission regulations, the rate of adoption remains poor with privacy the main concern. It is as though the tracing app has become the latest symbol of resistance in a pandemic that threatens to obliterate a cherished right.

Such distrust stands in marked contrast to the insouciance with which most people willingly entrust data about the most intimate aspects of their lives to the giant corporations with whom they have entered into a specific kind of collusion. We divulge how we feel and send data about our daily moods. We were fitness bands that carry information not only about our whereabouts and daily routines, but about the physiological rhythms and fluctuations of our bodies. We think nothing about letting them know whom we meet and what our political preferences are. All this in return for the kinds of digital services, apps and gadgets to which we have become addicted and without which life has become unimaginable. Shoshana Zuboff speaks about *Surveillance Capitalism,* an economic order in which we voluntarily give up our right to privacy in return for the economic benefits that we have learned to crave (Zuboff 2018).

This seems like the ultimate win-win situation, except that there is a reverse side to it. From one moment to the next the nightmare of a surveillance state in the form of a digitally upscaled Bentham's Panopticon could return and exercise total surveillance in decentralized ways. Information obtained through myriads of localized and decentralized electronic devices can be brought together, categorized and standardized in order to be measured against some kind of normative profile that prescribes who one has to be and how one has to act. However, as Zuboff's focus on capitalism makes clear, the main concerns are not so much related to a potential surveillance state but to the economic consequences of living in a capitalistic society. People fear possible discrimination by insurance companies or employers, of not having access to housing or other services that used to be communal and now are in the hands of private companies. Given the predictive power of algorithms and the potential accessibility of our data for employers, insurance companies, credit-rating firms, housing agencies and other private companies, regulation is an absolute necessity. It can only come from the state that has to include itself into the regulation. It matters that we know what it is we want to protect when we speak about privacy.

It is still left to each of us to download a tracing app or not, yet this was not the case for British students whose A-level exams had to be cancelled due to the COVID-19 crisis. During the summer the UK Education Secretary Gavin Williamson introduced a new procedure to review the A-level grades obtained by students. An algorithm should review the previous assessment by their teachers in order to prevent a potential bias in favour of upgrading student performance and to avoid grade inflation. Introduced as a 'moderation system' the algorithms that was deployed led to a reduction of almost 40% of the grades given by teachers. It disadvantaged high performing students from poorly performing schools and all students from schools whose results were improving. These disturbing results were obtained as the algorithm operated through OFQUAL included factors that had little to do with the students' performance and disproportionately affected students in schools located in disadvantaged areas. A public outcry followed as student university applications were seen as being unjustly denied. In the end, the algorithmic 'moderation' had to be cancelled and the students' previous grades were restored.

The incident may present nothing more than a minor, pandemic-related algorithmic hiccup. Yet, it highlights the issues of the increasing deployment of algorithms and machine learning procedures in various policy areas that go much deeper. As the example of the downgrading of teachers' assessment through a machine shows, decisions based on algorithmic results can have substantial implications for those who are affected. It raises issues of political accountability and legal compliance. To avoid outcomes that are patently unjust or in other ways considered biased or illegitimate, recourse is being sought in 'explaining' to users how machine learning systems are designed to improve if not real understanding, at least being informed about the 'black box' of algorithm-based decision-making. 'Explainability', as Diane Coyle and Adrian Weller (2020) argue, is treated as a technical problem, but it is far more.

A machine learning system is set up to optimize an objective function, the functional equivalent of human intention. It therefore must be made explicit what the system is expected to achieve and which are the explicit objectives, values and political choices to be incorporated in the design. In contrast, most policymaking relies on constructive ambiguity to pursue shared objectives. These are often the result of political compromises in order to achieve sufficient political consensus. Political and policy decisions therefore typically include trade-offs between multiple, often incommensurable aims and interests. The algorithms in machine learning systems, however, are utilitarian maximisers of what is ultimately a single quantity which entails explicit weighting of decision criteria.

If the demand for providing explanations about an algorithmic decision-making system prevails, the tension between human decision-making and the increased reliance on machine-supported decision-making will force greater clarity about choices and trade-offs that previously have been made only implicitly. It will be interesting to see how the political and policy-making system reacts to such a challenge. Unless digital machines will learn to observe and incorporate human contradictions, errors and ambiguities – which is far in the future – conflicting objectives and existing contradictions will have to be openly discussed. They need to be resolved in an unequivocal way, because only then are they quantifiable (Coyle and Weller, 2020). Once more, the COVID-19 pandemic offers a rich trove of examples of the lack of clarity about competing objectives. There was no time to seriously discuss priorities beyond slogans like 'whatever it takes' or 'we follow the science'.

Concluding Reflections: COVID-19 – the Disease of the Digital Age?

Science tells us that we will have to live with the virus for some time to come. Everyone will be affected by the long-term economic and social consequences, albeit not in the same way. Likewise, the impact of digitalization that is now percolating rapidly through society will be felt by all when it unleashes its unintended consequences. The predictive power of algorithms is likely to be at the forefront of many of these processes and developments. The wish to know the future is as old as humanity. All cultures practiced some form of divination to find out what the future holds in store. The convergence of access to an enormous amount of data, sophisticated algorithms and unparalleled computational power has enabled us to deploy predictive algorithms across a widening range of applications. Simulation models and complexity science let us see further into the future, but it is ever more urgent to reflect on what we are doing when we make sense of predictions and attribute meaning to them. The more we entrust agency to these algorithms, the more we need to carefully contextualize the outcome of their prediction. There is much to be learned from what worked and what not during the COVID-19 pandemic. The lack and weakness of data needed for reliable predictions is one of the important lessons.

The COVID-19 pandemic highlights in a flash the degree to which we have come to rely upon Artificial Intelligence. We put a huge amount of trust into AI when we ask for and follow the forecast of predictive algorithms. We entrust data to them that encode some of our most intimate desires. We let them follow our daily movements and queries. They have access to our eye movements and facial expressions from which they can infer attention and arousal of the nervous system. Human voices can be emotionally reconstructed so that they elicit emotions from those who feel addressed. We ask algorithms to look ahead and help us in planning, be it the daily routine or even our life. We share our most intimate aspirations with them and are willing to follow what they project for us. We rely on them to make predictions while they know nothing about the future towards which they are blind and don't care.

At the same time we distrust them as we are afraid of what might follow, especially when it comes to infringements of privacy. Yet, there is no contract that regulates these extraordinary gestures of trust and existing regulation to curb violations of privacy is patchy at best. No constitution lays down the fundamental principles of shared values on which rights and obligations are based. Debates around some of these issues are uncoordinated and far from providing sufficient common ground to become binding. As the process of co-evolution accelerates, Edward Lee exhorts us 'let us celebrate our humanity even as we digitalize our world' (Lee 2020). What could this humanity entail? It celebrates our contextual knowledge which is so much richer than anything a well-defined digitalized context provides. It includes tacit knowledge and thrives on the ambivalence that a digital entity abhors and must avoid. It is multi-sensorial in taking in the stimuli and signals it receives from the world around us while these are strictly preselected for an AI and the rest left out as irrelevant. It is therefore crucial to know what we are doing when we transfer the artificially defined and restricted context in which an algorithm places a prediction into the fluid, ambivalent and messy context in which our future will unfold.

From a historical perspective cholera epidemics were the disease of the industrial age. Repeated outbreaks occurred in densely crowded urban quarters where the most basic hygienic facilities and infrastructures were lacking. Perhaps future generations will look back and see the COVID-19 pandemic as the disease of the digital age. A previously unknown corona virus devised uncanny ways to attack multiple organs of the human body and to transmit the disease by infecting a-symptomatic carriers. The virus encounters a world that is globally interconnected and will remain so despite attempts to return to the nostalgia of national sovereignty. It is a highly complex world that brings together a global economy with its interdependent supply chains and a tightly interconnected financial system. Migration and the plight of migrant workers are likely to continue, just as global mobility is likely to resume, perhaps at a somewhat lower level. It is a world at the brink of a major environmental disaster in which we stumble forward towards one or several tipping points whose exact timing cannot be predicted. Meanwhile, we continue to drive whatever remaining wildlife closer into the already overcrowded urban habitats, opening them up to the viruses that will come with them.

In retrospect, the response to the cholera outbreaks and related diseases of the industrial age was a resolute introduction of hygienic measures and basic hygiene infrastructures as part of rapid urbanization and industrialization. In order to manage them, substantial administrative-bureaucratic capacities were built up, strengthening the nation-state at the same time. After many political struggles and social unrest the disease-causing bacteria and viruses associated with the industrial age were gradually brought under some kind of control through a health care system and welfare provisions intended to cover the entire population. In today's world, there are still large parts where these previously reached standards are lacking.

The restructuration and reforms that were undertaken in the wake of previous pandemics are a reminder of the huge challenges that we face in the digital age. We have the most advanced techno-scientific systems at our disposal and a highly efficient AI that we both trust and distrust. But such a dichotomy, as other dichotomies, will not bring us much further unless we develop and cultivate the kind of critical thinking and judgement that is needed to remain alert to what a digitalized world does to us being human. Algorithms and data are useless if they are not socially contextualized. We have become part of a complex system that includes viruses and digital objects, advanced mathematical simulation models as well as the care that must be given to patients and those who suffer. Our collective response to the COVID-19 pandemic has revealed that there is still a long way to better understand the directions into which digitalization pushes us, but also what needs to be done to maintain and perhaps redefine what it means to be human.

References

Caduff, C. (2020) What Went Wrong: Corona and the World after the Full Stop, *Medical Anthropology Quarterly*, vol.0, iss 0: 1–21, DOI: 10.1111/maq.12599.

Coyle, D. and Weller, A. (2020) "Explaining" Machine Learning Reveals Policy Challenges, *Science*, 26 June, vol. 368 (6498): 1433–1434, DOI: 10.1126/science.aba9647.

Lee, E. A. (2020) *The Coevolution: The Entwined Futures of Humans and Machines*, MIT Press: Cambridge.

Leonelli, S. and Tempini, N. (eds.) (2020) *Data Journeys in the Sciences*, Springer Open Access, <https://www.springer.com/gp/book/9783030371760>.

Nowotny, H. (2015) *The Cunning of Uncertainty*, Polity Press: Cambridge.

Prainsack, B., Kittel, B., Kritzinger, S. and Boomgaarden, H. (2020) 'COVID-19 affects us all – unequally. Lessons from Austria', *Medium Coronavirus Blog*, <https://medium.com/@bprainsack/covid-19-affects-us-all-unequally-lessons-from-austria-faf8398fddc1>.

Snowden, F. (2019) *Epidemics and Society: From the Black Death to the Present*, New Haven: Yale University Press.

Werthner, H. et al. (2019) Vienna Manifesto on Digital Humanism, viewed 20 June 2019, <www.informatik.tuwien.ac.at/dighum/>.

Zuboff, S. (2018) *The Age of Surveillance Capitalism: The Fight for a Human Future at the New Frontier of Power, Public Affairs*, New York: Hachette Book Group.

Eva Horn
Tipping Points: The Anthropocene and Covid-19

As I wrote this text in the spring of 2020, a large part of the world was under lock-down because of the outbreak of SARS-CoV-2. It was barely six months since the *Fridays for Future* demonstrations. So one could read quite a few articles dealing with the relationship between the coronavirus and the current ecological crisis which we have come to label the "Anthropocene." Are shrinking wildlife habitats, species migration and dangerously close human-animal contact directly or indirectly responsible for the Covid-19 pandemic? Or does the corona crisis rather present a temporary break in the otherwise relentless increase of greenhouse gases, a breather for air pollution hotspots, a chance for an ecologically sound reconstruction following the economic collapse? Due to reduced traffic and halted industry, blue skies have suddenly returned to many cities for the first time in decades. Many see Covid-19 as an opportunity to implement a completely new and more appropriate approach to environmental policy. The virus and its spread have taught us something about the fatal global interweaving of supply chains and tourist flows which are a driving factor in climate change. Is Covid-19, some columnists asked, not in fact a symptom of the Anthropocene (Scherer 2020)? Is it a "dress rehearsal" for the Great Climate Collapse (Latour 2020)? Or, looked at from a different perspective, does it offer, albeit by force of circumstances, an experimental space in which to test out how things might be done differently – proof that it is possible after all to limit travel and transportation, to reorganize work and communication, and to reduce the consumption of fossil fuels? Could it even present an opportunity to reinvent international cooperation in the face of a global threat?

These questions can hardly be answered at present. What I propose to consider here are epistemic links between the ecological crisis of the Anthropocene and the corona crisis. These are to be found, as I will argue, less in causal or metonymic relationships (the Anthropocene as the *cause* of Covid-19, or the pandemic as a *symptom* of the Anthropocene), than in temporal structures and event forms. What kind of caesura are we witnessing? What do the two crises – the ecological metacrisis of the Anthropocene and the global pandemic – have in common? In the case of the Anthropocene, this involves asking what it means to proclaim the beginning of a new geochronological epoch. How do we account for this beginning and on the basis of which historical thresholds? Which time scales come into view? A number of these questions have already been exten-

https://doi.org/10.1515/9783110713350-008

sively discussed (Hamilton 2016; Veland and Lynch 2016; Chakrabarty 2018; Horn and Bergthaller 2020). I will focus on a particular type of event that I deem emblematic of the Anthropocene: the *tipping point*. Both the Anthropocene and the SARS-CoV-2 pandemic are characterized by such tipping points, which combine slow latency periods with sudden rapid escalations. How does the structural, slow and barely perceptible crisis of the Anthropocene relate to the acute corona crisis which is occurring at breakneck speed but with an unclear time horizon? Where is their point of convergence, and what forms of planning for the future can be derived from it? Put simply: What can we learn from Covid-19 for the future of the Anthropocene?

In recent years, the Anthropocene has been discussed primarily as a geo-chronological concept: It has been established that humans have changed the Earth System to such an extent that the traces of these interventions can be found all over the world as a distinct sedimentary layer (Waters et al. 2016; Zalasiewicz et al. 2019). This also means that the state of the planet has changed so radically from the preceding 10,000 years of stability that it is no longer possible to speak of the present as the Holocene. The concept of the Anthropocene presents an ecological threshold, a break with the unusually stable ecological conditions of the Holocene (Hamilton 2016). Earth System science has shown that the earth has entered a state for which there is no parallel in its recent history (Moore et al. 2001).

The point of the term Anthropocene is thus to give an ecological diagnosis of the present – but one that locates it within the vast time scales of the history of the earth. This solicits a new understanding of history, with novel actors (such as fossil fuels), different kinds of narratives (along ecological lines) and unusual time scales. Both historical dimensions – the vast temporality of "deep time" and the rapid change brought about by threshold transitions – must be related to each other in order to understand how human history is inscribed in the larger framework of the Earth System. This also involves telling the history of humankind in a different way. A history of the Anthropocene tells of ecological transitions rather than political revolutions, of changing energy regimes rather than social change, and of technology rather than world-views. What it is interested in are the *material factors* involved in the threshold transition from the Holocene to the Anthropocene: first and foremost the change of energy sources (from renewable energy to fossil fuels), the rapid consumption of certain resources, the worldwide networks of trade and economic relations and, not least, the transfer and transformation of living organisms.

The Anthropocene: Thresholds and Tipping Points

As the "start" of the Anthropocene, the *Anthropocene Working Group,* along with many environmental historians, have proposed the "Great Acceleration," referring to the marked escalation of numerous parameters of consumption and environmental change from 1950 onwards (McNeill and Engelke 2016; Steffen et al. 2004; Steffen et al. 2015). The acceleration of social and economic change alongside the increasing consumption of resources are captured in a famous graph that visualizes this escalation in 24 curves, the common "hockey stick" shape of which is striking. On one side, the graph shows socio-economic developments, from the increase in the world's population to global GDP, urbanization and financial flows, water and paper consumption, transport and junk food. On the other, it shows ecological factors in the Earth System: the increase in greenhouse gases (nitrogen oxides, methane, carbon dioxide), the hole in the ozone layer, rising temperatures, species loss, deforestation etc. Even if in some of the curves there is a slight up-turn as early as the nineteenth century, it is this sharp escalation of socio-economic factors that has, within two generations, turned humankind from a small environmental factor into a large-scale force in the Earth System (Steffen et al. 2015: 94).

While the concept of the Great Acceleration impressively captures the parallel escalation of socio-economic trends and changes in the Earth System since the end of the Second World War, it cannot explain its own precondition – the switch to fossil fuels. The most serious consequence of this switch for the Earth System – the increase of CO_2 in the atmosphere – remained barely noticeable for a long time. This curve begins to rise gently but visibly in the last decades of the nineteenth century, grows significantly from the 1930s and then in the 1950s the sharp upward turn associated with the Great Acceleration occurs. The diagnosis of acceleration must therefore be supplemented by a different temporality – a slow, barely noticeable increase in side-effects that only come into view belatedly. The Anthropocene thus encompasses very heterogeneous temporalities: on the one hand, the rapid acceleration of consumption, technical innovation, mobility, global networking, etc., and on the other, latent, subtle changes in society and the environment that occur in imperceptible gradations – and thus are difficult to address politically.

The strange coupling of long, continuous, seemingly uneventful latency periods with moments of sudden acceleration and rapid change is captured in the concept of the "tipping point." The term stems originally from the social and economic sciences, where it denotes the abrupt change of a given development.

Yet in order to grasp the use of the concept in the context of the Anthropocene, it is necessary to consider the specific understanding in Earth System science of the relationship between human civilization and nature. Earth System science treats human life forms and human activity as part of a system of nature that is active and dynamic (cf. Lenton 2016). Nature is understood to be a planetary, self-regulating system. What emerges is a model of nature without a stable state. Thanks to new measurement and computing capacities, Earth System science today has a detailed understanding of the complex interaction of the various components of the Earth System. The biosphere – comprising all living organisms on the planet – has repeatedly acted as a stabilizer and "thermostat" in this system (cf. Lovelock 1991, 2006). However, this dynamic is inflected by sudden and profound changes in the overall system. With the Anthropocene, humankind as an agent of these changes is coming into focus. The founding document of Earth System science, the 2001 *Amsterdam Declaration*, is already informed by this perspective:

> Earth System dynamics are characterised by critical thresholds and abrupt changes. Human activities could inadvertently trigger such changes with severe consequences for Earth's environment and inhabitants. The Earth System has operated in different states over the last half million years, with abrupt transitions (a decade or less) sometimes occurring between them. Human activities have the potential to switch the Earth System to alternative modes of operation that may prove irreversible and less hospitable to humans and other life. ... The nature of changes now occurring simultaneously in the Earth System, their magnitudes and rates of change are unprecedented. *The Earth is currently operating in a no-analogue state.* (Moore et al. 2001)

What we are looking at here are tipping points – hard-to-predict moments of dramatic change in a complex self-regulating system. A tipping point occurs when a threshold value is reached at which a slight increase of a certain factor suddenly causes a massive change in the overall system, which thus irreversibly transitions to another state. At the tipping point, a small quantitative increase leads to drastic qualitative change in the entire system, or to the emergence of unpredictable new phenomena.

Tipping points refer to a type of event that lies beyond the difference between culture and nature, between human decisions and natural processes. Malcolm Gladwell's bestseller *Tipping Point* (2001) is for the most part concerned with social phenomena. His thesis is that certain emergent phenomena – from fashion trends, crime waves to bestsellers – are to be understood as epidemics: "Ideas and products and messages and behaviors spread just like viruses do" (Gladwell 2001: 5). According to Gladwell, social processes with tipping points have three basic characteristics: (1) They are contagious, i.e. they require participants to be in contact with each other and to pass on characteristics or opinions in increasing numbers; (2) in this process, small causes can have large consequences; and (3) after a long lead-up time, changes happen suddenly and quickly. Gladwell's examples are largely cheerful – the enforcement of fashions, the ebbing of crime, the effectiveness of drug and health policies. But of course, the idea can also be turned towards the catastrophic. "Catastrophe" – etymologically meaning "a sudden turn downwards" – is actually nothing other than a Greek word for tipping point. Accordingly, the term has become a catchword for the catastrophic tendencies of the present.

The problem is that tipping points are relatively difficult to predict. They come suddenly at the end of slow, seemingly continuous processes that solicit the deceptive expectation of further continuity. They begin as micro-trends that can hardly be measured and seem so minor that they can be ignored. Or they emerge from a new constellation of apparently unrelated factors whose interaction could not be foreseen. Self-regulating systems such as ecosystems, markets or societies can, over long periods of time and despite all crisis-like tendencies, repeatedly bring themselves into provisional equilibrium – until they reach that dangerous point of sudden change. Reaching a tipping point means that the system is "saturated" (to use a term from chemistry) or that a "critical mass" has been reached (in the terminology of physics). While a negative feedback mechanism had previously stabilized a given system, at a certain threshold the negative feedback tips over into a self-reinforcing cycle of positive feedback leading to escalation.

There is nothing new about rapid and radical breaks in social or economic trends – they are called revolutions or economic crises. Yet, the volatility of human culture has long been contrasted with the stability of nature. We long held the belief that while human life changes in leaps and bounds, nature does so only gradually, step by step and in scales of time so vast that they are hardly perceptible. Recent findings in climate research and Earth System science, however, make this image of a largely "inert" nature seem obsolete. The impression of a "stable nature" is a deception of the Holocene – that anomaly in the history of the earth that was characterized by extremely few climatic fluctuations. As recent research has shown, climate does in fact experience rapid and profound change (Warde; Robin and Sörlin 2018). According to Earth System scientist Tim Lenton, such change can dramatically transform the state of the entire earth system within decades:

> Whilst much of the behaviour of the Earth system can be described as "linear" and predictable with our current models, there is a class of "non-linear" change that is much harder to predict and potentially much more dangerous. It involves "tipping points" – where a small

perturbation triggers a large response from a part of the Earth system – leading to abrupt and often irreversible changes. Tipping points can occur when there is strong positive feedback within a system, which creates alternative stable states for a range of boundary conditions. When changes in the boundary conditions cause the current state of a system to lose its stability, a tipping point occurs, triggering a transition into the alternative stable state. (Lenton 2016: 100)

Perhaps the most important and threatening of these tipping points are the polar ice caps. These large white ice sheets increase the earth's albedo, counteracting the warming of the atmosphere by reflecting sunlight. As they melt away as a result of global warming, they expose the dark surface of sea water – which in turn further increases the warming of the climate. What was previously a stabilizing negative feedback against global warming, now becomes a dangerous positive feedback: the more the ice melts, the faster the atmosphere warms. This dynamic makes particularly clear the non-linear behavior of processes with tipping points. Everything changes when a single threshold is reached: the melting point of ice. In the range of a tiny temperature difference of a few degrees, the role of water in the system changes – and thus becomes a factor that severely affects the entire Earth System.

Unfortunately, tipping points rarely occur alone. They can influence each other and lead to convergences of complex escalating processes that are difficult to predict. This gives rise to domino effects in which several tipping points trigger or reinforce each other. It is precisely the combination of melting polar ice caps, rising sea levels and global warming that could trigger a dynamic which will accelerate climate change to a much greater degree than we can currently anticipate. Even the slight difference between 1.5 and 2 degrees Celsius could bring about serious and destabilizing changes to the habitability of coastal regions, the global water cycles, or ocean ecosystems.

Understanding the interaction of nature as a self-regulating system and the effective power of humans within this system thus provides insight into the *inherent instability* of the system. Climate, with its rapid and radical upheavals, is only one dimension of this volatility. Others relate to changes in the biosphere on land with the loss of habitats, migration and extinction of species, the loss of ecosystem services (through the disappearance of insects, for example) or even the changing world of microbes. If the Anthropocene is concerned with the geophysical power of humans, then the anthropogenic transformation of nature must be linked to its volatility: "Humans are more powerful; nature is more powerful," writes the Australian philosopher Clive Hamilton. "Taken together, there is more power at work on Earth" (Hamilton 2017: 45). An ever more irritable nature encounters increasing intervention from humans.

Processes with inherent tipping points thus connect two opposing types of events on different time scales. On the one hand, there are slow, continuous and gradual processes – latency periods. On the other hand, there are sudden, erratic upheavals that appear difficult to predict; they occur rapidly and bring about irreversible – often catastrophic – changes. The problem is that even this suddenness is barely perceptible, as long as one remains caught up within its dynamics. The concept of the Great Acceleration says nothing else. It ought to be understood less as a review of the recent past than as a prognosis: we are in the midst of an open-ended transformation that is progressing ever faster and only a small part of it seems to be foreseeable, shapeable or avoidable.

Catastrophe without Event

To situate oneself in the Anthropocene means to plunge "blindly," as it were, into a future that is arriving ever more rapidly and that is less and less predictable. What marks the consciousness of the present is the feeling of being at a tipping point, at the very moment a long latency period turns into quick disaster. "The idea of a tipping point introduces a perspective that the 'past' that led up to the current crisis is *only partially understood*, and that the *current transformation is a state of flux* where we have departed from past conditions, but have not yet arrived at a 'new normal'" (Veland and Lynch 2016: 4, my emphasis). The present is characterized by the opacity of the future; it consists above all in anticipating catastrophic upheavals – but without knowing exactly which ones. Thus, in the last twenty years, a wealth of non-fiction books, consulting literature, novels and cinema blockbusters exploring possible catastrophe scenarios have been produced – not a few of them under a title that sums up the sense of time in the 2000s and 2010s: "The end of the world as we knew it."

My diagnosis of this feeling was that the present felt the world was heading towards disaster, yet without having an idea of its concrete form (Horn 2018). There was a sense of foreboding that everything was driving towards tipping points, in ecosystems, climate, financial markets, the welfare states. One such tipping point was illustrated by the financial crisis of 2008/2009, both in its magnitude and the failure to predict it. While one might have foreseen the crash, no one could have anticipated nor prevented its consequences across the global network of financial markets, private credit and public finances. In the past decade, we were hypnotized by a diffuse set of possible worst-case scenarios – from climate collapse in a growing number of cli-fi thrillers to the total extinction of humanity, as in Alan Weisman's 2007 bestseller *The World Without Us* or Jan Zalasiewicz's enormously successful book *The Earth After Us* (2008), which takes up the concept of the Anthropocene from a geological perspective after the end of humankind.

These imaginaries appear to me to be symptoms of a deeper unease. The unease is a complicated mix of two fears: one referring to potential disasters, the other to the outlook that everything continues as before. Or, to put it differently, the prospects of growth and progress that we are constantly confronted with, are, in fact, the real catastrophe. We secretly dream of the big bang, the breaking out of the latency period into the manifest disaster. This conflation of a disruptive collapse and an eery, unhealthy continuity is most clearly embodied in the ecological crisis of the Anthropocene. The Anthropocene is a *catastrophe without event* (Horn 2018: 8 – 9, 55 – 88), both a disruption and (paradoxically) a continuity. It consists of gradual, yet profound changes. It does not take place in spectacular disasters, but in creeping environmental destruction, inconspicuous changes to biotopes, gradual transformations of water cycles and climate patterns. In the two decades since 2000, the present felt like the latency period before a looming collapse, the exact form of which, however, could only be imagined. This is why disaster movies had their heyday, and it is also why *Fridays for Future*, the only social movement that succeeded in putting climate change on the political agenda, relied heavily on apocalyptic rhetoric – even if this rhetoric is hardly appropriate to the structure of the problem. In order to counter the *catastrophe without event*, it was necessary to conjure up the ultimate event: the end of the world.

Today, with Covid-19, things look different. The arbitrariness of disaster scenarios has suddenly given way to something all too real: the pandemic. Not that there haven't been repeated warnings of precisely this scenario, including an eerily prophetic TED talk by Bill Gates in 2015 and repeated warnings by the WHO after the SARS, H5N1, and Ebola outbreaks. The question is how the *catastrophe without event* relates to the *catastrophe as event* that we experience with Covid-19. Is it a disaster movie come true? (The similarities to Soderbergh's *Contagion* (2011) seem uncanny.) Is the earth striking back? Quite a few commentators have tried to construct such a causal link: Increasing habit destruction and the consumption of "bushmeat" inevitably leads to zoonoses (Pascale and Roger 2020). Seen this way, the coronavirus would therefore present the revenge of the earth in the Anthropocene. But even if the disappearance of natural habitats does indeed increase the probability of zoonoses, assuming an immediate causality between the Anthropocene and Covid-19 oversimplifies the matter (cf. Ali 2020).

It is more plausible to understand the Anthropocene (and its structures, such as globalized travel, production and supply networks) as a framework facilitating the course of the crisis. As a worldwide pandemic, Covid-19 is clearly a phenomenon of the Great Acceleration. In 1950, the infection would not have travelled around the globe so quickly, nor would the shortages and global economic consequences have been so widespread. Yet most interesting to me are the epistemic parallels between the pandemic and the Anthropocene. Like the Anthropocene, the Covid-crisis is neither a purely natural disaster nor a purely social one. Bruno Latour welcomed the affirmation of the inseparability of nature and society in modern times (Latour 1993, Latour 2017) by Covid-19, and called the pandemic, not without a certain *Schadenfreude*, a "dress rehearsal" for the catastrophes that the Anthropocene still holds in store (Latour 2020). The pandemic exposes the vulnerability of the globalized world in the Anthropocene, but it also exposes the massive inequalities of this vulnerability. The point of intersection between Covid-19 and the Anthropocene is clearest from the viewpoint of statistics, which has become the main epistemic field of the pandemic. Following Foucault, Latour assigns this kind of knowledge to the nineteenth century as the epistemic field of biopolitics. Such a biopolitical interpretation of Covid-19 may be true for the interplay between political measures and the statistical recording of the population, as we have experienced in lockdowns, curfews, mass testing, and daily infection rates. etc. The curves themselves, however, are clearly not those of the biopolitical nineteenth century. They are the hockey sticks of the Great Acceleartion, visualizing global processes with sudden escalations.

It is no coincidence that the German climate scientist John Schellnhuber sees a parallel between the developments of Covid-19 and global warming: "[T]he ominous curve of the worldwide cumulative Covid-19 cases has an iconic counterpart, namely, the famous Mauna-Loa curve of the increase in atmospheric CO_2 concentration" (Schellnhuber 2020). Schellnhuber here points to the famous "Keeling curve", named after the chemist Charles D. Keeling who started documenting the increase in CO_2 at the Mauna Loa Observatory (Hawai) in 1958. While the Keeling curve starts only "after" a tipping point (which would have to be placed in the 1930s) and has since recorded an unstoppable rise in CO_2 levels in the atmosphere, in the Covid-19 curves we clearly see a long, flat latency period and then – in mid-March 2020 – a sudden upward turn and, since April, a weekly fluctuation in the daily cases, while the total number of infections worldwide is steadily increasing. In Europe, the curve slowly flattened in May (rising again for the "second wave" which started in August), while in the USA, Brazil, and India the number of infections continued to rise steadily, impressively documented on the website of Johns Hopkins University's Coronavirus Resource Center.

The epistemic similarity between Covid-19 and the Anthropocene lies in the type of event that characterizes both developments. Both are escalations following a long latency period and suddenly surging upwards. In the case of Covid-19 this escalation took place at a breakneck speed. Not years, but days decided the course of the curve – leading to rising infection rates and deaths, overburdened health care systems, stress on vital infrastructure and brutal economic consequences. The combination of tipping points, the domino effects of collapsing systems, to which climate scientists keep alerting us, are confirmed by the pandemic in a textbook manner. Covid-19 demonstrates how everything is connected: infection rates affect the world of work, consumption and health care, which in turn affect national budgets, global supply chains, production processes and labor markets. These linkages recognize neither the boundaries of nature versus society nor national or continental divides within a globally networked world.

Covid-19 is the Anthropocene in fast-forward – a model and an example. The pandemic can thus teach us a lesson about the dangers of ill-preparedness as well as about the risks of taking decisions in a state of highly incomplete and uncertain information. When the virus struck, even modern industrialized countries were not equipped in terms of their health systems and infrastructures, nor did decisions on lockdowns and/or social distancing always come at the right time or get implemented in a consistent way – some moved earlier and more efficiently, others more half-heartedly, others not at all. The failure to be prepared for something that had actually long been known to be a possible scenario once again reflects the structure of disaster thinking in the Anthropocene. While we have quite precise scientific knowledge of possible future threats we face so many options and conflicts of priority that governments and societies are incapable of carrying out concrete precautionary measures. What eventually prevails in the cacophony of disaster scenarios is precisely the principle of business as usual, an attempt to extend the present endlessly into the future. When things then all of a sudden tip, one has at once a feeling of complete unpreparedness and an uncanny sense of déjà-vu.

Sustainability in the Anthropocene

What could "sustainability" mean in a world of tipping points and escalations? Epistemically, the most interesting phase in tipping points is the latency period. It is a matter of both recognizing barely perceptible signs of an impending disaster and of acknowledging the global network of dependencies in which we are entangled. In the Covid-19 crisis we undoubtedly find ourselves beyond the decisive tipping point – maybe with more surprises to come. But where exactly do we stand in the slowly unfolding crisis of the Anthropocene? The *catastrophe without event* confronts every attempt to manage the future with the impossible task of including an unpredictable future in its precautionary calculations. If "sustainability" focuses on long-term strategies that can be extended into a foreseeable future, then it is definitely not the right keyword for the Anthropocene (cf. Horn 2017). Rather, the aim must be not only to anticipate radical changes, but to actively shape them. It is not about seeking to prolong the present but being ready to leave it behind consciously and in a controlled manner. It involves a different way of dealing with the future, which will in any case be different from and more volatile than the present. It is no coincidence that the politicization of climate change has not been carried out by adults, but by the next generation of politically silenced children and adolescents. They are looking into a fragile, radically different future that they cannot simply stand by and let happen. The question is how to give voice – and concrete power – to time horizons beyond the usual election cycles, ten year programs etc. Dealing with problems in the Anthropocene has to deal with much vaster time scales and much more unpredictable futures.

The Anthropocene thus needs a self-reflexive future management that is not only aware of the range of possible worst-case scenarios, but also of its incomplete knowledge of them. It requires a permanent reflection on those "unknown unknowns" (Horn 2018: 177), once famously ruminated by Donald Rumsfeld. On the one hand, this means an imperative of "preparedness," of being prepared for many different eventualities – Only a few months ago, this attitude would have been dismissed as alarmism. On the other hand, it also means being constantly alert and ready to revise one's hypotheses, which is the essence of scientific research – being aware of one's incomplete knowledge. It is extremely odd that these two attitudes – the gesture of being prepared and the admission of incomplete knowledge – have repeatedly given rise to the ridicule and biting criticism of the scientists consulted in response to the Covid-19 crisis. Anyone who appeared in March 2020 wearing a protective mask was derided as hysterical; anyone who laid down a few essential supplies was accused of being a toilet paper hoarder. Scientists who revised their knowledge based on more recent research findings were berated as being inconsistent. And any hospital chief or health minister who, concerned about a possible epidemic, purchased surplus medical equipment or set up intensive care beds beyond immediate requirements, would have been chased out of office for economic mismanagement.

But sustainability in the Anthropocene requires these two highly unpopular attitudes: Firstly, we need to accept "alarmism" as vigilance towards the possibilities and signs of future escalations. We need to etablish a precautionary principle not just towards technical and social innovations but towards the possibility of rapid changes to the very ground we stand on: nature. Secondly, we need to admit our incomplete knowledge about many non-linear processes. We have to develop forms of knowledge and awareness that constantly reflect on their own elements of blindness and ignorance. Alarmism and the awareness of ignorance, however, do not mean scepticism towards established science such as the IPCC reports or the findings of epidemiology. The difficulty of precisely anticipating non-linear processes applies to climate as well as to social systems, to economics as well as to contagions. But these two attitudes – vigilance and epistemic self-reflection – require a significant degree of imagination. For this reason, the philosopher Hans Jonas advocated an "ethics of the future" based on what he called the "heuristics of fear." As a "compass" or inspiration for such an ethics of the future, he proposed imagining the anticipated danger as precisely as possible: "What can serve us as a compass? The envisioned threat itself! It is only in its *lightning flash from the future* – in the recognition of its planetary scope and profound implications for mankind – that it is possible to discover the ethical principles from which we can derive the obligations that our newfound power demands" (Jonas 1984: 7–8, my translation). Jonas' advice is both complicated and simple: the idea is to assume a standpoint in the future and to look back from that future onto the present as its prehistory, its latency period. Such a glance from the future onto the present cannot be done without imagination. Possible future developments, to the extent that they are now visible at best in small indicators or unspectacular curves, must be extrapolated, fleshed out and highlighted into full-blown scenarios of a world, as it were, *beyond* the tipping point.

This is not only a problem of knowledge, but also one of agency. It is about not only *knowing* something, but also *believing* it – and acting on this conviction. The French philosopher of science Jean-Pierre Dupuy has described this attitude as "enlightened catastrophism," which helps us move beyond denial or paralysis in the face of a threat: "Let's suppose we are certain, or almost certain, that catastrophe lies ahead [...] The problem is that we do not believe it. *We do not believe what we know*" (Dupuy 2002: 141, 144 f., my translation). To believe what we know means to make it an integral part of the reality we live in, to translate it into practical measures or demands. Warnings of global pandemics had been around for a while, but nobody 'believed' in them. Today we hear Lenton or Schellnhuber and their colleagues warn us of the complex web of escalations right ahead of us. Yet the governments that Schellnhuber advises, for example, only partly believe in what they know. The point is to understand threats not as a mere hypothesis but as a *fact* – like a prophecy that says what *will* come, not what might come. For it is only by believing the prophecy, as Dupuy explains using the biblical story of Jonah, that it can become an instrument of its own prevention. This requires that a possible threat becomes credible, tangible, concretely imaginable – not as a possible future, but as the *given* one. "The future," wrote

Jorge Luis Borges, "is inevitable and exact, but it may not happen. God lurks in the intervals" (1999: 223). Humans, one might add, have no other option than to make good use of these intervals.

If the pandemic can teach us a lesson for managing the future in the Anthropocene, it is not only about the possibility of tipping points. It is also about the immense cost of dithering and of scepticism towards scientific findings. Covid-19 also teaches a lesson regarding the wealth of possibilities we are facing – for the best and for the worst. With the pandemic, we have been caught up in a global catastrophe that was considered unthinkable outside of movie theatres. We have learned that within days and weeks our lives and livelihoods can be uprooted. However, Covid-19 has also shaken many of the iron laws of what was deemed politically and economically feasible. It can therefore be seen as an experiment in the scope of possible action that is afforded societies and individuals in the face of global crises. It has awakened an awareness of contingency, making possible that were previously considered unthinkable. The only thing that is now no longer possible is to carry on as before.

References

Ali, S. (2020) How the Current Coronavirus Pandemic Links to Questions of Ecological Sustainability in the Anthropocene, accessed: 10.05.2020, https://sustainabilitycommunity.springernature.com/users/183121-saleem-ali/posts/63681-how-the-current-pandemic-links-to-broader-questions-of-sustainability-in-the-anthropocene.

Borges, J. L. (1999) The Creation and P.H. Gosse. In: E. Weinberger (ed.) *Selected Non-Fictions*, trans. E. Allen, S. J. Levine, and E. Weinberger, New York: Viking. 222–4.

Dupuy, J.-P. (2002) *Pour un catastrophisme éclairé. Quand l'impossible est certain*, Paris: Éditions du Seuil.

Gates, B. (2015) The Next Outbreak? We're Not Ready, accessed: 10.05.2020, https://www.ted.com/talks/bill_gates_the_next_outbreak_we_re_not_ready.

Gladwell, M. (2001) *Tipping Point. How Little Things Can Make a Big Difference*, New York: Little Brown.

Hamilton, C. (2016) The Anthropocene as Rupture. *The Anthropocene Review* 3 (2) 93–106.

Hamilton, C. (2017) *Defiant Earth. The Fate of Humans in the Anthropocene*, London: Polity Press.

Horn, E. (2018) *The Future as Catastrophe: Imagining Disaster in the Modern Age*, trans. Valentine Pakis. New York: Columbia University Press.

Horn, E. (2017) Jenseits der Kindeskinder. Nachhaltigkeit im Anthropozän. *Merkur* 71 (814), 5–17.

Horn, E., and Bergthaller, H. (2020) *The Anthropocene: Key Issues for the Humanities*, London: Routledge.

Jonas, H. (1984) *The Imperative of Responsibility*, transl. H. Jonas, and D. Herr, Chicago: Chicago University Press.

Latour, B. (1993) *We Have Never been Modern*, New York: Harvester Wheatsheaf.

Latour, B. (2017) *Facing Gaia: Eight Lectures on the New Climatic Regime*. Cambridge: Polity Press.

Latour, B. (2020) Is This a Dress Rehearsal? *Critical Inquiry*, 26.03.2020, accessed: 10.05.2020, https://critinq.wordpress.com/2020/03/26/is-this-a-dress-rehearsal/.

Lenton, T. (2016) *Earth Systems Science: A Very Short Introduction*. Oxford: Oxford University Press.

Lenton, T. et al. (2019) Climate Tipping Points – Too Risky to Bet Against. *Nature* 575 (7784), 592–5.

Lovelock, J. E. (1991) *Gaia. The Practical Science of Planetary Medicine*, London: Gaia Books.

Lovelock, J. E. (2006) *The Revenge of Gaia. Why the Earth is Fighting Back and How We Can Still Save Humanity,* London: Allen Lane.

McNeill, J. R., and Engelke, P. (2016) *The Great Acceleration. An Environmental History of the Anthropocene since 1945*, Cambridge, Mass.: Belknap Press of Harvard University Press.

Moore, B. III et al. (2001) Amsterdam Declaration on Earth System Science 2001, accessed: 10.05.2020, http://www.igbp.net/about/history/2001amsterdamdeclarationonearthsystemscience.4.1-b8ae20512db692f2a680001312.html.

Pascale, F. De, and Roger, J.-C. (2020) Coronavirus: An Anthropocene's Hybrid? The Need for a Geoethic Perspective for the Future of the Earth, *AIMS Geosciences* 6 (1), 131–4.

Schelling, T. C. (1971) Dynamic Models of Segregation, *Journal of Mathematical Sociology* 1 (2), 143–86.

Schellnhuber, J. (2020) Seuchen im Anthropozän. Was uns die Krisen lehrten. *Frankfurter Allgemeine Zeitung*, 15.04.2020, accessed: 10.05.2020, https://www.faz.net/aktuell/feuilleton/debatten/seu-che-im-anthropozaen-die-lehren--der-corona-krise-16726494.html.

Scherer, B. (2020) Die Pandemie ist kein Überfall von Außerirdischen, *Frankfurter Allgemeine Zeitung*, 03.05.2020, accessed: 10.05.2020, https://www.faz.net/aktuell/wissen/geist-soziales/leben-im-anthropozaen-die-pande-mie-ist-kein-ueberfall-von-ausserirdischen-16744840.html.

Steffen, W. et al. (2004) *Global Change and the Earth System. A Planet Under Pressure*, Berlin: Springer.

Steffen, W. et al. (2011) The Anthropocene. Conceptual and Historical Perspectives. *Philosophical Transactions of the Royal Society* 369 (1938), 842–67.

Steffen, W. et al. (2015) The Trajectory of the Anthropocene. The Great Acceleration. *Anthropocene Review* 2 (1), 81–98.

Veland, S., and Lynch, A. (2016) Scaling the Anthropocene. *Geoforum* 72, 1–5.

Warde, P., Robin, L., and Sörlin, S. (2018) *The Environment. History of an Idea*, Baltimore: Johns Hopkins University Press.

Waters, C. et al. (2016) The Anthropocene Is Functionally and Stratigraphically Distinct from the Holocene. *Science* 351 (6269), aad2622.

Weisman, A. (2007) *The World without Us*, New York: Thomas Dunne Books.

Wilkinson, B. H. (2005) Humans as Geologic Agents. *Geology* 33 (3), 161–4.

Zalasiewicz, J. (2008) *The Earth after Us. What Legacy Will Humans Leave in the Rocks?*, Oxford: Oxford University Press.

Zalasiewicz, J. et al. (eds.) (2019) *The Anthropocene as a Geological Time Unit. A Guide to the Scientific Evidence and Current Debate*, Cambridge: Cambridge University Press.

Bryan S. Turner

The Political Theology of Covid-19: A Comparative History of Human Responses to Catastrophes

In this chapter I consider the human need for meaning-making vocabularies in response to catastrophes and disasters. Human responses to catastrophes in the past often took the form of theodicies, that is, attempts to vindicate the will of God in the face of traumatic catastrophes. These disasters could be either natural, such as earthquakes or political-social, such as warfare. Recent debates on the risk society may suggest that catastrophes may increase with modernization (Beck 1992; Giddens 1990: 124–5). One might conclude that globalization and technical change have made our world increasingly vulnerable. Covid-19 is an obvious example of the risks of open borders and globalization. However, the ancient world was not exempt from such world-changing events and there are certain historical similarities between Covid-19 and previous pandemics. We can identify four parallel developments. The very idea of social distancing and quarantine were invented in reponse to the Black Death. In 1348, the port authorities of Venice established a forty-day period before ships could unload sailors and goods, which gives us 'quarantine'. Similar measures were adopted in English ports in the same period. Secondly, previous plagues have resulted in considerable social and political disturbance in response to economic hardship. Plagues uncovered obvious differences in contagion and mortality rates between different social strata, thereby adding fuel to social unrest. Thirdly, plagues and natural disasters had deep effects on collective consciousness and memory with considerable generational differences in terms of beliefs and values. With the Covid-19 pandemic, we can see the similarities with the plagues of the past. We have yet to see how the collective consciousness around generational differences between pre-Covid-19 and post-Covid-19 might evolve. Will there be a post-Covid-10 era? Perhaps this brings in a possible fourth similarity. The bubonic plague is still active and on 7 July 2020 the World Health Organization released a report to say that an outbreak of bubonic plague ('the Black Death') had been identified in Inner Mongolia. Covid-19 is a zoonotic disease, that is, an infection transferred from animals to humans. As our natural environment is further corrupted, we can expect more global plagues. In short, we are not in a post-bubonic plague era and, as with influenza, we may never be entirely free from Covid-19 outbreaks.

https://doi.org/10.1515/9783110713350-009

Catastrophe, Fortune and Theodicy

From a sociological perspective, it is the social change brought about by pandemics that is of particular interest. Major disasters of the ancient world often conjured up episodes of major historical change. In the ancient world of the Middle East, after three centuries of peace and stability, Jerusalem fell, in 614 CE, to the Persian army of King Khosroes II. A major disruption of power relations ensued and foreshadowed the Muslim seizure of the city in 638 (Bowerstock 2012). The problematic history of Jerusalem may also illustrate the uncomfortable fact that the consequences of specific catastrophes can stay with us for centuries.

In addition to wars, there is ample evidence of devastating plagues from the past. The Old Testament provides a record of the plagues of Egypt and the Four Horsemen of the Apocalypse have provided a dramatic representation of death and famine (Grell 2000). From the perspective of reflections on the meaning of the Covid-19 pandemic, we might begin an inquiry with the Book of Job, which is traditionally regarded as the origin of theodicy, in which Job confronts God with the question: why do the innocent suffer? (Gutiérrez 1988). In the early modern period, the Black Death or the Pestilence from 1346 to 1353 had a devastating impact on the European population and gave rise to dramatic representations of suffering, for which there was no rational explanation (Ziegler 1969) when around twenty million people died from the plague. An early reference to the gruesome idea of the *danse macabre* came from the poet Jean Le Fevre in 1376. The *danse macabre* portrayed the plague as a hideous attack on the human population, regardless of rank, wealth or gender (Huizinga 1996: 156–72). There were many literary responses that included Geoffrey Chaucer's 'The Pardoner's Tale' in the *Canterbury Tales*, written between 1382 and 1400, and Giovanni Boccaccio's *The Decameron*, composed between 1348 and 1353. Goethe's *Faust* was based on the Book of Job. In his analysis of the figure of Faust, Alfred Hoelzel (1979: 6) asks: 'And what is Goethe's *Faust* if not theodicy? …no author prior to Goethe, not even Marlowe, had ever employed the Faust story explicitly to challenge God's role itself and to question the very value of Creation'.

The Black Death was the origin of various manifestations of theodicy. It was typically regarded as a punishment for human sins, for which regular confession was recommended by the bishops of the Church. By contrast, the Flagellants, a sect that attracted large numbers in northern Europe in 1349, gathered in groups and paraded in white gowns flagellating themselves with three-pronged whips.

Unsurprisingly such catastrophes in early and early modern Europe had significant social and political consequences. The most obvious was the Peasants'

Revolt of 1381, also known as Wat Tyler's Rebellion. With the decimation of the working population, wages and prices were rising. To control wage inflation, the Ordinance of Labourers fixed wages and introduced price controls. The revolt was in response to these restrictions. This political and economic crisis was also influential in the work of John Wycliffe (1330 – 84), who was critical of the ruling elites and the wealth of the Roman Catholic Church. His translations of the Bible into the vernacular inspired his followers at the University of Oxford, who became known as the Lollards. It was his attack on the eucharistic doctrine of transubstantiation that forced him to retreat to his rural rectory. He came to be regarded as the predecessor of the Protestant Reformation. The division of Christianity with Martin Luther's theses in 1517, the translation of the Bible into vernacular German and the rise of Lutheranism can be traced back to the catastrophe of 1346 – 53. At this stage we can only speculate about the long-term consequences of the catastrophe of 2020.

These brief examples suggest that the distinction between socio-political and natural catastrophes is somewhat arbitrary; political disasters often attend or follow natural disasters. What they have in common is the human response, namely, that humans often want some meaningful interpretation over and above the factual description of a disaster. Theodicies have been part of the human repertoire of cultural responses to disastrous episodes with the ambition of clothing them with a meaning system and offering some grounds for hope in a future free from catastrophe. Perhaps utopia can be seen as yet another aspect of theodicy as an expression of hope or at least the fantasy of a luxurious existence free of pain and want. In that regard, Cockaigne or the Land of Plenty was a common theme in medieval art and literature, depicting a land of plenty in contrast to the harsh and laborious world of the peasantry. Cockaigne was not exactly a theodicy. but it expressed the hope for a better, richer and safer world beyond the harsh conditions of the peasantry under feudalism. Such utopian responses may aim to provide intellectual and emotional comfort, and possibly hope for a better future. As I will indicate, Christianity, with its belief in a Second Coming and the promise of salvation for the pure at heart, has been a rich source of theodicies of hope. By contrast, theodicies in the modern world, especially after Auschwitz, have been theodicies of despair and rage. Existing as we are on the cusp of the Covid-19 catastrophe, it is unclear what, if any, theodicies will emerge, and whether they will offer hope or only despair. The suspicion must be that, as with Auschwitz, they are more likely to be characterized by confusion and anger, especially in the context of populist political cultures.

In referring to the human capacity for meaning-making in the face of extreme circumstances, I am drawing freely on Max Weber's comparative sociology of religion, especially his interpretation of theodicy. In the *Sociology of Religion*

(Weber 1966 [1920]), he identified three ideal type theodicies. The first included the doctrine of karma in Indian spirituality and the second type explored examples from Gnosticism and Manichaeism. In his third type, he gave more attention to monotheistic beliefs regarding predestination in Judaism, Christianity and Islam. Within that cluster, his discussion of the ascetic version in various forms of Protestantism is germane to my argument. Given the belief in a caring and omnipotent God, human suffering presents a critical challenge to religious belief. Ultimately there is no rational theology to resolve the contradictions in belief and the quest for a religious meaning breaks down.

Of additional importance to my argument, I refer to Weber's comparative studies of world religions as a contribution to what became a debate about the long-term civilizational consequences of the Axial Age (800 – 200 BC). On the basis of Weber's comparative studies, Karl Jaspers published his *The Origin and Goal of History* in 1949 (Jaspers 1953 [1949]). This period has been called 'the age of criticism' (Momigliano 1975: 9), when prophets, philosophers and religious charismatics grappled with the meaning of the harshness and injustice of everyday life and developed critical visions of alternative possibilities. There has been much dispute around claims that ideas about 'transcendental visions' emerged in this period, suggesting that there was an 'age of transcendence' (Schwartz 1975). A more modest conclusion is that the axial thinking was 'associated chiefly with heightened attention to morality and self-reflection facilitated by a conception of other and better worlds' (Torpey 2017: 9). I introduce this debate to suggest that the basic components of theodicy were forged in the first millennium.

One leading figure from the Axial Age is Aristotle (384 – 322 BC). A key theme of his moral teaching was the idea of *Eudaimonia* or happiness. In his *Nichomachean Ethics* (Aristotle 2011), he confronted the problem of human well-being or happiness, in which, after much deliberation, he proposed that virtue rather than wealth and health was a crucial feature of human satisfaction. While virtuous activity is important, he nevertheless concluded that luck or good fortune could never be entirely excluded (Nussbaum 2001). Virtue strengthens our capacity to cope with bad luck. Furthermore, when faced with the possibility of misfortune, it was not until the end of life that a person could be judged happy. In conclusion, we might also note that it is only the vulnerability of humans to external threats that makes them especially susceptible to unhappiness, as we have observed in the extreme case of plagues.

In this introduction, therefore, I need to reflect more systematically on the significance of catastrophe, fortune, unhappiness and political theology as the framework for this chapter. There would be little argument with the proposition that Covid-19 is a catastrophe in terms of its impact on the health of its victims and, in particular, with respect to their mental well-being. We might pause briefly to consider the literal and implied meanings of the Greek *cata-strophe* which formed the conclusion to a dramatic sequence of *strophes*. The *cata-strophe* formed the final act of a drama or its denouement. These issues were raised in Greek philosophy and drama long before the rise of Christianity, in which one might argue that, in its catastrophic theology, the denouement is both the crucifixion and the resurrection. In his *Poetics*, Aristotle (2013) notes that a *cat-astrophe*, in provoking fear and pity, concludes the set phases of a tragic drama. By the seventeenth century, *cata-strophe* had also acquired the meaning of an overturning or overthrowing of a given order in society. In other words, catastrophe defines a revolution in social and political terms.

In thinking of catastrophe, it is crucial to realize that we only have theodicies, including political theologies, because societies and the humans who live in them are permanently exposed to risk and uncertainty. If the world had been constructed by a divine Watch Maker that ran smoothly on time, we would not, in fact, could not, have catastrophes. In a perfect world, running smoothly through time, there could not be any unexpected catastrophic events to destroy the Divine Clock. If the world was completely predictable, offering human societies ample time to prepare for disasters, the scale of human suffering would be greatly reduced. Lack of preparedness for a pandemic on the scale of Covid-19 has been all too obvious in the advanced societies of the West. What I regard as our ontological vulnerability only compounds the hazards of our environment, such as the risks of natural calamities and the failure of governments to allow for future disasters through contemporary expenditure. The Californian authorities might make rational plans for a second wave of Covid-19 infections, but what precautions could they make with limited resources against an anticipated yet unpredictable catastrophic earthquake?

In early European societies, a prominent metaphor for the unpredictable character of the lives of individuals was the Wheel of Fortune. Uncertainty characterized the lives of people in 'feudal society, an uncertainty which deepened as the internal contradictions of this society grew more acute, was bound to encourage a belief in fate or destiny. Countless illustrations show the Wheel of Fortune. She herself sits in the centre, crowned as the 'sovereign of the world', and keeps the wheel turning' (Gurevich 1985: 142). *Fortuna* became a well-established trope of western culture and was famously explored, for example, in the medieval poems that are collected in the *Carmina Burana* from 1230 onwards. The cycles of the wheel capriciously determined the fate of individuals who were destined to rise and fall at her will. The female figure who controls the wheel was blindfolded and was deployed to signify how the world was under her control in the idea of *Fortuna imperatrix mundi*. The obvious conclusion is that without bad fortune, there would be no theodicy. What better example of fortune than Covid-19? The two most plausible candidates to explain the origin and spread of the pandemic are either that the virus was accidentally transferred from an animal to humans in the wet market of Wuhan or that it was leaked accidentally from an experimental laboratory to humans. Are these accidents a turn of the Wheel of Fortune?

The sense of random fortune is deepened by an awareness of radical social change. An all-pervading sense of crisis was, for example, characteristic of the baroque world, stretching over the first half of seventeenth-century Europe, and especially in Spain, which was challenged by chronic economic uncertainty, the impoverishment of the majority of the population, and consequent instability in personal lives. Fortune became the 'rhetorical image of the idea of the world's immutability' and as 'the world was a stage of changes, the idea of fortune was seized upon to explain those changes whose succession did not seem to correspond to a rational order' (Maravall 1986: 189). Christine Buci-Glucksman (1994: 23) insightfully observed that the ' primary images of the baroque were in fact the ruin, the labyrinth and the library; all of these phenomena are based upon deception, complexity and artificiality', hence the political culture of the baroque 'expressed a deep sense of alienation from society, self and nature'.

Niccolò Machiavelli (1469–1527), that great political theorist of the Baroque, in *The Prince* (1908 [1517]) interpreted the success or failure of cities and their ruling elites as a precarious relationship between power and fortune. Machiavelli analysed fortune in terms of the availability of resources for a ruler, the role of destiny or fate, and the more general idea of uncertainty (Airaksinen 2009). As with the medieval Wheel of Fortune, Machiavelli's Fortune was a woman. Roman rulers of the past were thought to have enjoyed power or virtue with fortune on their side. By contrast, Machiavelli complained that in his day the Italian princes were weak and stupid, and also lacked good fortune. Machiavelli had a second metaphor for destiny as a flowing river than can sweep everything before it. We can only protect ourselves from the unpredictable nature of a cascading river by maintaining the dykes that can contain its force. In the metaphor of the river, it is possible for the prince to master fate by his own power and virtue. It is only man's incapacity to govern his own nature and to foresee the changes ahead that stand in the way of his mastery of fortune (Hornqvist 2004: 240). Machiavelli's advice to princes regarding foresight has an unfortunate relevance to the inadequacy of contemporary political responses to Covid-19.

In my argument, these are all elements of a theodicy in the seventeenth-century European crisis. Perhaps unsurprisingly the crucial theorist of theodicy was the Baroque philosopher, Gottfried Wilhelm Leibniz (1646–1716). His famous

Theodicy: Essays on the Goodness of God, the Freedom of Man and the Origin of Evil (2005 [1710]) was composed in response to a natural disaster, namely, the Lombardy floods. He famously argued that we live in the best of all possible worlds, one that is complete and rich in its complexity. However, his attempt to defend the goodness of God collapsed when his legacy was confronted by the Lisbon earthquake of 1755 which destroyed much of the city and created a tsunami that travelled to the shores of Ireland. The earthquake put an end to any convincing notion that catastrophes could be explained by reference to human sinfulness. Critical scrutiny of Leibniz's theory supports Weber's view that, in the long run, there is no rational solution to theodicy based on the idea of a loving and caring God.

Nevertheless, theodicies, however imperfect, also contained a message of hope that a future was possible leading to a conclusion that ushered in a world without suffering. It has been argued that melancholy was the dominant trope of the Baroque (Benjamin 1998) and hence Leibniz's optimism was in fact out of kilter with the Baroque fascination with death and ruins. If Leibniz's *Theodicy* jars with modern secularism, his *Monadology* (1991 [1714]) continues to intrigue postmodern philosophers (Deleuze 1993). The theory of monads gave further support for his theodicy in claiming that everything that exists is better than non-existence. I refer to this debate from the eighteenth century to make the obvious point that in the year of Covid-19 there is ample scope for a philosophy of melancholy rather than optimism.

The Political Theology of Catastrophe

With secularization, explicit theological explanations of catastrophe begin to lose any traction in the wider society. In this chapter, I propose therefore to consider the prospects for secular theodicies of Covid-19. The secular form of theodicy has been called a *sociodicy* (Lyman 1995) and further developed around the theme of suffering (Morgan and Wilkinson 2001). The general inspiration for this development came from Peter L. Berger's sociology of religion. In *The Sacred Canopy*, Berger (1967) treated religion as a world-building exercise in clothing reality with meaning. Following many of the assumptions of philosophical anthropology in his early work, Berger argued that our instinctual structure offers us little for survival in a hostile environment (Turner 2018). We have to build our worlds with culture rather than instincts. However, the social world is inherently unstable, and we need theodicies to make sense of the suffering that is the lot of all humans. I would add that the sacred canopy comes into play because humans are rarely satisfied with bald factual or descriptive accounts of disaster.

We are meaning-making and meaning-needing creatures. But meaning systems change and the wrath of God of traditional theodicies is replaced, if only partly, by a sociology of catastrophe, with an implicit or explicit moral message that describes, for example, the indifference and unethical behaviour of political leaders and their elites.

Because theodicy occupies an important part of my argument, I want to define it and to offer some justification of it in my account of the causes, development and possible consequences of Covid-19. My aim is to distinguish where possible between religious and secular theodicies. However, my approach to secular theodicies is not to dwell on the idea of sociodicy as the secular equivalent of theodicy, but rather to adopt the idea of 'political theologies' of Carl Schmitt (1985). Schmitt argued, among other things, that modern political theory (of sovereignty, for example) is simply a secularized version of its theological ancestors. Specifically, 'all significant concepts of the modern theory of the state are secularized theological concepts not only because of their historical development – in which they were transferred from theology to the theory of the state – but also because of their systematic structure' (Schmitt 1985: 36). In my adoption of this idea. I argue that religious theodicies of hope are being transformed into political theologies of despair in response to Covid-19.

The implication here is that sociology itself often promotes a typically hidden theodicy, albeit of a secular character. In my 'Theodicy, the career of a concept', I argued that, 'Any sociology which comes up against pain and death, accident and misfortune, inequality and injustice in social life, must necessarily find itself confronted by the problem of theodicy ... While the term "theodicy" is not regularly and routinely employed by modern sociologists, the problem of social theodicy is present in any sociology which attempts to raise the question of the origins and causes of inequality' (Turner 1981: 170 – 1). I adopt the idea of a 'political theology' rather than sociodicy, because the cut-off from religious to secular idioms is not a clean break, and secular vocabularies of catastrophe typically retain an undercurrent of theology.

It is convenient to think of the history of theodicy and political theology around the themes of catastrophe, fortune and human responses by an examination of the evolution of the concept in several stages through various transitional periods. The Lisbon earthquake spelt the death of traditional theodicies of human sinfulness, but in reality there was a long transition to a fully secular politics of catastrophe. I argue that Auschwitz was a critical turning point in the emergence of a theodicy of rage based upon the idea of the death of God. Despite the secularization of responses to catastrophe, religious themes continue to inform human understanding of politics. In my conclusion, I consider the political theology of George W. Bush and evangelical Christian support for Donald Trump in times of crisis. I conclude by looking at the political theology of Covid-19 with special reference to extremist political accounts of the pandemic among white evangelical Christians. Can we fashion a modern theodicy to give it meaning beyond the mere facts of infections and deaths? I conclude that there is to date no discernible consensus of meaning-making in response to the global crisis; there is only a growing political theology of rage against both the pandemic itself and government responses to the crisis, especially in terms of lockdowns, social distancing and the wearing of masks. Opposition to these regulations appeals less to freedom of religion than to human rights or the rights of 'sovereign citizens'.

The Transition to a Secular Theodicy: William Blake and Antinomian Politics

An important transition to a secular critique of emerging capitalism can be found in the work of William Blake (1757–1827) . His poetry and illustrations reflect the deeply unsettled time in which he was living – the French Revolution and the wars that followed, the America War of Independence, and political and social unrest in English towns. The Gordon Riots of 1780 began as an anti-Catholic protest but quickly developed into urban violence, including attacks on Newgate Prison and the Bank of England.

Blake can be read as a key figure in responses to the development of the factory system and the transformation of the English countryside. The poet, while walking in the countryside from Lambeth to the City, was shocked by the vision of the Albion Flour Mills that had been destroyed by fire from an arsonist attack. These buildings may have been the 'the dark satanic mills' of Blake's great poem *Jerusalem*. There is, however, no settled interpretation of Blake's religious and political ideas, which is one additional reason for regarding him as a transitional figure (Kuntz 2000). Blake was strongly influenced by the antinomian theology of the Protestant sects, which emphasized grace over the law and morality. In that respect, Blake adhered to the legacy of Paul and the New Testament in which the legalism of the Old Testament was replaced with a doctrine of love, not law. Blake's vision of the world followed a particular passage in Paul's *Letter to the Romans* 8 – 'Because the creature itself also shall be delivered from the bondage of corruption into the glorious liberty of the children of God. For we know that the whole creation groaneth and travaileth in pain together until now.' Blake interpreted Paul to mean that there will come a new form of justice that exists outside the limitations of human law (Mueller 2012).

Blake had no time for the establishment of the Church of England, which was, in his view, socially and politically oppressive. He was specifically critical of the theodicy of Bishop Watson's *The Wisdom and Goodness of God, in Having Made Both Rich and Poor*. In the second of *The Four Zoas*, he satirizes any appeal to 'The Wisdom and Goodness of God', but Blake's personal vision is far more complex than simple agnosticism. He retained a notion of providence at work in history (Dawson 1987). As a transitional figure, Blake combined support for the French Revolution and embraced a powerful biblical view of human destiny.

Blake has been identified with the growth of socialism, especially socialist humanism, through the work of E.P. Thompson, whose *The Making of the English Working Class* (1968) is regarded as the classic account of the origins of political radicalism in England. He challenged the view that the Methodists had exercised an influence on the emergence of secular radicalism. Blake, not John Wesley, was the key figure in growing political radicalism. Thompson was a Marxist historian but his classic study of the working class was not hostile to all religious movements and indeed his historical studies sought to reject the 'condescension of posterity', including the deluded followers of Joanna Southcott (1750 – 1814), who claimed to be in possession of supernatural gifts and eventually declared herself to be 'Woman of the Apocalypse'.

Undoubtedly Blake drew inspiration from the dissenting sects, and in fact he was influenced by a variety of radical trends in Christianity, including the Swedenborgs (Rix 2007). There is a connection between Blake's antinomianism and emerging working-class radicalism. He has often been identified as an early precursor of English socialism (Morton 1958; Mee 1992). Thompson in *Witness against the Beast: William Blake and the Moral Law* (1993) connected Blake with an obscure dissenting sect, the Muggletonians. This movement emerged from the tradition of the Ranters and emerged in 1651 with two London tailors, Lodowicke Muggleton and John Reeve, who claimed to be prophets. They believed that God did not intervene in the mundane affairs of society but would intervene eventually to bring the world to an end. The Muggletonians were antinomian, egalitarian and pacifist. While they were anti-clerical and critical of the Church in general terms, they also fell out with the Quakers whom they regarded as the enemies of religion.

Why were Blake and the Muggletonians important for Thompson and why should I dwell on this period in the evolution of socialism in a chapter on Covid-19? The answer is that in socialism, especially in socialist humanism, we can detect a secular theodicy which has a vision of a perfect society or, in Blake's terms, a 'Garden of Love'. This aspect of my argument was precisely expressed by Robert Fine (1994) in a tribute to Thompson, when he identified what he claimed were the 'contrasted states' of law. Reflecting on the character of law, Fine referred to an Enlightenment tradition or juridical stream that focused on rights and citizenship and its opposite, the Anti-Enlightenment antinomian interpretation of law, which emphasized justice, responsibility, alterity and love. From my perspective, these radical dissenting sects adhered to a theodicy that was evolving towards a political theology, in which the coming socialist society would destroy elite corruption, bring in a society of equal rewards, and establish a world of peace and plenty. The danger of Covid-19 in our time is that the necessity of lockdowns and social distancing, which, while based on good science, may damage the community of citizens that is based on civility and intimacy as much as on the law. In short, Covid-19 deepens the contrast between these two traditions.

Auschwitz and the death of God: The End of Optimistic Theodicies

If Blake and the dissenting sects were transitional moments in the evolution of secular thought on the disasters of an industrial civilization and the urban squalor that attended its emergence, Auschwitz was the catastrophe from which no religious explanation of human suffering could survive. Religious responses to Nazi Germany and the Shoah or Annihilation represent a significant (and perhaps final) turning point in the history of traditional theodicies. For many Jewish intellectuals, it was no longer possible to continue with existing religious traditions that had been followed for centuries before the Shoah. Of course, Jewish reflections on the meaning and significance of the Shoah produced a wide range of conflicting responses. The responses included attempts to cling to a traditional theology, but these were silenced by authoritative figures in the community. Rebbe Menachem Mendal Schneerson, who was regarded by his Hasidic followers as the Messiah, rejected any attempt to suggest that the Shoah was caused by Jews departing from their traditional ways and beliefs. For Schneerson, the Annihilation had no rational explanation. Richard Rubenstein went further in *After Auschwitz* (1966) to propose that the only honest and coherent response was to reject God, and to accept the conclusion that all existence is meaningless. His views were widely read in the 1970s when his idea that 'The death of God is a cultural fact' gained attention. The view that the Shoah was not susceptible to human understanding was challenged by Hannah Arendt (1994). She argued that it was simply difficult to understand, especially when the Nazi effort to construct and run the extermination camps had no military rationale.

Hannah Arendt was a crucial, if controversial, figure in the post-war debate about the meaning of Auschwitz. Her *Eichmann in Jerusalem* in 1977 gave rise to acrimonious debate in part because she questioned the role of the *Judenräte*, the councils that were set up to regulate Jewish communities in Poland and other East European societies. She is also a crucial figure in the evolution of notions about theodicy and the character of evil in human societies. The sub-title of her report on the Eichmann trial was 'A Report on the Banality of Evil'. She once described evil as the problem that 'will be the fundamental question of postwar intellectual life in Europe' (Arendt 1994: 134). She distinguished between the evil and demonic by insisting that evil was comprehensible and, once understood, allows us to anticipate its recurrence in the future. Her treatment of Auschwitz and the Shoah in general has been appropriately described as a theodicy (Neiman 2001). For Arendt, Auschwitz did not spell the end of theodicy; evil was banal not incomprehensible. Despite her religious sensibilities that were related to her doctoral dissertation on Augustine, it was a secular theodicy (Moyn 2008).

American Exceptionalism

In contemporary responses to Covid-19 in Europe, there is little overt attention in public debate to explicitly religious issues. It has been argued that Far Right populists have 'hijacked' religion (Marzouki, McDonnell and Roy 2016). However, the largely secular culture of the continent, with the possible exception of Catholic societies on the eastern border such as Poland, stands in sharp contrast to the United States, where populism has found ample support from charismatic Christian communities. In order to understand this religious trend and its enthusiastic support for the populism of Donald Trump, it is necessary to begin a sociological inquiry with the presidency of George W. Bush and the rise of the Christian Right. This discussion then turns to the religious basis of opposition to lockdowns, social distancing and the scientific advice of Dr Anthony Fauci.

President Bush was the third Methodist to become President of the United States, but Bush has been noteworthy for his explicit commitment to Christianity as the basis for both his domestic and foreign policies. His Christian beliefs include ideas about providence, divine grace, and good and evil. Bush adheres to a dispensational theology, which is a doctrine about God's interventions throughout history that has created a series of special dispensations (Turner 2017). These ideas were first articulated by John Nelson Darby (1800 – 1882), but the final dispensation will involve Israel and the End Times. A further addition to this theology is the 'pre-tribulation rapture' whereby the Church and its faithful followers will be taken up into heaven through a rapturous experience before the final catastrophic destruction of the world.

Although dispensational theology influenced Bush's foreign policy, including the invasion of Iraq, his early presidency was taken up with a faith-based domestic policy to assist the role of the churches in American society, where it was thought they were losing ground in the provision of welfare services. Beginning with *Unlevel Playing Field* in 2001, an administrative audit from the White House, Bush worked to develop a new policy to give the churches greater prominence in welfare and education (Daly 2008). The initiative was based on two ideas of sovereignty and subsidiarity which support the idea of independent churches based on self-rule in a free society with a limited state. Behind these principles, Bush maintained a commitment to capitalist enterprise, free markets and individual responsibility.

This domestic policy was overwhelmed on September 11, 2001 by the attack on the Twin Towers. Bush rapidly acquired a new vocabulary in the 'war against terrorism' and 'to rid the world of evil' as Bush's dispensational theology was transformed into the 'theology of empire' (Wallis 2004). The endless wars in Iraq and Afghanistan were seen in biblical terms to fulfil America's calling to defeat 'the axis of evil'.

Antinomian Populism

One might have imagined that with the presidency of Barack Obama (2009 – 17) that the dispensational theology had been replaced by more secular and pragmatic domestic and foreign policies. While the Tea Party changed the role of grass-roots organizations in Washington in 2010, their influence also appeared to decline both nationally and in key Republican constituencies. Although Bush and Trump have very different personalities and perspectives, Trump has also been successful in winning the support of evangelical Christians and Roman Catholics due to his support for pro-life policies and the separation of church and state, alongside his opposition to evolution and sex education in the school curriculum, and abortion. A Pew Research Center for Religion in Public Life issued a report on March 12, 2020 that affirmed 'White evangelicals see Trump as fighting for their beliefs, though many have mixed feelings about his personal conduct.'

Cultural grievances rather than strictly economic and political ones have been a significant part of America's conservative politics and it is on these cultural and status issues that Trump's political message has been effective. He has managed to combine conservative Christian support, on the one hand, and far-right populism, on the other. With his populist attacks on the 'Washington swamp', East Coast intellectuals, migrants, Muslims and, in general terms, the outside world, his rally speeches take the form of religious revivalism. His foreign policy objectives and the promise to Make American Great again constitute a political theology. It has been described as a 'white political theology' that aims 'to build on the racialist Anglo-Saxon thesis, one whose defining narrative is that of a "magistrate of God" under siege by the generally perceived ills of mixity, migration, and multiculturalism' (Mukherjee 2018: 2).

In the months leading up to the November election, Trump has lost support over his management (or mismanagement) of the Covid crisis, and trailed behind Joe Biden. Trump's views on masks, lockdowns, vaccinations, the WHO, the severity of the crisis and its origins, and the importance of social distancing have been inconsistent. Nevertheless, his version of political theology continues to win support from his base, but his political credibility has been compromised by his unpredictable responses to the policies that are necessary to bring the pandemic under control. There are various factors, some of which are peculiar to the United States, that make it difficult for any president to achieve consistent control over the pandemic. These include federalism, individualism, business interests, fake news, the Second Amendment, and populist hostility to government over-reach.

In response to the pandemic, economic decline and lockdown, charismatic Christian groups have taken up the theme of messianic dispensations and welcomed Trump's support of Israel where the Second Coming will take place. Working with the media, evangelical Christians have embraced the conspiracy theories promoted by QAnon, 4Chan, and 8Kun to accept the idea of a 'deep state', supported by the hostile media and working to undermine Trump's presidency. They go further to recognize Donald Trump as a Messiah to bring about the Kingdom of God on Earth. Following from my discussion of the Muggletonians, we could regard the charismatic Christian opposition to what they perceive to be excessive government interference in their lives by restrictions on their individual freedom as an antinomian political theology.

Conclusion: The Enclave Society

As of writing this chapter in early September 2020, we have no idea if or when the pandemic might come to an end through the development of a successful vaccine or by the development of 'herd immunization' as more people recover from the infection, or by changes to behaviour through lockdowns, social distancing, closure of political borders, and quarantine. We do not know how many societies such as Yemen or Lebanon might may not survive the pandemic or what the long-term consequences for the global economy might be. Will there be new outbreaks or old outbreaks? While there are no definite answers to such questions, what we can reasonably assume is that the phase of globalization that has been a marked feature of recent history will come to an end.

After the Vietnam War (1955–75), the United States began to enjoy a period of peace and prosperity Samuel Huntingdon wrote about 'democracy's third wave' (1991), and the fall of the Berlin Wall commenced in 1989 and was completed in 1991. In retrospect, globalization theory, with the publication of Roland Robertson's influential *Globalization: Social Theory and Global Culture* (1992), envisioned an emerging cosmopolitan world based on international co-operation. Three catastrophes have shaken that world. The attack on the Twin Towers on September 11, 2001 transformed America's relationship to the outside and led to the invasion of Iraq and the destabilization of the Middle East. The financial crisis of 2008–11 underlined the dangers of the financialization of capitalism and the austerity packages that followed exposed the fragile relations between states in the European Union and played a role in Brexit. Covid-19 of 2020 is the third catastrophe to destabilize the western democracies.

The pandemic of 2020 exposed the constraints on the democracies in enforcing quarantine measures and other regulations over erstwhile free citizens. The pandemic has confirmed the principle that while commodities can travel with relative ease, humans do not. Covid-19 has brought in a raft of measures, technological, legal and social, that are deemed necessary in response to the highly contagious nature of the virus. Enclave societies may come to replace open borders and the free movement of people within the European Union (Turner 2007). Interestingly, Giorgio Agamben (2020) in an article 'L'invenzione di un'epidemia' in the Italian journal *Quodlibet* has argued that the shut-down in Italy was unwarranted and irrational and that the emergency measures extended the role of the state in regulating the daily lives of individuals. Human relationships had been degraded as citizens became merely 'virus carriers'. In other words, Italy, which witnessed the earliest forms of quarantine, has become an enclave society. The irony is that in Italy the populist Five Star Movement in 2015 led a campaign condemning mandatory mass vaccination programmes only to be challenged by a major outbreak of measles in 2017 (Lasco and Larson, 2020).

While Agamben's views were severally criticized, many on both the political left and political right have regarded the closures, lockdowns and related measures as undemocratic authoritarian interventions into daily life. This view on the political left is ironically consistent with the antinomian views of conservative evangelical Christians in the United States who regard the closures as the over-reach of a governments that is now socialist and the work of the devil. Although Agamben has also been criticized for his negative and pessimistic view of politics, Jessica Whyte (2013) in her *Catastrophe and Redemption* claims that there are redemptive moments in his work where something good can emerge from the rubble of sovereignty and law.

On the Far Right, the closures are consistent with their views that migration needs to be stopped or controlled, that globalization has destroyed local communities and their economies, and that global elites are indifferent to the suffering of the people. The arguments emerging are part of a broad populist critique of remote and heartless elites. However, no consistent sociodicy or political theology is emerging, and instead the media offer an endless space for competing world-views. Attitudes and beliefs are shifting and contradictory, because we do not yet know when and if the pandemic may come under control through a combination of vaccines, lockdowns and herd immunity, or whether, like influenza, it will remain embedded in the human population. But are there deeper reasons that explain why our meaning-making capacity has so far generated no convincing narrative of the pandemic? Religious theodicies will win little support, but will a secular sociodicy have much greater success? Max Weber and Alasdair MacIntyre (1967) may be right for different reasons in saying that we no longer have the intellectual apparatus to formulate convincing and coherent vocabularies and values with which to construct meaningful responses to a catastrophe on the scale of Covid-19.

References

Agamben, G. (2020) L'invenzione di un'epidemia. *Quodlibet* 26 February.

Airaksinen, T. (2009) Fortune is a Woman: Machiavelli on Luck and Virtue. *Homo Oeconomicus* 26(3/4): 551–68.

Arendt, H. (1977) *Eichmann in Jerusalem: A Report on the Banality of Evil*, New York: Penguin Books.

Arendt, H. (1994) *Essays in Understanding, 1930–1954*, New York: Harcourt Brace.

Aristotle (2011) *Nichomachean Ethics*, Chicago: University of Chicago Press.

Aristotle (2013) *Poetics*, Oxford: Oxford University Press.

Beck, U. (1992) *Risk Society: Towards a New Modernity*, London: Sage.

Benjamin, W. (1998) *The Origin of German Tragic Drama*, London: Verso.

Berger, P.L. (1967) *The Sacred Canopy: Elements of a Sociological Theory of Religion*, New York: Anchor Books.

Bowerstock, G.W. (2012) *Empires of Collision in Late Antiquity*, Waltham, MA: Brandeis University Press.

Buci-Glucksman, C. (1994) *Baroque Reason*, London: Sage.

Daly, L. (2008) The Political Theology of George W. Bush's Faith-Based Initiative, *Theoria* 115(1): 32–63.

Dawson, P.M.S. (1987) Blake and Providence: The Theodicy of the Four Zoas. *The Blake Quarterly* 20(4): 134–43.

Deleuze, G. (1993) *The Fold: Leibniz and the Baroque*, London: Athlone Press.

Fine, R. (1994) The Rule of Law and Muggletonian Marxism: The Perplexities of E.P. Thompson. *Journal of Law and Society* 21(2) 193–213.

Giddens, A. (1990) *The Consequences of Modernity*, Cambridge: Polity Press.

Grell, O.P. (2000) *The Four Horsemen of the Apocalypse: Religion, War, Famine and Death in Reformation Europe*, Cambridge: Cambridge University Press.

Gurevich, A.J. (1985) *Categories of Medieval Culture*, London: Routledge & Kegan Paul.

Gutiérrez, G. (1988) *On Job: God-Talk and the Suffering of the Innocent*, New York: Orbis Books.

Hoelzel, A. (1979) Faust, the Plague and Theodicy. *The German Quarterly* 52(1): 1–17.

Hornqvist, M. (2004) *Machiavelli and Empire*, Cambridge: Cambridge University Press.

Huizinga, J. (1996) *The Autumn of the Middle Ages*, Chicago: University of Chicago Press.

Huntington, S.P. (1991) Democracy's Third Wave. *Journal of Democracy* 2(2): 12–34.

Jaspers, K. (1953 [1949]) *The Origin and Goal of History*, London: Routledge & Kegan Paul

Kuntz, P.G. (2000) William Blake and the Ten Commandments. *Soundings* 83(2): 427–45.

Lasco, G. and Larson, H.J. (2020) Medical Populism and Immunization Programmes: Illustrative Examples and Consequences for Public Health. *Global Public Health* 15(3): 334–44.

Leibniz, G.W. (1991 [1714]) *Monadology*, Pittsburgh, PA: University of Pittsburgh Press.

Leibniz, G.W. (2005 [1710]) *Theodicy: Essays on the Goodness of God, the Freedom of Man and the Origin of Evil*. La Salle, IL: Open Court.

Lyman, S.M. (1995) Social Theory and Social Movements: Sociology as Sociodicy. In: S.M. Lyman (ed.) *Social Movements: Critiques, Concepts, Case-Studies*, London: Macmillan, pp. 397–435.

Machiavelli, N. (1908 [1517]) *The Prince*, London: J.M. Dent & Sons.

MacIntyre, A. (1967) *A Short History of Ethics*, London: Routledge and Kegan Paul.

Maravall, J.A. (1986) *Culture of the Baroque: Analysis of a Historical Structure*, Manchester: Manchester University Press.

Marzouki, N., McDonnell, D. and Roy, O. (eds) (2016) *Saving the People: How Populists Hijack Religion*. Oxford: Oxford University Press.

Mee, J. (1992) *Dangerous Enthusiasm: Blake and the Culture of Radicalism in the 1790s*, Oxford: Clarendon.

Momigliano, A. (1975) *Alien Wisdom: The Limits of Hellenization*. Cambridge: Cambridge University Press.

Morgan, D. and Wilkinson, I. (2001) The Problem of Suffering and the Sociological Task of Theodicy. *European Journal of Social Theory* 4(2): 199–214.

Morton. A.L. (1958) *The Everlasting Gospel: A Study of the Sources of William Blake*, London: Lawrence and Wishart.

Moyn, S. (2008) Hannah Arendt on the Secular. *New German Critique* 105: 71–96.

Mueller, J.C. (2012) Creatures against the Law: Blake's Antinomian Renderings of Paul. *Interdisciplinary Studies in Literature and Environment* 19(1): 123–41.

Mukherjee, S.R. (2018) Make America Great Again as White Political Theology. *Revue LISA* XVI(2): 1–16.

Neiman, S. (2001) Theodicy in Jerusalem. In: S. E. Aschheim (e.d) *Hannah Arendt in Jerusalem*, Berkeley, CA: University of California Press, pp. 65–90

Nussbaum, M. (2001) *The Fragility of Goodness: Luck and Ethics in Greek Tragedy and Philosophy*, Cambridge: Cambridge University Press.

Rix, R. (2007) *William Blake and the Culture of Radical Christianity*, Farnham: Ashgate.

Robertson, R. (1992) *Globalization: Social Theory and Global Culture*, London: Sage.

Rubenstein, R. (1966) *After Auschwitz*, Baltimore, MD: Johns Hopkins University Press.

Schmitt, C. (1985) *Political Theology*, Cambridge, MA: MIT Press.

Schwartz, B.I. (1975) The Age of Transcendence, *Daedalus* 104(2): 1–7.

Thompson, E.P. (1968) *The Making of the English Working Class*, London: Victor Gollancz.

Thompson, E.P (1993) *Witness against the Beast: William Blake and the Moral Law*, New York: The Press.

Torpey, J. (2017) *The Three Axial Ages: Moral, Material, Mental*, New Brunswick, NJ: Rutgers University Press.

Turner, B.S. (1981) Theodicy, the Career of a Concept. In: B.S. Turner, *For Weber: Essays in the Sociology of Fate*, London: Routledge& Kegan Paul, pp. 142–76.

Turner, B.S. (2007) The Enclave Society: Towards a Sociology of Immobility. *European Journal of Social Theory* 10(2): 287–303.

Turner, B.S. (2017) Dispensational Theology, Nationalism and American Politics. In: P. Michael, A. Possamai, and B.S. Turner (eds.) *Religions, Nations and Transnationalism*, New York: Palgrave Macmillan, pp. 135–52.

Turner, B.S. (2018) Vulnerability and Plausibility Structures: Peter L. Berger, Arnold Gehlen and Philosophical Anthropology. In: T. Helm (ed.) *Peter L. Berger and the Sociology of Religion*, London : Bloomsbury Academic, pp. 13–25.

Wallis, J. (2004) George W. Bush's Theology of Empire. *Mississippi Review* 32(3): 60–72.

Weber, M. (1966 [1920]) *The Sociology of Religion*. London: Methuen.

Whyte, J. (2013) *Catastrophe and Redemption: The Political Thought of Giorgio Agamben*, New York: SUNY Press.

Ziegler, P. (1969) *The Black Death*, London: Collins.

Daniel Chernilo

Another Globalisation: Covid-19 and the Cosmopolitan Imagination

In this chapter, I offer a reflection on recent transformations of globalisation and cosmopolitanism that have been triggered, or have become more readily visible, during the Covid-19 pandemic. My argument is twofold: on the one hand, the rapid development of Covid-19 allows us to think through some of the dislocations between the national, international and global dimensions of modernity. On the other, the pandemic offers us an opportunity to reconsider new challenges for the cosmopolitan imagination. On both counts, I do not think we can underestimate one novel feature of this pandemic: this is arguably the first global phenomenon in human history in which the majority of the world's population is experiencing a *similar event at the same time.*

The structure of the chapter is as follows. I start by looking at how ideas of the national, the international and the global are all relevant in our understanding of modernity. I then use Ulrich Beck's risk society thesis in order to highlight some key dimensions of the current Covid-19 crisis. I close with some reflections on new possibilities this affords for our cosmopolitan imagination.

The Rise of Modernity: National, International and Global

The success of early sociological theories in capturing the most salient trends that gave shape to modern society was crucially dependent on their ability to offer a dual account of their national and global dimensions (Turner 2006). The transitional period of the rise of modernity, between the 1870s and the 1930s, was marked by how industrial technologies, means of transport, ideas of democracy and racial supremacy, mass political parties, and even the organisation of university education itself, co-evolved both as national and global trends. At the same time, a systematic flaw of this period was the extent to which there was no concomitant development of solid *international* institutions that were able to mediate between the newly found strength of nation-states and the dynamism of global trends themselves. Indeed, the weaknesses of international institutions are now seen as one of the key causes of World War I, while the failure of the League of Nations in the following decades seems somewhat overdetermined by its inability to carve out a significant role vis-à-vis na-

https://doi.org/10.1515/9783110713350-010

tional governments and global capitalism (Tooze 2015). The canonical works of Marx, Weber and Durkheim were all interested in this dialectic between the national and global (Chernilo 2007), but remained conspicuously silent about ideas of international law, governance and institutions. No idea of a genuine an international order springs out of their pages.

The period that commenced with the end of World War II, in 1945, may be characterised by the disintegration of overseas European empires and the emergence of dozens new nation-states in Africa, South-East and the Middle East. There appeared at the time to be a long-lasting correspondence between a political organisation that cohered on a bureaucratic and territorial state, a belief that technological innovations were to be manufactured nationally and for the benefit of the national economy as a whole, and the rise of new cultural industries that wittingly or otherwise helped reinforce that sense of national unity (Wagner 1994, Habermas 1988). In fact, the sociological imagination at that time was captured by the idea that the emergence of independent nation-states equalled the definitive constitution of modern societies. Among its many shortcomings, this form of *methodological nationalism* reified the allegedly natural ability of novel nation-states to develop and, in so doing, it lost sight of the fact that this development was in itself a global trend (Chernilo 2011, 2020). At the same time, the establishment of a more solid international system, under the umbrella of the newly established United Nations, was a major innovation insofar as it created a network of rules, practices and institutions that now seemed abler than before to both 'globalise' national trends and 'nationalise' global ones. Yet the very notion of the international eventually helped reinforced the view that nation-states were the best and only legitimate vehicle for modernity to deliver on its promises: progressive taxation for a sound national economy, the development of national infrastructure, and indeed international cooperation itself could be regarded as global in scope, but their ultimate organisational drive was to remain attached to the nation. Indeed, the key feature of this period was a clear primacy of the national, together with a partial disappearance from view of modernity's global dimension – or at least its dissolution into the international.

The collapse of the Soviet Union and the end of the Cold War in the early 1990s are commonly referred to as marking the beginning of contemporary globalisation. For our purposes here, we can concentrate on three main trends that signal the rise of globalisation as a new historical epoch. The first has to do with the role of *economic globalisation* as its primary drive. While the early sociology of globalisation was quick to add that contemporary transformations could not be reduced only to the economy – and must also include culture, migration and even legal globalisation in the form, say, of human rights regimes – free trade agreements and global financial transactions remained cornerstone in explaining the rise of globalisation (Sassen 2007). The transformations in economic activity – quantities, volume, speed, rewards – became the primary drive that made global times what they have become.[1]

A second argument in the turn of the century literature on globalisation was that these trends were able to move faster, go deeper and reach further than all previous global processes because they were coupled with the *rise of information technologies*. There was a renewed view on the primacy of technology that more than merely echoed the technological determinisms of old: society and culture have changed in the way that they have because of the material possibilities that have been opened up by the technological transformations that underpin them (Castells 1996). Time-space compression, unlimited storage, immediate availability, ubiquity, portability, individualisation: the rise and main features of all these trends that now characterise contemporary culture are defined by the technological transformations themselves. The third trend that I should like to mention is *the weakening of the nation* and *the crisis of state sovereignty*. The end of the mythical image that nation-states are the natural and necessary representation of a modern society was seen as a fundamental expression of global ideas of epochal change. This predicted decline of nation-states has not come to materialise, however, and recent revivals of nationalistic politics the world over need to be understood no so much as a reaction against globalisation but as one of its very expressions: the reappearance of the language and symbols of nationalistic politics is itself an illustration of nationalism's own global success. Within this context, the national appears as the one thing people can hold on to – however misguided that belief might be – the international is looked at with scepticism as idealistic at best and ineffectual at worst, whereas conceptions of the global are crisscrossed by a tension between dynamism and promises, on the one hand, and fear, anxiety and self-destruction, on the other.

From a sociological point of view, this was roughly the situation we were in at the time a new virus infected the word: national, international and global trends that did not complement each other but appear disjointed and work in a dysfunctional way. Yet the fact that they are disjointed historically does not mean that, analytically, we do not need them all in order to comprehend, let alone handle, crises of the kind we currently face.

---

1 In historical terms, there are different versions of this argument as well: from late 20th century globalisation being wholly unprecedented, to the longer-term view that sees it as the most recent incarnation of the development of the world economy that began with slave traffic in the 17th century (Wallerstein 2011). Either way, the key argument remains that the prime mover of globalisation is the economy.

Ulrich Beck's Theory of the Risk Society

Ulrich Beck's (1992) theory of risk society was arguably among the most sophisticated within the sociology of globalisation at the turn of the last century. It successfully highlighted how the three dimensions we have just mentioned – an accelerated globalisation of the economy, equally fast technological transformations of our everyday lives through information technologies, and a redefinition of state sovereignty and national identities – configured a new epochal constellation. In Beck's theory, contemporary modernity is defined by new technologies that require huge economic investment and international cooperation and, because of that, they also pose unprecedented risks to the environment and human life itself. At the same time, these technological transformations open up new forms of social action which, because they transcend previous state borders and national identifications, also open the door for more cosmopolitan kinds of politics and identity. The Covid-19 pandemic has brought a new lease of life to Beck's risk society theory, as the challenges we now face are intimately related to the global dynamics of the modern economy and culture, international cooperation in science and technology, and the ways in which nations and states are able to respond to these while maintaining the sources of its democratic legitimacy. Indeed, the underlying trends for both risks *and* their potential solutions are undistinguishable and belong equally in our exacerbated global times.

Beck's risk society theory is based on the presupposition that 'nature', 'society' and 'culture' are separate domains and that our task is to develop better ways of looking at how they actually intersect and interact. Both his notions of globalisation and risk are construed around the view that these are self-contained spheres and that changes in any one of them will trigger changes and have implications in all others. Thus, the idea of risk underscores the extent to which institutional changes (for instance, in environmental regulations), technological innovations (new irrigation techniques) are able to trigger both natural disasters (draughts, deforestation) and social crises (famine, riots, etc.). Contemporary problems all have complex causes and their consequences are felt, equally, in these several domains at the same time. While the ability to connect them was seen as one important strength of Beck's theory, some difficulties remain. For instance, the actor-network literature that we associate with the work of Bruno Latour (1993) has been making for some time now the convincing argument that society, culture and nature are *not* separate and self-contained domains. In fact, they are best understood as composites of complex interrelations that not only change over time but, above all, have no stable core that remains unchanged. A major strength of Latour's outlook is that we ought to revise the ways in which we look at technology: the conventional view of technology as tools that mediate between, say, humans, society and nature does not really hold (Latour 2020). After Covid-19, it is hard to disagree.

In Beck's theory of reflexive modernisation, all modern challenges have science and technology at their core, and their eventual resolution, even if imperfect, equally relies on scientific and technological innovations. The ways in which scientific knowledge and its applications have entered all domains of life makes modern societies wholly dependent on them. It is impossible to step outside the relentless stream of technological developments that have become key to how we produce and consume our food, travel, educate our children, carry out our politics and even fall in love. Whatever new challenges modern societies may face, science and its various institutions – universities, health systems, bureaucratic and planning units of all kinds – are almost universally at the centre of the practical possibilities for their solutions. At the same time, however, technology is a permanent source of fears, worries and concerns, as technology remains an endless source of dystopic possibilities and scenarios. Given that it is not possible to step outside the technological world we live in, all problems are to be corrected by more rather than less technology, more rather than less modernity itself. Even the side- and unintended-effects of rapid social change are to be tamed only by even *more rapid* social change.

Yet for all its interest in the role of science and technology at both the national and global levels, there is little in Beck's theory about their international dimension in its own right: international cooperation, networks of collaboration, funding opportunities and several layers of regulatory standards are all crucially dependent upon the international. This is not altogether surprising if we consider that Beck's (2000) idea of globalisation is built on the problematic premise that an incremental significance of global trends is to be matched by a concomitant reduction in the significance of the national dimensions of social life. Beck's sociological and normative investment in the idea of Europe is a clear instantiation of this critique of national modernity (Beck and Grande 2007). Against Beck's own best intentions, this emphasis on Europe made his cosmopolitan project somewhat parochial rather than genuinely global, and rather naïve rather than actually anchored in the national traditions that have shaped the modern world. Eventually, his theory settled for a flat idea of globalization that exaggerated its novelty as well as underplayed the interaction between global, international and national. And while the idea of Europe as an emergent transnational formation is a progressive normative project, it prevented Beck from reflecting more explicitly on the need to articulate national, international and global levels – each one of them having their own unique contribution to make. The rise of global risk society was eventually understood as a zero-sum game between national and global forces and with no clear role for the international.

From Risk Society to the Anthropocene: Enter Covid-19

Economic globalisation, ever-changing technological developments, transformations of state sovereignty, international institutions whose role remains ambiguous, risks of environmental implosion at a planetary scale: all these challenges are central to our understanding of the risk societies of the present. The Covid-19 pandemic may well be seen as the latest, and arguably most sobering, of global crises that the theory of the risk society was already predicting three decades ago. In fact, during this time we have also witnessed a major paradigm shift in various natural sciences that now speak of the 'Anthropocene' as a new geological era that is defined by the fact that humans have become the major force of nature, with a proven ability to alter the normal cycles of the earth's climate and all its eco-systems (Crutzen 2002, Lewis and Maslin 2018). Rather than separate 'health', 'economic', or 'environmental' crises, the Covid-19 pandemic may need to be seen as a complex civilizational transformation that includes every aspect of human life in every region of the world and which will continue to define our life for the foreseeable future. The paradigmatic shift the anthropocene suggests has also reached the humanities and the social sciences (Chakrabarty 2009, Delanty and Mota 2017). Crucially, it invites us to reconsider some deepseated epistemic, temporal and indeed normative presuppositions about how we understand modern times (Chernilo 2017).

In fact, as a problem of global health, Covid-19 is a typical disease of the age of the anthropocene because it speaks of a particular way of interaction both among humans themselves and between humans with their various environments. In turn, this triggers unintended effects on all domains of life (Hirschfeld 2020). Indeed, despite inevitable arguments regarding its conceptual precision and normative implications (Doshi 2011), the World Health Organisation's definition of a pandemic includes both dimensions that have proved central to my argument so far: the idea of the global and the need to account for the complex relations between the natural and the social. The definition reads as follows:

> A pandemic is the worldwide spread of a new disease. An influenza pandemic occurs when a new influenza virus emerges and spreads around the world, and most people do not have

immunity. Viruses that have caused past pandemics typically originated from animal influenza viruses WHO 2010[2]

Because it is global, and because it highlights the complex interactions between nature, society and our humanity, the very idea of a pandemic speaks to the core of how we are able to confront our most pressing contemporary challenges both in theory and in practice. My main argument in this section is that the force with which the Covid-19 pandemic has hit everywhere in the world has to do with the limits and dead ends of contemporary globalisation.

As we mentioned above, the sociology of globalisation at the turn of the century underscored the extent to which we witnessed an intensification of global trends – these were triggered by but cannot be reduced to economic trends. One major difficulty, it seems to me, lies in that the empirical growth of global trends that undermine national sovereignty is fundamentally misunderstood if we seek to explain it primarily, let alone exclusively, through a global prism. In the first section I also argued that the salience of the global is not in itself a global phenomenon, but one that includes also national and international processes and institutions. We are unable to understand how global dynamics have intensified, and have become more prevalent in recent decades, if in our explanation of those very trends we focus exclusively on the global. Instead, their elucidation requires us to embrace rather than discard the national and the international. The equivocations here remind us of what the philosopher of science, Alfred N. Whitehead (1953), referred to as the *fallacy of misplaced concreteness:* for us to understand certain empirical trends – in our case, the rise and main features of globalisation – we cannot turn empirical facts themselves into the concepts with which we are to explain these processes. More concretely, this means that we misconstrue the global if we treat it as detached from the long-term national, international *and* global dynamics that have structured modern societies for over 200 years. If Covid-19 is a global crisis, this is the case because it is not only a global crisis, but it is a national and international one as well. Another way of saying this is that there is no such thing as a global crisis because the national and the international are built into the global itself. In the rest of this section, I should briefly like to describe some key trends of the Covid-19 pandemic at these national, international and global levels.

First, all corners of the world are now definitively part of a global economy with an irresistible capacity to make people, goods and services travel the world over at an unprecedented speed. Covid-19 started off in China, it travelled fast

---

2 https://www.who.int/csr/disease/swineflu/frequently_asked_questions/pandemic/en/

within Asia and then expanded to Europe, the US before reaching Africa and Latin America. It took just over 3 months between its outbreak in Wuhan, China, and the moment when the WHO declared it to be a pandemic – that is, a novel global disease against which humans have no immunity (1 Dec 2019 and 11 March 2020). By the middle of April 2020, well over 180 sovereign units all over the world had reported active cases and implemented restrictions to travel, work and education. But while its rapid global expansion is certainly one of its most salient features, the ways in which this has taken place is not only caused by global forces. In some respects, Covid-19 is not necessarily exceptional; AIDS in the late 20th century and SARS in the early 21st display comparable features with regards to the reconfiguration of health problems as global ones. If Covid-19 may be portrayed as the most global crisis to date, this is because it brings home the realisation that we have *reached the globalisation of the very globalisation processes that started in the 1990s*. Neither the causes nor the best practices for handling the crisis has come from 'the West'. Europe and the US have lost a great deal of traction as global players and, for long periods of time during the evolution of Covid-19, they have agonisingly looked for answers on what to do. If this is the case, a main lesson from the Covid-19 crisis is that how it demonstrates that globalisation is not so much an autonomous logic of its own. It developed, expanded and will eventually be curbed through the interplay of national forces, international institutions and global trends themselves. It has included all three right from the start.

In terms of its national dimension, Covid-19 has left us in no doubt that the health systems that have struggled to cope with it worldwide are to a large extent still confined to national borders and respond to national budgets, guidelines and traditions. The decision to implement and enforce lockdowns, while many were taken at the local level, depended mostly on national legislations, and the quality of critical infrastructure at the national level. Equally, the rise in unemployment and poverty figures that have followed are fundamentally national problems for nation-states that continue to be overburdened by a wide range of different demands that they find difficult to meet due to chronic fiscal crises. In fact, the provisional argument can be made that a major difference in the ability to face to the pandemic between those Asian countries that have fared well (Singapore, South Korea, Taiwan and Hong Kong) and those European ones that have not (Italy, Spain and the UK) is that the former had not faced the downward trajectory of the latter in terms health spending during past couple of decades. Furthermore, whether relations between states and civil societies are more democratic or authoritarian may have also impacted on how different populations responded to requests (or commands) of staying indoors.

A fuller picture of the Covid-19 crisis must equally include the role of international institutions such as the WHO. These institutions are highly competent in their areas of expertise but remain unable to put their recommendations into practice without state support. As mentioned in the first section of this paper, the history of the second half of the 20th century was marked by the constitution of a system international institutions that focuses on different aspects of modern life. UNESCO, WTO, INTERPOL, and indeed several others, are able to monitor, compare and orient states' actions in their different domains (Brown 2019, Brown, Cueto and Fee 2006). International institutions are able to guide states on what to do and have huge amounts of technical and practical knowledge to disseminate. Yet we have also witnessed that their capacity to act autonomously from nation-states is quite weak, so in order to deploy their expertise they depend – juridically, politically and economically– on what states let them do. In these critical times, these contradictions have been dramatically exposed.

The Rise of a New Cosmopolitan Imagination?

Insofar as the contemporary obsession with the global is concerned, one possible reaction to this pandemic is to suggest that it may signal the beginning of the end of globalisation. After all, in a weakened global economy, countries that are more self-sufficient in their access to raw materials and natural resources may prove more resilient, be able to turn the page more quickly, and even gain a comparative advantage in the case of a global recovery. The case of New Zealand, the one country that was able to control Covid-19 relatively early and with just a handful of deaths when most were counting their deceased in their thousands, seems to prove that point: a small island that is also geographically isolated.

From what we have argued so far in this chapter, however, the idea that we are to witness an end to globalisation of strikes me as the wrong lesson to learn from the Covid-19 crisis. In the short term, it is hard to see how members of the international community may be able to step outside the global economy without the alleged solutions causing even more pain than the potential remedy. The expectation, indeed hope, for a vaccine against the virus is a clear example of this: pooling resources globally offers better prospects for success. If it were to work at all, any possible dismantling of the global economy will have to be a part of a global endeavour itself. A better approach, it seems to me, is to underscore that while our global condition itself may be irreversible, globalisation itself has no preordained form. If the past thirty years have been characterised by an approach to globalisation that was driven by the economy and technological innovations, as an historical trend this is a contingent rather than a necessary process. Furthermore, our understanding of it has mistakenly treated the relations between the national and the global as a zero-sum game, so we must now redraw the balance between them – not least by reintegrating the role of international institutions in a much more fundamental way.

A starting point may be to avoid the twin dangers of, on the one hand, exaggerating the novelty of our current situation in order to speak of a dramatic epochal change while, on the other, falling back to a premature sense of normalcy and business as usual as soon as the current crisis appears to be over. Here, the reconfiguration of our cosmopolitan imagination should play a key role (Delanty 2009, Fine 2007). As a conclusion to this chapter, therefore, let me highlight four potentially cosmopolitan implications of the global events of 2020.

First, in relation to the economy, the current pandemic has had the unprecedented feature of simultaneously affecting *all areas of the economy and society as well as all regions of the world.* Whether we see economic globalisation as a long-term trend that began in the 17th century, or as a recent one that only goes back a couple of decades, the fact remains that we had never experienced a simultaneous contraction of the world economy where no actor – be it a state or a private corporation – remains in an unquestionable position to lead the path to recovery. In previous global recessions – 1929, 1973 or 2008 – the US, oil production, or China's soaring demand were able to take that leading role. Nowadays, however, most big businesses have had huge loss of revenue, most areas of the economy have contracted, and most states have accrued greater fiscal debts as a result of the pandemic. The fact that such a severe disruption of the economy has taken place in the midst of an increased awareness of the ecological challenges we face as a species must surely be an opportunity to imagine a different type of globalisation that ought to be organised around a more sustainable approach in our relations with the planet's natural resources.

Second, we may witness a revalorisation of state institutions. As we mentioned above, the argument can provisionally be made that the ability of national health services to respond to the Covid-19 crisis was to a large degree dependent on their previous fiscal trajectory in the past 10 or 20 years. Thus, for instance, health systems in South Korea, Singapore and Japan coped better than those of Spain, Italy or the UK and this may well have to do with the fact that fiscal trajectory of the latter had for some time now pointed towards reduction, contraction and downsizing. Of course, this is not a universal law, as Greece and Portugal have done better than many of their wealthier partners in Europe, so more evidence would have to be gathered before reaching definitive conclusions. Yet the fact remains that questions about the general health of the nation are likely to remain at the forefront of national politics for some time. As the experience of the World Wars shows, greater state expenditure and new welfare institutions seem to be a recurrent trend after traumatic events bring to the fore the collective responsibility we have for each other. Crucially, in many parts of the world the medical staff of 'national' health system is already highly international, and this opens an opportunity for a revalorisation of the role international migration play in the *strengthening* of national institutions.

Third, the strengths and weaknesses of international institutions such as the World Health Organisation have been laid bare during this pandemic. This is not the place to attempt a full balance sheet of its behaviour, of course, but I think it would be difficult to argue that, at a global scale, we would have been better off without its presence and advice.[3] If this is the case, the most significant lesson for international institutions is relatively straightforward: we need as resilient a version of them as possible. A 21st century WHO needs more resources, more autonomy vis-à-vis national politics, and greater technical capacity to act on the ground. Indeed, this argument is very much aligned with the view that we need a comprehensive reform of the United Nations for its ability to remain a relevant global actor to be fulfilled. Yet both conditions, financial resources and autonomy in relation to nation-states, have been stuck for too long within a restrictive framework that emphasises the role of states themselves in its functioning and legitimacy. Time has come for a new charter of the United Nations that incorporates global civil society more decidedly (Habermas 2008, Archibugi 2008).

Fourth, and finally, we seem to witness a paradox in the fact that lockdowns and the dramatic reduction of international travel worldwide may well become, in years to come, be construed as our first truly cosmopolitan *experience* in real time. To be sure, global events are nothing new in the history of modernity. The Lisbon earthquake on 1 November 1755, the very tragedy that inspired Kant (1991) to write on the rise of a new cosmopolitan consciousness in the 1790s, the opening of the Panama Canal in 1914, the Chernobyl disaster in 1986, or the terrorist attack on the World Trade Centre in New York in 2001, have all gone down in history as such global events. The Covid-19 pandemic is different from these because it cannot be encapsulated in one single instance or indeed one geographical location. More significantly, this is the first global crisis that simultaneously includes the great majority of human beings in the planet: never before in human history had we experienced the same events in the first person and the same time. At its peak, lockdowns, quarantines, restrictions of travel, work and education reached around 80% of the world's 7 billion of inhabitants.

---

3 Comments by Presidents Trump and Bolsonaro against WHO have remained the exception and even these have mostly fallen on deaf ears.

As Robert Fine (2012) put it, we are still in need of an idea of 'cosmopolitan solidarity' that may translate a cosmopolitan outlook, which is necessarily abstract, into practical political action. A standard criticism of a universalistic or cosmopolitan morality has been its inability to gather motivational force given its disconnection with people's direct experiences and everyday life. In this case, lockdowns have been imposed by states and governments but have had to rely on people's willingness to comply. To many of us, the most significant social and political action of 2020 has been restraint, our 'not-to-do' most of the things that we are normally free to do and feel entitled to do. Elections have been postponed, demonstrations have been cancelled, long-awaited transformations have had to wait. People all over the world have understood remarkably well that there is a greater good at stake.

It is obviously too early to tell how significant these changes may become or what their long-term consequences will be. Yet a new type of cosmopolitan solidarity may be in the making: global and national actions, and indeed *inactions,* that have brought people together by staying at home; a sense of commonality that is based on our refraining from doing. We may be witnessing the remaking of global bonds and duties by reasserting their interdependence with the national and the international: people's behaviour in one country and region have a clear and significant impact on how the pandemic spreads in other parts of the world. Somewhat paradoxically, we are only being able to slowly regain control of this global experience by not moving; our best form of global action as citizens of the world has been, for the time being at least, staying put. A different type of cosmopolitanism may hopefully be in the making.

References

Archibugi, D. (2008) *The Global Commonwealth of Citizens: Toward Cosmopolitan Democracy,* Princeton: Princeton University Press.

Beck, U. (1992) *Risk Society. Towards a New Modernity,* London: Sage.

Beck, U. (2000) *What is Globalization?,* Cambridge: Polity Press.

Beck, U. and Grande, E. (2007) *Cosmopolitan Europe,* Cambridge: Polity Press.

Brown, C. (2019) The Promise and Record of International Institutions. *International Relations* 33 (2) 143–56.

Brown, T. Cueto, M. and Fee, E. (2006) The World Health Organization and the Transition from "International" to "Global" public health. *American Journal of Public Health* 96 (1) 62–7.

Castells, M. (1996) *The Rise of the Network Society,* Oxford: Blackwell.

Chakrabaty, D. (2009) The Climate of History: Four Theses. *Critical Inquiry* (Winter) 197–222.

Chernilo, D. (2020) Beyond the Nation? Or back to it? Current Trends in the Sociology of Nations and nationalism. *Sociology* 54 (6) in press

Chernilo D. (2017) The Question of the human in the Anthropocene Debate. *European Journal of Social Theory* 20 (1) 44–60.

Chernilo, D. (2011) The Critique of Methodological Nationalism: Theory and History. *Thesis Eleven* 106 (1) 98–117.

Chernilo, D. (2007) *A Social Theory of the Nation-State*, London: Routledge.

Crutzen, P. (2002) Geology of Mankind. *Nature* 415: 23.

Delanty, G. (2009) *The Cosmopolitan Imagination: The Renewal of Critical Social Theory*, Cambridge: Cambridge University Press.

Delanty, G. and Mota, A. (2017) 'Governing the Anthropocene: Agency, Governance, Knowledge. *European Journal of Social Theory* 20 (1): 9–38.

Doshi, P. (2011) The Elusive Definition of Pandemic Influenza. *Bulletin of the World Health Organization* 89: 532–8.

Fine, R. (2007) *Cosmopolitanism*, London: Routledge.

Fine, R. (2012) The Idea of Cosmopolitan Solidarity. In: G. Delanty (ed.) *The Routledge Handbook of Cosmopolitanism Studies*. London: Routledge

Habermas, J. (1988) *Legitimation Crisis*, Cambridge: Polity Press.

Habermas, J. (2008) The Constitutionalization of International Law and the Legitimation Problems of a Constitution for World Society. *Constellations* 15 (4): 444–55.

Hirschfeld, K. (2020) Microbial Insurgency: Theorizing Global Health in the Anthropocene. *The Anthropocene Review* 7 (1) 3–18.

Kant, I. (1991) *Political Writings*, Cambridge: Cambridge University Press

Latour, B. (1993) *We Have Never Been Moderns*, Cambridge, Mass.: Harvard University Press.

Latour, B. (2020) *Where to land after the pandemic? A paper and now a platform.* http://www.bruno-latour.fr/node/852.html Last access 8 Sept 2020.

Lewis, S. and Maslin, M. (2018) *The Human Planet. How We Created the Anthropocene*, London: Penguin.

Sassen, S. (2007) *A Sociology of Globalization*, New York: WW Norton.

Tooze, A. (2014) *The Deluge. The Great War, America and the Remaking of the Global Order 1916–1931*, London: Penguin.

Turner, B. S. (2006) Classical Sociology and Cosmopolitanism: A critical Defence of the Social. *British Journal of Sociology* 57 (1) 133–55.

Wagner, P. (1994) *A Sociology of Modernity*, London: Routledge.

Wallerstein, I. (2011) *The Modern World-System I: Capitalist Agriculture and the Origins of the European World-Economy in the Sixteenth Century*, Los Angeles: University of California Press.

Whitehead, A. N. (1953) *Science and the Modern World*, New York: The Free Press.

Frédéric Vandenberghe and Jean-François Véran

The Pandemic as a Global Social Total Fact

Epidemics occur when a contagious disease spreads rapidly to a large number of people in a given population in a short period of time. Epidemics turn into pandemics when the infectious disease is not contained and spreads through whole regions of the world. When contagion reaches all the continents (with the exception of the Antarctic) and potentially affects each and every person on earth – as is the case with the new coronavirus – the pandemic turns into a global pandemonium. Fear spreads through all ranks of society, emergency measures are taken, implemented and contested, everyday life is disrupted, and the social order unravels rapidly. While some people hope that the interdependence and mutual vulnerability of all will lead to a higher level of unity and consciousness, others fear the advent of the Hobbesian nightmare of a war of all against all, between individuals and groups, and at the international level.

The pandemic triggers an 'omnicrisis' (Negri and Hardt 2000: 189, 201), reinforcing pre-existing ecological, economic, political, social, cultural and personal strains, fusing them into an all-encompassing crisis of multiple institutions that takes on a humanitarian dimension and evokes dystopian scenarios that plunge us back, if not into the Middle Ages (the plague and the quarantine), then certainly to the bleakest days of the twentieth century – the First World War (and the 1918 flu), the economic downturn of 1928 – 29, and the emergence of totalitarian regimes in Europe and Asia.

The global outbreak brings whole societies over the edge, and possibly over it. The looming omnicrisis comes with a strong sense of decline, decay and collapse – as if we have seen nothing yet and the worst is still to come. From the point of view of the humanities and the social sciences, there is not just one virus, but multiple pathogens running at the same time through the population: neoliberalism, populism, post-truthism and the Anthropocene. Since the end of the 1970s, monetarism, free market ideologies and corporatist interests have spawned an economy that is increasingly untethered from democracy ('post-democracy'). By increasing inequality and vulnerability among the masses, the liberal economy has triggered a populist backlash against the elites that has led to the authoritarianism of 'illiberal democracies'. The resurgence of virulent nationalisms in many parts of the world has in turn strengthened anti-globalism, undermined cosmopolitanism and pulled the rug from multilateral agreements to control climate change and other ecological risks of the coming Anthropocene. With the political polarisation that splits the citizenry into antagonistic factions, one by one all limits of political decency have been transgressed. The pandemic

https://doi.org/10.1515/9783110713350-011

and lockdown fatigue have only radicalised the tensions. Post-truths, fake news, conspiracies and 'epidemioideologies' have completely unhinged representations of reality from reality. As Baudrillard (1976) had anticipated, fact and fiction mingle and reality has turned into 'hyperreality'. Everything happens as if the postmodernism of the 1980s has now come back with a vengeance. Not depoliticised, as with Baudrillard, but hyperpoliticised and combative.

Both authors of this chapter are European academics who have settled in Brazil and work at the Federal University of Rio de Janeiro. One is an anthropologist, the other a sociologist. During the Covid-19 emergency, one was in Rio, the other on a sabbatical in Paris. Together, we will analyse the processes of contagion and degeneration from two angles (social theory and applied anthropology) and two locations (Paris and Rio de Janeiro).

In Brazil, since the onset of the pandemic, one of us (FV) analysed the political situation (in weekly gatherings on Zoom) with a group of doctoral students (GRAF 2020). We have witnessed how the crisis has exacerbated the authoritarian tendencies of President Jair Messias Bolsonaro. Instead of confronting the virus head on, implementing and coordinating public health policies, he has doubled down on his historical and ecological revisionism with an open denial of scientific evidence. Not only does he negate two decades of military dictatorship in Brazil, which he conceives of as the apex of democracy, but he also denies the Amazon is on fire and he has seized the threat of Covid-19 as an opportunity to foment a military coup – as if it were still possible to return to the twentieth century.

In Paris, the other (J-FV) had, with *Médecins Sans Frontières*, embarked on operations during the two-month lockdown, aimed at delivering medical assistance to the most precarious populations (illegal immigrants, asylum-seekers, homeless, drug addicts, sex workers, etc.). The anthropologist-fieldworker was expected to conduct outreach activities to follow the fast-expanding frontiers of vulnerability during the weeks of lockdown, as resources, coping mechanisms and resilience were depleting, transforming the deserted streets into a disaster zone.

In this chapter, we adopt a neo-Maussian perspective on the pandemic and analyse it as a 'global social total fact'. With Durkheim, we assume that it can be analysed not only as a biological, but also as social fact, i.e. as a complex of collective acts that impose themselves on individuals from without (*epi-demics*, literally, that which comes down from above onto the demos) and regulate their ways of thinking, feeling and acting. With Mauss, we will further assume that it is a total fact that affects all societies and all individuals (*pan-demics*, literally, that which affects all people) that has to be analysed in all its dimensions, from the biological to the political, from the symbolic to the economic, from the aesthetic to the existential.

The Pandemic under the Sociological Macroscope

The spectacle of disarray and desolation is difficult to bear, both collectively and individually. However, when one is right in the eye of the storm, from a social scientific point of view, it is a boon. It offers a unique opportunity for analysis, diagnosis and therapeutics. It is the equivalent of a large-scale experiment in real time that reveals in all its clarity and with all its brutality how the whole of humanity, all societies, all groups and every individual are potentially affected by the coronavirus. The virus itself may be tiny and microscopic but its social effects are gigantic and, as it were, puts the whole of society under the 'macroscope'. As happens in revolutionary times, structures, cultures and practices that were taken for granted now become conspicuous. The system unravels in relations, processes and events. Local events can have immediate repercussions on global structures, while global structures can immediately percolate down to the local level. Large-scale tendencies and long-term processes burst into the open and come to the surface. Notwithstanding a general sense of contingency and uncertainty, the social dynamics become readable when the conflicts between social groups become exacerbated and the social order undergoes a serious crash test.

The plague fractures populations from within, increasing tensions between rich and poor, black and white, nationals and immigrants, believers and sceptics. It also introduces at once the whole of humanity as a unit of analysis and diagnosis. Reverting to old philosophies of history that conceive humanity to be a single acting and suffering subject, humankind is brought in once again as a single species with a living biological substrate that is both unique and coextensive to all individuals, yet also open to interference with other species. The causes of the pandemic are complex and, therefore, difficult to determine, almost *indécidable*, as Derrida would say. Not only do different sciences have different interpretations of, and explanations for, the phenomenon, but because they affect everybody epidemics also trigger psycho-social and socio-political epidemics. With the result that at the limit everybody also tends to come up with their own explanation and interpretation, diagnosis and critique. As a result, it is not clear whether one has to blame globalisation, the president of the United States or a bat in Wuhan.

Viral outbreaks occur when microorganisms are able to cross the species barrier when human societies open up to each other either by accident, warfare or regular social and economic intermixing, and when the ecosystem is troubled by human interference (Epstein 1995). Any approach to the pandemic has necessarily to take into account three dimensions: the processes of viral contagion, the response of individual organisms to the virus, and its repercussions on collective human behaviours in all spheres of life (religion, politics, the economy, etc.). While epidemiology deals with the distribution and the patterns of diffusion of the virus among populations, medical clinicians focus on the individual biological reaction to viral infection. The social sciences for their part investigate how individuals and collectives react and respond to the epidemiological and biomedical realities, discourses and practices. The three dimensions are obviously interrelated. One cannot analyse the Covid-19 crisis without taking into account the statistics of contagion (the number of infected people, the number of deaths, the curves, etc.), the health policies that are implemented (from social distancing and lockdown to masks, ventilators and vaccines) and the whole gamut of psychological, cultural, social and political actions and reactions to the havoc that comes with the collective attempts, and the failures, to bring the viral spread under control.

The Gift of Marcel Mauss

Although we fully recognise that the epidemiological and clinical dimensions have their autonomy, we think, however, that the social sciences need to investigate the social aspects of both the biological and the clinical reality. For the sake of the argument, as an exercise in social theorising coupled to a multi-sited ethnography, we adopt in this article the perspective of the Durkheimian School. We will conceive of the *anthropos* as a totality (*l'homme total*): a living being with a consciousness who is a member of society (Mauss 1989: 280 – 310, 329 – 330). As a bio-psychic and social entity that is part of a larger whole, the human being cannot be decomposed, but has to be taken in all its complexity: "Body, soul and society: everything here is mingled" (Mauss 1989: 303). We assume that the pandemic is a social fact and that even the biological, the medical and the scientific dimensions of the Sars-Covid-2 virus are susceptible to social analysis.

Drawing on one of Marcel Mauss's most imaginative concepts, we analyse the pandemic as a global total social fact that affects all the people(s) on Earth and "brings the totality of society and its social institutions into movement" (Mauss 1989: 274) or, as is the case, to a standstill. We follow Mauss's lead and investigate the morphological, physiological and symbolic aspects of the outbreak of Covid-19, interweaving bodies, representations and practices in dialectical fashion. While the pandemic is observed nationally (like the World Cup and Olympic Games), we will draw out its global aspects – following the actors, narratives, discourses, policies and practices as they move through space, unify humanity, transform societies and fracture communities.

In his famous essay on the gift, Mauss (1989: 143–279) uncovers the moral foundations of gift exchange. By looking at how the gift weaves together various populations in circles of reciprocity (for example, with the Kula in Melanesia) or investigating how hierarchy is reproduced and reinforced in political tournaments of generosity (for instance, the North American potlatch), Mauss has most convincingly shown that the exchange of gifts is not just an economic phenomenon. If anything, its moral and political dimensions are preeminent (Caillé 2000). It is enough to violate the norms of reciprocity and to fail to honour one of the triple obligations ('to give, to accept and to return the gift') to put the community under tension. The gift is an operator of peace, but may also lead to war.

Of course, the virus is not a gift. If anything, it is a curse, but it is also a living cursor that interconnects groups and individuals into a single community of fate. Like the collars and shells of the Kula or the animal furs of the potlatch, it circulates freely within social relationships and brings into movement the whole of society, the totality of their members and their institutions. Because infection by Sars-Cov-2 requires physical and therefore social proximity, its epidemiology is the biological imprint of hyper-connected social networks. In the global era, the extensity, intensity, velocity and impact of the contagion has been aggravated by the economic interdependence of whole regions in a single commodity chain that connects industrial production in Wuhan with consumption in London, New York and São Paulo.

Pandemics are nothing new in the history of humankind. Humans have always been social beings and therefore have always contaminated each other. This plague is different however. As indicated by Gerard Delanty in the introduction to this volume, the current contagion is not the first one of modernity, but it is the 'big one' that epidemiologists have been expecting for decades. Although we are still officially living in the Holocene, everything indicates that the current plight is one that humanity inflicted on itself. More contagions will follow because they are the result of at least two centuries of intensive extractive industrialisation of the planet. If the current rate of deforestation of the Amazon forest continues, the next zoonosis may well come from Brazil.

If the essay on the gift exemplifies marvellously the concept of the global social total fact, its most elaborate theoretical systematisation is to be found in a more confidential text in which Marcel Mauss tries to reorganise the various sections of the *Année Sociologique*, the famous journal of the Durkheimian School. In 'Divisions and Proportions of Divisions in Sociology', Mauss (1969: 42–80) followed his uncle (Durkheim 1970: 136–159) and divided social phenomena into social morphology and social physiology. Social morphology refers to the material and quantifiable substratum of society, consisting of 'men and things', 'masses and numbers', 'groups and their structures' that can be graphically represented (geography) and statistically measured (demography). Physiology contains the elements that set it in motion ('collective representations and social practices'). Starting from their material and morphological base, the analyst must systematically integrate the collective practices that make up societies and the symbolic representations that structure and orient them by linking them to the totality. In synthesis, the analyst must: "seek the acts under the representations and the representations under the acts, and under both, the groups" (Mauss 1969: 60).

Morphological Analysis

Morphological analysis studies the social group as a material phenomenon. It looks at the substrate of society – at bodies (human and animal) and things (temples, factories, hospitals, etc.) and studies how they form a mass, with volume and density, and how they are distributed in time and space. Let us start with the geographical aspect of the pandemic and follow its spread through time and space, using Facebook's Timeline and Google's Earth to underscore its direct connection to globalisation (Grésillon 2020). From a geographical and geopolitical perspective, the pandemic appears as a product of the systemic interconnection of industrial and commercial urban regions into a global network that can be analysed as a single network of interconnected nodes through which flows of people, goods, money, information, images, discourses, and now also viruses, circulate. In the information age, 'networks constitute the new morphology of our societies' (Castells 1996: 469).

Networks of contagion

To understand the spread of the contagion of the coronavirus from the province of Hubei, via Europe and the US, to almost each of the 500,000 villages of India, one only needs to introduce a microscopic virus into the network of flows of people and things, while scaling up the analysis to the global level, to see that the clusters of contagion explode first in the nodes of the network (gigantic production poles, global cities, technological valleys, corridors of innovation) and then move from there via its spokes to its rims.

Although the hypothesis still needs to be confirmed, the pandemic is said to have originated in an exotic food market in Wuhan where a pangolin that had been infected by a bat transmitted it to a human sometime in late 2019. From Wuhan, it followed the merchandise and spread to China's business partners in the Far East (Taiwan, Singapore, Hong Kong and South Korea) at the beginning of the year. On the 21st of February, the first cluster (not the first case) of contagion was detected in the economically most affluent region of Italy, so-called 'Third Italy' with its innovative industries and flexible specialisation. The scenes of mass transportation of coffins in Bergamo are unforgettable. By the beginning of March, it had spread to the rest of Europe.

Everywhere, the grammar of diffusion is the same: within every country, the economic hubs (Milan, Paris, London, Madrid) are the 'super-spreaders'. With the exception of Sweden, Lithuania and Hungary, all European countries put their populations in lockdown. By April, Covid-19 arrived in the USA. The hospitals of New York and Seattle collapsed. By May, the contagion was completely out of control in the USA, Russia and Brazil. The numbers are staggering. The images are heart breaking. By September, India had become the new epicentre of the outbreak while the rest of the world was bracing for a second wave.

By now, it is evident that the diffusion of the virus is a direct function of the intensity of human interactions. Human interactions are most intensive where economic and commercial activities are concentrated. A general deduction can then be drawn at three geographic scales: Geopolitically, contagion follows the routes of global commerce and migration. That explains why Africa, with the exception of North and South Africa, has been relatively spared so far. Nationally, it circulates in the urban conurbations, and from there, it keeps on spreading along the regional and local transport lines, with workers who were required to sustain 'essential' economic activities transmitting the virus while the majority of the population was under lockdown. This is how contagion reached the poor suburbs of all European capitals within a few weeks. In India, when the Modi government put the whole country on lockdown with hardly any advance warning, millions of poor workers went into 'reverse migration', walking in droves for days and nights, bringing the virus to their native villages.

Now that the 'trickle-down effects' are better understood, we can expect a systematic scaling down of contagion measures to regional local clusters targeting and controlling the smallest geographical unit of analysis. During the pandemic, social morphology was transformed at its very base: the pandemic has triggered a change in social density similar to a seasonal variation. Like the Inuit in summer, in an early study by Marcel Mauss (1989: 387–477) on the rhythms of social life, the social relations that animate society were loosened and became sparser. As people fell back on their family units, with apartments and houses akin to the dispersed tents of the Inuit in summer time, social and psychic life slowed down significantly and societies worldwide went through a protracted 'phase of languid and depressed sociality' (Mauss 1989: 471). Had it not been for an uptake in phone calls and video conferences, life in hyper-connected societies would have shrunk down to the micro-local pockets of interaction that characterises societies with segmental differentiation.

The hyperconfined and the unconfinables

Morphological analysis studies how individuals and groups are distributed over the territory. Drawing from human geography, Mauss stresses the importance of the spatial organisation of society and considers its limits, its transport channels, its density, the rural/urban contrast etc. as precious indicators of a given society's morphology. Indeed, satellite observation of shipping activity in ports, cars parked at shopping centres or night-time lights in urban areas, has shown how the pandemic provoked a sudden change in the patterns of human activity. The 'mass' of societies became, as it were, 'liquefied' with the arrival of the coronavirus. In the beginning, the mass flowed along major traffic routes. To ward off the fear, many joined family in their homesteads. The images were reminiscent of Ebola when extended West African families gathered, bringing back their relatives from different countries. The global lockdown also provoked an urban exodus. To flee the crowds and the stale air, a process of 'counter-urbanisation' was unleashed with a surge of house prices in the suburbs as a result. Made jobless by strict lockdowns throughout the globe, the 'wretched of the earth' who had moved to cities for work, returned home spurring a massive 'reverse migration'. In Asia as in Latin America, the interminable processions of families on foot and with hardly any luggage remind us of the war exodus of 1940 or, more recently, that of the Syrian refugees. And then, suddenly, social life came to a standstill and 'froze'.

In many countries worldwide, the lockdown was decreed in the form of an injunction with almost immediate effect, applying to all in a rather undifferentiated manner. Soon a significant difference appeared between two parts of the population who had quite a different experience of the lockdown. Based on our fieldwork in applied anthropology with Médecins Sans Frontières (MSF) in Paris, we distinguished two distinct populations: the 'unconfinables' (the 'locked-out') and the 'hyper-confined' (the 'locked-down') (Véran and Viot 2020).

During the lockdown (March 17 to May 11), the unconfinable went into a paradoxical hyper-mobility. For the homeless, the street disappeared as a space of survival. The streets were suddenly empty and so were the rubbish bins. When the bars and restaurants closed, they lost access to leftovers. The toilets of McDonald's or the neighbourhood library also closed. The homeless had to be constantly on the move to survive: from a water access point to a point of food distribution. As the city centre became dangerous overnight, some walked all the way to the terminals 2E and 2F of the distant airport of Charles de Gaulle to find a secure place to sleep. When definite categories of activities were declared essential (pharmacies, supermarkets, etc.), the working class also started to move. The subways and buses coming and going from the popular suburbs to the urban centres never stopped. In Paris, the metro line 13 to Saint-Denis was extremely busy. With delivery services such as Uber-eats and Ifood, the überexploited were continuously transiting on their motorbikes and bicycles (sometimes rented). Since no one was going anywhere, they had to be everywhere. We found them in total burnout, close to panic attacks or feverishly fighting their symptoms of Covid-19 in the waiting lines of our mobile clinics.

The 'hyper-confined' for their part remained cloistered at home. Since March, they have been living in a goldfish bowl. The elderly, those with a medical condition of co-morbidity, the middle classes in their home office who order their food online, people trapped by fear and anxiety all remained sheltered at home, even after the easing of the sanitary measures. In many places of the world, the hyper-confined devoted themselves to an 8:00 PM ritual: they opened their windows and clapped hands in gratitude to the health and other front-line workers. After the lockdown, some hyper-confined people remained homebound, like those soldiers who spent years in a bunker after the end of the Second World War.

During the lockdown, the public space lost its anonymity. Without the protection of the crowds, it became a space of hyper-visibility and, therefore, also of overexposure. In a squat, MSF found 85 transsexual sex workers who had systematically avoided the street as a risk mitigation strategy against discrimination and violence. Similarly, many illegal migrants had retreated from the streets, revealing a cross logic of fear of contamination and of police harassment. In the name of safety, they had given up a decent diet and were not seeking medical help when they needed it. The outreach team also gave medical assistance to dozens of people living in tents in the heart of the Bois de Vincennes: to protect themselves from the virus, they had chosen to live like Robinsons, often with the price of renouncing care.

Physiological Analysis

In the old-fashioned language that Durkheim transposed from biology to sociology, 'social morphology' refers to the structure of society, while 'social physiology' refers to structures in movement, that is, to dynamic totalities. It includes both social representations and practices that are tied together in living institutions. Institutions are established ways of thinking, feeling and acting that are transmitted from generation to generation. The great contribution of Marcel Mauss is to have adapted and shifted the language away from Durkheim's collective representations to symbolic representations of society (Tarot 1999). The symbolical is the great discovery of Marcel Mauss. It influenced the whole tradition of French structuralism and post-structuralism, from Benvéniste to Bourdieu, from Lévi-Strauss to Descola, from Lefort to Castoriadis and Gauchet. For Mauss, everything is significant, and everything signifies. As a consequence, the morphological substrate also takes on meaning, and everything and everyone are interrelated with everything and everyone else. "There is no social phenomenon that is not an integral part of the social whole" (Mauss 1969: 51). As all parts are interrelated in a totality, sociological analysis is always holistic. Thanks to symbolism, societies are able to project their unity and their division outside of themselves and these representations directly structure the social practices from within. Symbolic representations therefore not only represent, but by commanding acts, they also perform the collective: they bring it into existence and into movement.

Holism, individualism, co-immunism

When one analyses complex societies in a holistic fashion, one quickly comes to realize that their individualism is also a social product and a moral fact. The individual is sacred, as Durkheim (1970: 261–278) and Goffman (1967: 47–95) have amply shown, at the macro and micro levels of society respectively. The initial consensus established within the World Health Organization's area of influence confirmed the principle of the sacredness of the individual. This explains why, at least at the beginning of the pandemic, individual health became the one principle that unified societies and led to international institutional convergence. Because each individual counts and survival is the highest value, only one course of action seemed possible: 'flatten the curve', don't overburden hospitals, save lives.

Almost everywhere in the world, all institutions and all subsystems of society were brought under the imperative of health. Complex societies started to de-differentiate and returned to segmental differentiation: "Never before has our life been so simple and never again, after these few weeks are over, will it be that simple again" (Stichweh 2020: 9). The economy was no longer the dominant system. Utilitarianism was discarded and *homo economicus* was put back in his place. For a moment, politics were handed over to the experts (virologists, epidemiologists, even sociologists) who took crucial decisions based on science. Scientific research itself became monothematic. The news turned into a collective funeral. Sports and concerts, the equivalents of folklore, were suspended. So were the most elementary freedoms, including the right to come and go.

The curtailment of individual liberties was accepted because people become conscious of their interdependence. They knew that Covid-19 is a relational hazard and that to protect others they had to accept limitations to their own freedom. Breaking with the vision of independent individuals, modern individualism showed its holistic imprint. The *homo clausus* of economic and political liberalism, theorised by Norbert Elias (2001) in *The Society of Individuals,* opened up to fellow citizens. The knowledge that the newly infected became the new infectors linked individuals into a chain of transmission in which the weakest link inversely determines the force of the chain: as the weak links multiply, the force of contamination gets ever stronger. The pandemic showed that the individualism of modern societies is a moral and political one. Willingly relinquishing social contact to protect each other, moral individualism appeared as a form of 'co-immunism' (Sloterdijk 2011) that prolongs, but also inverts, Marcel Mauss's convivialism (*Internationale convivialiste,* 2020): individuals can only 'live together with their differences' and demonstrate their organic solidarity if they accept the rules of physical distance.

Epistemocrats and magico-populists

For a moment, there was a sense of interdependence and unity. However, after a couple of weeks of lockdown the unity quickly started to fracture. A period of what Victor Turner called 'structural liminality' opened up (Turner 1969): the old structures ceased to function and societies entered a protracted moment of 'anti-structure' in which old norms and conventions lost their sway and the new ones seemed both artificial and unnecessary. The social distancing had led to isolation, the isolation to atomism, and the atomism to anomie. Dark volcanic undercurrents came to the surface. The symbolic representations of unity were undercut by diabolic representations of division within the population.

Populist leaders pitted the scientific establishment and their elites against the common people who were afraid not only of losing their life, but also their livelihood and their jobs.

As always happens during epidemics, the outbreak of disease was doubled by a psycho-social contagion of fear and panic, ignorance and agitation that ripped through both isolated individuals and the social body, disrupting everyday practices, undermining faith in established authorities. With Philip Strong's model of an 'epidemic psychology', which tracks the "waves of individual and collective panic, outbursts of interpretation as to why disease has occurred, rashes of moral controversy, and plagues of competing control strategies" (Strong 1990: 257), Mauss's vision of a 'collective psychology', or, as he phrases it, a 'psychological sociology' (Mauss 1989: 289) took on a more sinister turn.

As 'sad passions' spread through society, dynamogenetic currents of negative effervescence progressively took hold on some parts of the population. At first, to conjure the panic, politicians and the people put their faith in science. Everywhere, 'scientific committees' were set up. Every country designated a prominent (male) epidemiologist, a great clinician, a 'knower', who became the face and voice of Reason. Politicians sought advice from the experts in their 'war against the virus'. Like their predecessors who had consulted the oracles before a fight, the politicians now entrusted their policies of public health to the scientific experts. They were the ones who had to devise and implement the most efficacious strategies to contain the viral contagion, through lockdown, contact tracing, testing, etc. In a frantic rush against the clock to develop the vaccine, exclusive contracts with the pharmaceutical industry were signed in haste.

Then came a six-syllable 'miracle': hydroxychloroquine. In his *Outline of a General Theory of Magic*, co-written with Henri Hubert, Mauss (1989: 1–141) had already analysed the magical substrate of miracle drugs, which they considered 'a real fabric of symbolism, sympathies, homeopathies and antipathies' (Mauss 1989: 12). With Didier Raoult, the French *bricoleur* in the white coat, the world discovered the magico-scientific superpower of symbolic enactment. With his oppositional style and his anti-establishment discourses, he re-enchanted medicine, replaced doubt by certainty, and instantly became a folk hero. Against the psycho-social contagion of fear, people were adhering to science-engineered hydroxychloroquine as a mimetic ritual conjuring of fear. And then the populists plugged into this energy and transformed it into a magico-political performance. Mauss knew that magic is a substitute for science and that it does not pass the test of truth. It is therefore not surprising that Bolsonaro and Trump, two major preachers of post-truthism, began to peddle hydroxychloroquine in the same way that in the past bonesetters would sell elixirs of youth. As one cannot prove that it is efficacious, one cannot disprove it either. It was produced en masse by the military in Brazil and President Trump also sent to Brazil over 200 million doses.

The corona-scepticism of Jair Messias Bolsonaro

While most politicians were happy to coordinate the execution of public policies hiding behind the protective shield of their 'knowers', some autocrats and would-be dictators, like Alexander Lukashenko (Belarus), Gurbanguly Berdymukhhamedov (Turkmenistan), Daniel Ortega (Nicaragua) and Jair Bolsonaro (Brazil), refused to take the virus seriously and systematically played down the risks. Here we will focus on Brazil and we will treat it as an extreme case – an 'ideal type' or, closer to the truth, a real dystopia – that shows in all brutality the real distortions of the populist politics of fear (Graf, 2021).

Giving priority to economic growth over health, Bolsonaro took the position that unemployment was worse than Covid-19 itself. Following Trump, he kept repeating 'the medicine is worse than the disease'. Since the beginning of the scourge, he has ignored safety measures, joined political rallies without mask and actively sabotaged social distancing. While other countries were locking down their populations, Bolsonaro wanted them to go back to work: 'Brazil cannot come to a halt'. The result of his irresponsibility became visible in the streets. Social distancing lasted only a couple of weeks. By mid-April, most businesses in Rio de Janeiro had reopened, at first hesitatingly behind half-closed doors, but then, under pressure from commerce and industry, officially and openly. Informal trade spilled over into the streets with ambulant vendors occupying the pavement. In the midst of the sanitary crisis, the president fired two of his ministers of health, who refused to sign off on hydroxychloroquine, only to replace them by an army general without medical experience, but with expertise in logistics. As soon as the general took over, the statistics started to be manipulated. Eventually, a private consortium formed by the main newspapers had to take over the production of reliable epidemiological data. As there's no longer any real health policy, every Brazilian citizen is now his or her own minister of health, deciding whether to wear a mask or go to the beach at the weekend.

In Brazil, corona-scepticism became the official position. The attack against science and the universities is a frontal one. Here, biopolitics and necropolitics are part of an ugly ideological war that is waged in the name of the religious truth itself and with support from the military against communism, science, education, culture, ecology and indigenous populations. The pandemic is unchecked, the Amazon forest is once again on fire, genocide against indigenous populations is taking place and, yet, nothing happens. With his insulting speeches and his bad manners, Brazil's strongman is perceived as authentic. His followers call him the 'myth' and even though he destroys the country, he's cast in a messianic aura as the one who will save the country. He tells lies like a fascist and has even installed a propaganda cell in his presidential palace. In the midst of a pandemic, he created one political crisis after the other and even tried to foment a coup (Vandenberghe, 2020). He failed, at least for now. Thanks to the financial relief of 600 reais (100 euros) per month, he has actually increased his popularity. As part of the elites who voted him into power have changed their mind, he is now increasingly dependent on the poorest fractions of the population to support him

Rituals of the Blame Game

A rash of accusations invariably follows disasters. As Paul Farmer (2006) found in his study on AIDS in Haiti, which we will extend here to Covid-19, there are three ways to perpetrate an accusation: sorcery, moral condemnation, and conspiracy. Covid-19 is often read in popular religions as a divine punishment for sin that announces the end of times or as a curse that is attributed to witchcraft. To undo the spell, the formulas have multiplied. In the Philippines, volcanic ash was said to kill the virus. In parts of China, saltwater has been used. In India, it was cow dung and urine. In the US, bleach and UV light. Meanwhile, over 700 Iranians have died from drinking methanol, which they believed would cure the virus (Gusterson, 2020). Accusations are also built around an unstoppable moral argument. Responsibility for the contamination rests on each and every one of us. Social distancing must be respected. Masks must be worn all the time. Everyone is thus potentially responsible for the death of a family member or a friend. Individual consent to lockdown stems to a large extent from this devolution to individual behaviour of moral responsibility for the epidemic. Finally, by moving from the level of interpersonal relationships to that of social groups, the accusation of witchcraft turns into an accusation of conspiracy. The Chinese Communist Party contaminated the world, the virus is being spread through G5 networks, Bill Gates wants to insert microchips into vaccines, etc. These complex mechanisms of accusation are not to be understood here as cultural atavisms. They reflect an overall dysfunction of contemporary societies in addressing their people's basic needs and so they express the shifting balance of global power.

Conclusion

The pandemic is not a parenthesis. It is a transition point that indicates a rupture. In many parts of the world, the pandemic is already becoming an endemic disease. Its fluctuations and waves are difficult to understand, even for epidemiologists. Its repercussions on politics and society are unpredictable. We consider the pandemic a symptom of a global modernity that has gone awry. From a geological perspective, it may not be the 'golden spike' that opens the Anthropocene, tipping the scales from globalisation to planetarisation. Yet, we all sense that an epoch is coming to an end. We know that other pandemics are inevitable and that the sanitary crisis is only a harbinger of major structural, cultural and personal transformations. All signs point dangerously to another Great Transformation, similar to the one that Karl Polanyi talked about. Only now it is not the nineteenth century civilisation that has collapsed, as indicated in his famous opening line (Polanyi 1957: 3), but the twentieth century one.

In this chapter, we have investigated the pandemic as a global total social fact. To understand a social fact as a total fact implies (ideally) that one reveals the totality of social relations that constitute it. We have treated the Covid-19 crisis as a microscope of societal currents that come from the depths of society, may crystallize in social institutions (social physiology) and materialise in social structures (social morphology). With the Durkheimian School, we have analysed societies as 'dynamic totalities' that are continuously subject to 'movements of structuration, destructuration and restructuration' (Gurvitch 1967: 19). To capture the ambivalence and negativity of the present, we have shifted the analysis from a functionalist consensus theory to a more dialectical conflict theory.

From the material distribution and circulation of bodies and things (Durkheim's 'social structure') via functions and dysfunctions of the economy, politics, law, etc. (the 'institutions') and via symbolic and diabolic representations ('collective representations'), to creative and destructive currents ('effervescences'), we have tried to capture the societal consequences of the pandemic in all its depth, complexity and volatility. As we are still in the midst of a period of liminality, this strange time between 'separation' (the 'old world') and 'reintegration' (the 'new world') when everything can shift for better or for worse, we are well advised to avoid conjectures about the future. We do not even know what will happen in three weeks' time. With the horizon blocked, time itself seems to have warped.

Instead of global scenarios of the turbulent times of transition, we will finish on a more phenomenological note. Mauss did not hesitate to use his personal experience in the trenches as a basis for understanding how 'techniques of the body' (Mauss 1989: 383–386) adjusted to the context of war. Our own experience of retrenchment has not been easy either. Like everyone else, we had difficulties adapting to the 'new normal'. As we went into social distancing, we were breathing less, moving less and consuming less, while continuously tracking the latest news on our tablets. With a lot of anxiety, we had to move our classes on line and we learned new ways of suffering: while J-FV had frosted glass lesions in his lungs, FV went through the anguish of social disaffiliation. We were experiencing, perhaps, the inversion of Sartre's formula: hell, after all, might be the absence of other people.

While we were experiencing the frailty of the human condition and rediscovering our humanism, the world of non-humans began to reclaim urban spaces: rabbits in the centre of Paris, wild boar in Barcelona, dolphins in Mediterranean ports. Meanwhile in Brazil, jaguars in the wetlands and forest trees in the indigenous territories of the Amazon were consumed by fires, lit by farmers, miners and other criminals who felt encouraged by Bolsonaro's ruthless promotion of the extractive economy. The fauna and the flora would no doubt be better off without us. But if we, humans, are to survive we will have to expand our humanism to include social relationships with other species – including viruses and bacteria – and learn to live with them in the web of life.

References

Baudrillard, J. (1976) *L'échange symbolique et la mort*, Paris: Gallimard.

Caillé, A. (2000) *Anthropologie du don. Le tiers paradigm*, Paris: Desclée de Brouwer.

Castells, M. (1996) *The Rise of the Network Society*, Oxford: Blackwell.

Durkheim, E. (1989 [1897]) *Le suicide. Etude de sociologie*, Paris: PUF.

Durkheim, E. (1970) *La science sociale et l'action*, 261–278. Paris: PUF.

Elias, N. (2001) *Die Gesellschaft der Individuen*. In: *Gesammelte Schriften*, vol. 10. Frankfurt am Main: Suhrkamp.

Epstein, P. (1995) Emerging Diseases and Ecosystem Instability. New Threats to Public Health, *American Journal of Public Health*, 85(2): 168–172.

Goffmann, E. (1967) *Interaction Ritual. Essays on Face-to-Face Behavior*. New York: Pantheon Books.

GRAF (Gabinete de reflexão antifa) (2020) Análise da disjuntura ao longo da pandemia: Um experimento de escrita sem partitura, *Dilemas. Reflexões sobre a pandemia,*17 de Setembro, 1–17.

Graf (Gabinete de reflexão antifa) (2021): "Brazil: The Real Dystopia Project", forthcoming in Digithum.

Grésillon, B. (2020) "Géopolitique du Covid-19", *AOC Média*, May 7.

Internationale convivialiste (2020) *Second manifeste convivialiste. Pour un monde post-néolibéral*, Paris: Actes Sud.

Gusterson, H. (2020) Covid-19 and the Turn to Magical Thinking, *Sapiens, Anthropology Magazine*, May 12.

Gurvitch, G. (1967) Objet et méthode de la sociologie. In: Gurvitch, G. (ed.), *Traité de sociologie*, Vol. 1, 3–27. Paris: PUF.

Mauss, M. (1989) *Sociologie et anthropologie*, Paris: PUF.

Mauss, M. (1969) *Essais de sociologie*, Paris: Seuil.

Negri, A. and Hardt, M. (2000) *Empire*. Cambridge, MASS: Harvard University Press.

Polanyi, K. (1957 [1944]) *The Great Transformation*, Boston: Beacon Press.

Stichweh, R. (2020) An diesem Imperativ kann die Politik scheitern, *Frankfurt allgemeine Zeitung*, April, 7, 9.

Sloterdijk, P. (2011) Co-immunité globale. Penser le commun qui protège, *Multitudes*, 45 (2): 42–45.

Strong, P. (1990) Epidemic Psychology: A Model, *Sociology of Health and Illness*, 12 (3): 249–259.

Tarot, C. (1999) *De Durkheim à Mauss, l'invention du symbolique. Sociologie et science des religions,* Paris: La Découverte.

Turner, V. (1969) *The Ritual Process. Structure and Anti-Structure*, Chicago: Aldine.

Vandenberghe, F. (2020) Demokratur in Brasilien. Versuch einer Lehre vom Systemzusammenbruch, *Leviathan. Berliner Zeitschrift für Sozialwissenschaft*, 48 (4).

Véran, J.-F. and Viot, M. (2020) On avait tout prévu sauf l'humanitaire: précarité et Covid-19 en Ile-de-France. Paris: Médecins Sans Frontières.

Part 3: **The Social and Alternatives**

Sylvia Walby
Social Theory and COVID: Including Social Democracy

How does thinking about COVID change social theory? In reflecting on the impact of COVID on society, what aspects of social theory are illuminated and what revisions are needed? How does COVID change social theory of science, crisis, and our categories of alternative social formations?

The UK government claimed to be 'following "the science"' during the COVID crisis. But 'the science' was deeply divided, with Independent Sage (a coalition of independent scientists) (Independent Sage 2020) challenging the official government Scientific Advisory Group for Emergencies (a committee of scientists engaged by government) (Sage 2020). The policies and forms of governance to address COVID varied at different moments of the crisis and between different countries. The sickness and death rate varied between countries and between social groups. At the time of writing, there is no cure or vaccine, so the key policies concern how to separate infected from not-infected people. What model of justice underlies the relationship between individual and society in the policies to stop spread of the infectious deadly virus? How is society and governance being restructured in the 'crisis'?

Delanty's (2020a) review of the response of social theory to the impact of COVID on society identifies six political philosophical positions on the coronavirus pandemic: utilitarian; Kantian; libertarian; biopolitical securitization; post-capitalism; and behaviouralism. These theorists address the relationship between the individual and society in the development of policy through the lens of justice. They invoke concepts concerning science, crisis and alternative forms of society.

Agamben (2020) is positioned by Delanty (2020a) as if he were pivotal to this debate, flanked by Žižek (2020) and interpretations of Foucault (1977). In Agamben's work, COVID is constructed as if it were a crisis manipulated to legitimate a state of emergency, a state of exception, in which the executive could seize control over the usual instruments of governance to discipline society in the search for a perceived security. Foucault (1977) is invoked to interpret measures of lock down, distancing and masks used to stop the spread of the virus as if they were forms of authoritarian surveillance and disciplining. Žižek offers alternative outcomes of the crisis as if only barbarism or communism is possible and sees deep challenges to capitalism. Delanty is right to reflect on issues of justice and the relationship between individual and society. But are the interventions to –

https://doi.org/10.1515/9783110713350-012

separate the infected from the not-infected really best characterised as authoritarian, and are the alternative forms out of the crisis actually restricted to barbarism and communism?

Into this debate, I insert the concept of 'social democracy', which is curiously absent, though Delanty notes the significance of democracy. Social democratic visions and practices underpin the theory and practice of 'public health' interventions into COVID as well as other health issues. Social democracy is the model of society that informs the public health project, in which 'if one is sick, we are all potentially sick' and in which the risks and costs associated with sickness are shared by the whole society, not only the individual who is sick. It is a social model which insists that justice and efficiency are linked together, rather than being opposed in a zero-sum trade off. Interventionist social democratic practices can be contrasted with neoliberal polices that pursue more minimal intervention to (mistakenly) reduce damage to the economy. Interpreting public health interventions as authoritarian rather than as social democratic is a mistake. Addressing the social theory relevant to COVID requires understanding the multiple facets of COVID in the relationship of science and governance, crisis and governance, and alternative social formations.

COVID has killed hundreds of thousands of people around the world and made millions sick, already by September 2020. Death rates vary with inequality. Death rates are higher among the poor and Black and minoritized ethnic groups (ONS 2020). The routes of transmission of COVID are shaped by inequalities: some forms of employment, some forms of caring generate forms of contact that are conducive to catching the virus. The response to COVID has generated further adverse effects on people as activities are curtailed. COVID is a virus which spreads through droplets carried in the air and the touching of contaminated surfaces. While health care alleviates some aspects of the ensuing illness, currently, the only preventative interventions are non-pharmaceutical and involve some form of separation of the infected from the non-infected. Achieving separation is central to reducing and eliminating the virus. Policies to achieve separation reduce social and economic activities. Achieving separation is challenging in a context in which not all carriers of the virus show symptoms and tests for the virus are difficult, so it involves engagement with those at risk of having the virus rather than those who are visibly sick. Reducing the rate of reproduction of the virus, represented as 'R', is central to reducing and eliminating COVID. The UK has one of the highest death rates from COVID in Europe and the world (John Hopkins University 2020). The death rates vary between social groups, in general higher among the poorer, and especially high in the sick, the old, black and minority ethnic people.

Delanty (2020a) offers an important, agenda setting, early review of different approaches to the relationship between individual and society that is central to theorising the COVID crisis. How are the interests of individuals and of the social whole actually and potentially being balanced in public policy towards COVID? In utilitarianism (Singer), the interests of the whole are greater than that of any individual (as in the examples of the 'herd immunity' approach, and of lockdown and isolation). In Kantian philosophy (illuminated by Habermas), the value of every individual human life is primary and utilitarian solutions are unwelcome. The libertarian approach condemns any encroachment on personal freedoms, even if there is an identified public interest. The use of biopolitical securitization, theorised by Foucault, in the context of the COVID crisis is condemned by Agamben as an unjust extension of state powers under the guise of an unwarranted claim to a state of emergency. Žižek offers a vision of postcapitalist futures that are polarised between barbarism and communism, suggesting that new forms of solidarity are emerging from the crisis. The approach of behavioural science (Sunstein and Thaler 2008) focuses on the individual, who can be nudged into compliance with government priorities. Intriguingly, Delanty picks up the theme of democracy in his conclusion, which is rather subdued in the political philosophy that he has been discussing.

As Delanty notes, different approaches to COVID by social scientists contain different visions of society and principles of social justice. Here, I widen the spectrum of approaches, to include the social democratic vision that contests the neoliberal orthodoxy. The social democratic vision is fundamental to the public health response that is currently actively contesting the individualistic, neoliberal understanding of society found in UK (and US) policy and is actively rejecting the false polarity between individuals and society as a zero-sum game. Making visible the social democratic vision allows for a better understanding of the arguments ongoing within science over COVID and their interpretation within social theory. Making social democracy visible in social theory allows for a better theorisation of the COVID crisis and its alternative outcomes. It allows for a better grasp of multiple intersecting inequalities within social theory, especially when combined with a complex systems approach to society. This social democratic perspective contests the neoliberal restructuring of society.

The article addresses key areas of social theory relevant to COVID – alternative forms of societal organisation; the nature of crisis and its relationship to governance and society. It offers revisions to social theory informed by the underestimated significance of social democratic projects, governance and social formations embedded in public health. It addresses the tension between the real and the socially constructed in the COVID crisis; the relevance of multiple intersecting inequalities, not only class; and advances in complexity science approach to systems for developing a theory of society.

Society: Including Social Democracy as a Societal Formation

COVID poses challenges in how social theory addresses the alternative forms of society. Since COVID generates a crisis, it potentially generates a time of rapid change. The identification of alternatives and the differences between them affects the understanding of actions taken during the COVID crisis. In order to understand these potential changes, it is necessary to specify the alternatives. A theory of society is needed (Delanty 1995; Dubet 2020; Walby 2020).

Several ways of thinking about differences in forms of society are found in the texts identified by Delanty as central to the COVID debate, but these do not include social democracy. The differences between Delanty's texts focus on freedom versus authoritarianism (Agamben 2020; Foucault 1977), and on barbarism versus communism (Žižek 2020).

There are alternative ways of making distinctions between forms of society, found, for example, in macro-sociological debates on varieties of capitalism and on varieties of gender regimes. A key distinction has been made between social democratic and neoliberal forms of society. This is not the same division as that between freedom versus authoritarianism.

In the context of COVID, both typologies are in play: freedom vs authoritarianism; and social democracy vs neoliberalism. At stake is the interpretation of state intervention, as democratic or authoritarian.

In the political philosophies identified by Delanty, the main focus is on the relationship between individual and society, with a special focus on justice. The main line of disagreement is between a libertarian focus on individual freedoms and a statist focus on authoritarian. Further currents of discussion in this literature include utilitarianism (discussed by Habermas) and 'nudge' behavioural science (Halpern), though these are not full alternative societal formations.

Agamben distinguishes between freedom and authoritarianism, drawing on Foucault's work on surveillance in times of plague. Following Foucault, state interventions against plagues that involve increased knowledge by state agencies on individuals are conceptualised as surveillance. This is then further interpreted as the loss of individual freedoms and an increase in authoritarianism.

Žižek distinguishes between barbarism and communism in his vision of alternative futures that might follow the COVID crisis. He suggests that current political developments engaging in progressive ways with COVID constitute a fundamental challenge to capitalism itself.

Other literature on variations in societal formations has focused on different lines of differentiation for comparison. A key line of difference is between neoliberalism and social democracy, which is found in the varieties of capitalism (Hall and Soskice 2001; Hanké, Rhodes and Thatcher 2007) and varieties of gender (Walby 2009, 2020) regime literature. Sometimes further categories are added, for example, conservative corporatist (Esping-Andersen 1990; Shire 2020). But the nuances in this body of literature do not deflect from the significance of identifying variations in forms of society that contrast major types of social organisation that differ in the depth of democracy and level of inequality.

There are debates as to how best to conceptualise conservative and authoritarian forms (Delanty 2020b). One approach considers authoritarianism to be a sub-set of neoliberalism (Bruff 2014), rather than a separate category. However, it is more appropriate to consider authoritarianism and securitisation as a logical extension of the intensification of the neoliberal form (Walby 2018; Wacquant 2009). The definition and conceptualisation of neoliberalism is the issue here, with debate as to the extent to which the term is focused on liberalism and free markets or has developed to include the utilisation of the power of the state to restructure markets and capital/labour relations (Gane 2014). When neoliberalism is understood to routinely include authoritarian state forms, there is no need to distinguish between neoliberal and authoritarian society forms (Walby 2009, 2018).

Whatever the boundaries to the concept of neoliberalism, its 'other' is social democracy.

Social democracy is a project, form of governance and a societal formation. It has a distinctive logic, intellectual heritage, and set of institutional locations and practices. It can be identified in the economy, polity, civil society and violence. It is a more democratic and less unequal form of capitalism and gender regime than neoliberalism. At its core is the notion that justice and efficiency go together and are not in opposition in a zero-sum game; that sharing the risks of modern life (Beck 1992, 2009) among all people rather than allowing them to be borne by the individuals immediately affected is both just and productive.

Social democracy emerged as a theory of society during the twentieth century in the context of the development of suffrage and the use of democratic power to tame capitalism (Berman 2006). It is associated with the development of the welfare state (Beveridge 1944; Titmuss 1958; Crossland 1956), citizenship (Marshall 1950), the regulation of economy including of capital (Keynes 1936; Minsky 2008 [1986]), education (Klasen 2002), the social investment state (Morel, Palier and Palme 2012). It has synergy with Kantian (1795) approaches to peace through peaceful means rather than the deterrence of larger violence at both inter-state and inter-personal levels (Galtung 1966; Haas 1958).

There are controversies as to the proper location of the boundary between social democracy and neoliberalism, not least concerning the place of the market in discussions of the Third Way (Giddens 1998). There are debates as to how democracy engages with plural multi-culturalism and the rights-based approaches to justice (Habermas 1996 [1992]) and, in the context of COVID, whether there are limits to rights to life and to dignity (Habermas and Günther 2020). The application of social democratic principles that were originally centred on class and nation to multiple intersecting inequalities including gender, ethnicity and nation is ongoing rather than settled (Walby 2011).

Social democracy is also a set of practices that are varyingly embedded in institutions and societies. After the big mid-twentieth century crisis of financial crash, economic depression, rise of fascism, holocaust and war, social democracy emerged as a powerful governmental project contrasted not only with neoliberalism but also with fascism and communism. Its institutional development is linked to the institutionalisation of democracy and projects led by the labour and trades union movement, feminism, and internationalist anti-colonialism. It was core to a new set of political parties, some of which gained access to state power.

The social democratic project won sufficient governmental power to shape society in Nordics in 1930s, in Western Europe after 1945, and the EU. Within the UK, which is overall more neoliberal than many other countries in western Europe, it is lodged in specific institutions, especially health, including public health, education, and other institutions of the welfare state. It is embedded in international institutions including the UN, EU and the practice of multilateralism (Walby 2009).

The importance of social democracy as an alternative form of societal organisation in the COVID crisis takes an acute form in the disputed significance of 'public health' as a practice, institution, and vision of societal formation.

Public health interventions aim to eliminate COVID by stopping transmission of the virus by the practices of test, trace, isolate, and support. This requires state intervention at a significant scale, with public expenditure on a network of institutions embedded at local, national and international levels. Public health combines philosophy, science, governance and a theory of society. Its philosophy can be summarised as 'if one is sick, all are potentially sick'; so, the risks and costs of COVID and its elimination are to be shared through society. As a theory of society and justice, it understands the simultaneity of justice and efficiency, since if the infected are only supported in acute care, but not materially when asked to isolate, all are at risk of being infected. It is a form of intervention that depends on democratic governance for its legitimation and practice. It is based on enlightenment understandings of rationality and science, broadly conceived, to include data, multiple disciplines, and a precautionary preventative approach to disaster with planning, not just acute care in hospitals for those who are most sick. It is a theory of society that understands the significance of social connections for both transmission and for support for those isolating for the good of the rest of us; and which embeds the technical and biological into the approach to the social (Independent Sage 2020; Women's Budget Group 2020).

The theorists considered by Delanty don't get public health. They do not recognise this social democratic, science-based approach, and miss this critical alternative societal formation and understanding of justice. Social democratic public health goes beyond individual versus society, freedom versus authoritarianism; it is a democratic and scientific collective mobilisation of state capacity. There is enormous variation between countries in the extent to which government responses to COVID have mobilised either neoliberal or social democratic strategies. Higher death rates are found in countries that have had strategies informed by neoliberalism rather than social democracy (John Hopkins University 2020).

COVID has generated a society-wide crisis, which is potentially a moment of rapid change to an alternative form of society. The COVID crisis has different effects on societies that partly depend upon the pre-existing structure of society. Identifying the alternative forms of society at stake is necessary to understand the significance of practices and events.

In the UK, there is both a government-led attempt to restructure provision using neoliberal practices – state awarded contracts to large private corporations rather than funding existing local public health institutions. And there is a vigorously articulated alternative, which can be seen to coalesce around the concept of public health: among scientists in independent sage, among local political leaders such as the northern mayors, and in grass-roots mobilisations at neighbourhood level.

At the international level, the WHO (2020) embeds a social democratic response, and is under attack from the US, which has withdrawn funding. Understanding the nature of these contestations matters.

Social theory is potentially important in identifying the big strategic alternatives in collective responses to COVID. This needs to include the social democratic, which in COVID is articulated through public health practices and institutions. The loss of individual freedoms in reducing the social contacts that drive the reproduction and spread of COVID is not best understood in a binary of libertarian/authoritarian axis. The contestations in the COVID crisis are better understood as part of a neoliberal/social democratic contestation.

Crisis

COVID has generated a crisis. How is 'crisis' best understood in social theory? What does reflection on this concept and its inclusion in a theory of society offer social theory (Beck 1992, 2009; Gilbert 1998; Schumpeter 1954; Walby 2015)? Is it real or constructed (Buzen et al 1998; Hay 1996; Mirowski 2013)? Does crisis allow a political executive to legitimate use of emergency powers (Klein 2007)? Is the crisis a critical turning point (Gramsci 1971, Habermas 1975), or a catastrophe (Diamond 2005), or is it stabilised and absorbed (Engelen et al 2011; Minsky 2008), or will it cascade through further social systems (Haas 1958; Perrow 1999; Walby 2015)? Is there more than one crisis (Delanty 2020b)? If it is a critical turning point, between what and what is the change (Esping-Andersen 1990; Žižek 2020)? Is the social democratic alternative made sufficiently visible in current debates? How does interrogating the COVID crisis take forward these debates on the place of the concept of 'crisis' in social theory? How does improving the concept of crisis and its place in social theory allow better understanding of the COVID crisis?

In discussing COVID in relation to crisis, Delanty (2020a) draws attention to the work of Žižek (2020) and Agamben (2020), which addresses these issues. Since Agamben's (2020) text on the process of the COVID crisis circulated widely (Diken, and Laustsen 2020), structured ensuing debate (Delanty 2021), and is based on a pre-existing body of work on crisis (Agamben 2005), this is point of departure here.

Žižek (2020) argues that the crisis is real, is generating social struggle, and is a potential turning point between barbarism and communism. Hence, he disputes the notion that the crisis is only a social construction, means authoritarian governance by the political executive, and is a turning point between freedom and authoritarianism. He understands that the crisis may have a long way to go. However, he does not discuss social democracy as an active project in the crisis nor discuss its potential to constitute an alternative form of society.

Agamben (2020) argues that the crisis is socially constructed rather than real, is manipulated to give greater power to the executive branch of government, thereby generates a more authoritarian form of governance, and constitutes a critical turning point. Each of these claims is contested. The crisis is real rather than confected. The executive branch has not (by September 2020) gained many excessive new powers. The contestations over the form of governance is not between freedom and authoritarianism but between neoliberalism and social democracy. The crisis is still cascading through society and it is too soon (in September 2020) to announce that there has been a critical turning point.

Agamben (2020), on 26 February 2020, described the response to COVID as 'disproportionate', 'frenetic, irrational and entirely unfounded emergency measures adopted against an alleged epidemic of coronavirus' and suggested that the media was 'provoking an authentic state of exception with serious limitations on movement and a suspension of daily life in entire regions'. He considers this to be 'the tendency to use a state of exception as a normal paradigm for government'. He considers the epidemic a 'pretext' and that 'It is almost as if with terrorism exhausted as a cause for exceptional measures, the invention of an epidemic offered the ideal pretext for scaling them up beyond any limitation.' While this account by Agamben might be considered an unfortunate early wrong call based on insufficient evidence of the infectiousness and deadliness of COVID, it is nevertheless an exemplar of this approach, and has been used as a point of reference by many others. But, even by 17 March 2020, when the scale of the deaths had become clear, Agamben remains consistent to his earlier position: 'A society that lives in a permanent state of emergency cannot be a free one. We effectively live in a society that has sacrificed freedom to so-called "security reasons" and as a consequence has condemned itself to living in a permanent state of fear and insecurity.' In these texts, Agamben has effectively positioned himself as a libertarian opposed to state actions, even when state actions save lives.

There are several points of contention in these texts by Agamben that offer sites of discussion of important issue for social theory of crisis.

Is a crisis, such as COVID, understood as a social construct, or as real? Or indeed is it both simultaneously? Agamben sets up a dichotomy between the crisis as a social constructed and as real. He argues that the crisis is a 'pretext'; that measures taken by the state are 'irrational' and that the basis for them is 'entirely unfounded'. This draws on earlier work (Agamben 2005) in which he theorised crisis as a claim by the executive branch of government (President, Premier, Prime Minister, cabinet) for enhanced powers because there was a state of emergency that justified a state of exception from the usual political processes in which there were multiple checks and balances (legislature, parliament, courts) to the exercise of power. This approach finds resonance in the new security studies (Buzen et al 1998), which analyses the extension of the powers of the state legitimated by the claim to existential threat to national security. It has parallels in analysis of crisis using the concept of 'narrative' (Ricoeur 1984), as something that can be manipulated by political authorities (Hay 1996).

Agamben is wrong to suggest that there is not a real crisis. Hundreds of thousands of people have died from COVID and millions more have been sick. The modern era is not devoid of crises generated by the intersection of society and environment (Diamond 2005), indeed aspects of modernity may exacerbate these tendencies (Beck 1992, 2009). Plagues have long generated crises for humanity (McNeil). The structure of the environment in which the crisis occurs can affect the outcome of the crisis (Gilbert 1998).

A crisis can be both real and socially constructed. A real crisis can have disputed origins and remedies. The contestation of the narrative of the crisis can have significant implications (Gramsci 1971; Klein 2007, 2020; Mirowski 2013). The existence of a struggle over the meaning and implications of a crisis does not need to entail a claim that the crisis is not also real (Diken and Laustsen 2020; Engelen et al (2011).

Agamben is right to suggest that governments referred to COVID to generate a state of emergency. It is the case that governments attempted to control the narrative of the crisis in order to legitimate policies that they wished to pursue. This is not incompatible with the crisis being real. The COVID crisis was both. The dichotomy between socially created and real is mistaken.

Does the declaration of crisis as a state of emergency result in the political executive exercising excessive power? The crisis offers an opportunity for the executive to legitimate a claim for more power on the grounds that in such exceptional circumstances these powers are needed to counter an existential threat (Agamben 2005, 2020; Buzen et al 1998). But are these powers 'excessive'? The libertarian critique leaves little space for reasonable use of increased state powers on behalf of social democratic project.

Agamben is right to argue that governments declared a 'state of emergency' or a state of exception, which enabled greater legitimacy for powers taken by the executive branch of government. But the way these powers exercised saved lives. The social democratic public health project used its power and influence to save lives and improve health outcomes. Without lock-down, many more people would have died. The powers were not unlimited in extent or duration – lock downs were temporary. There has been significant contestation over the powers used by government. There is still space for a wider politics (Diken, and Laustsen 2020). Agamben assumes that increasing the powers of the state means increasing authoritarianism. He sets up a dichotomy between 'freedom' and state actions. This can be characterised as a left libertarian position. However, this dichotomy is mistaken. State actions can be consistent with freedom and justice. A better distinction is between neoliberal and social democratic forms of governance. Social democratic public health should be included, not excluded, in these debates on the mobilisation of the power of the state.

The crisis is a state of emergency; powers were taken; but they were not, generally, excessive, even though they were not performed competently. The theorisation of these practices requires the mobilisation of the concept of social democracy in order to conceptualise public health interventions, rather than to reduce this to a contrast between libertarianism and authoritarianism. The 'other' to the mobilisation of local public health social democratic interventions has been the outsourcing of testing to global corporations under a neoliberal model of governance.

Is the crisis a critical turning point, a catastrophe, or absorbed or cascading? A crisis can have one of several different relationships to society (Walby 2015). It may be a temporary aberration followed by a return to normal; a disaster or catastrophe; a single critical turning point to a new form of societal formation; or the crisis may cascade from one societal domain to another and another.

In Agamben's account, the state of emergency is treated as if it were a critical turning point towards authoritarianism. For Žižek, the crisis will lead to barbarism or communism. The changes in the form of governance are highly contested and not yet re-stabilised.

The crisis may be absorbed, and the society return to equilibrium, as is the case for small economic crises, such as bubbles (Keynes 1936), though re-stabilisation may require significant state action (Minsky 2008 [1986]), or massive societal reorganisation (Polanyi 1957). The crisis may be a disaster or catastrophe in which many people die and from which recuperation is not possible (Chase-Dunn and Hall 1997; Diamond 2006). A crisis may be a moment in which major structures change, in which the old is destroyed and new institutions emerge (Schumpeter 1954). Crisis may be understood as a positive component of social and political restructuring (Haas 1958) or negative (Klein 2007, 2020). These structural changes maybe systemic (Gramsci 1971). Further, a crisis in one social system may or may not cascade into another social system, depending on how closely coupled they are (Perrow 1999, 2011; Haldane and May 2011). The crisis may cascade through multiple societal domains leading to a major change in the societal formation (Walby 2015). The temporality of crisis needs to be taken into account before judgements are made as to whether it is a critical turning point. This analysis of crisis requires a theory of society; of how changes in one institutional domain may change others; of how societal domains are interconnected.

If the crisis is a critical turning point, between what alternative societal formations is it turning? For Agamben, the alternatives appear to be freedom or authoritarian. For Žižek, barbarism or communism. A different set of alternative societal formations is that of neoliberal or social democratic. The neglect of the social democratic societal alternative is a mistake. Social democracy should be included, in general, and also specifically for the COVID crisis because of the importance of the public health project which is informed by social democratic principles.

There a crisis; but its interpretation is not settled. This matters for understanding the COVID crisis; and the discussion matters for social theory. Interrogating the COVID crisis can help take forward debates on the place of the concept of 'crisis' in social theory. Developing the concept of crisis and its place in social theory allows for better understanding of the specificity of the COVID crisis.

The COVID crisis is both real and its contours are socially interpreted. Both aspects of the crisis coexist and both aspects matter. Over-stating one or the other is counterproductive for analysis. Agamben under-estimated the real aspects of the crisis in which people were and are dying. Being socially constructed does not negate the possibilities of a crisis being real at the same time.

In the COVID crisis, increased power has been taken by the executive, which was legitimated by the state of emergency. These increased powers were both justified and contested. The extent of parliamentary scrutiny and the mobilisation of criminal sanctions rather than welfare support shows how important is the depth of democracy in considering the implications of these powers. Agamben is right to draw attention to the way that a state of emergency is treated as a state of exception in which exceptional powers are taken by the executive branch of government. While right to ask the question as to whether these powers were justified; he is wrong to suggest that increased powers were not justified.

In the COVID crisis, Agamben made contrasts between freedom and authoritarianism as the main societal alternatives; while Žižek contrasted barbarism and communism. Both these sets of alternatives are mistaken. Raising the question as to the alternative forms of society that might be the outcome of the crisis was correct, but the alternatives presented were not. Social democracy needs to be added back into the theoretical vocabulary when thinking of societal alternatives.

The COVID crisis is a potential critical turning point. But it is not over yet. It may be the case that there is a recuperation back to pre-COIVD forms of society; the social democratic moment of Keynesian support for the economy may end. It may become a catastrophe in which millions more die. It may be a turning point to intensified neoliberalism with outsourcing of previously state-run health institutions; it may be a turning point to social democracy as grassroots initiatives coalesce with reinvigorated party politics. It is more likely, but not certain, that it is not a single critical turning point, but the start of a prolonged series of linked crises, which cascade through economic recession, intensified cleavages in civil society, political and constitutional crisis, to violence. Theorising these forms of change requires complex systems analysis, which can address the non-linear forms of change involved (Walby 2007, 2015).

Conclusion

Social democracy should be included in the discussions of the COVID crisis in contrast to neoliberalism. Social democracy is a project, form of governance and societal formation, in which if one is sick we are all potentially sick, a risk to one is a risk to all, so solidaristic provision of welfare to support the infected and possibly infected, is both efficient and just simultaneously. It contrasts with neoliberalism that permits the poor, the old, and the minoritized to bear the brunt of the crisis. In science, social democracy is represented in public health institutions and practices, in comparison with 'herd immunity'. In the crisis, social democracy is relevant to the Keynesian style economic intervention to prevent the cascade of the crisis, in comparison with the neoliberal outsourcing of health and social care services.

COVID illuminates debates on the relationship between individuals and society and the alternative forms that society can take. Delanty offers an agenda setting review of the zero-sum approaches of political philosophers from utilitarian, Kantian, and libertarian perspectives on justice. Agamben offers a contrast of freedom and authoritarianism. Žižek offers a choice between barbarism and communism as future forms of society. But the range of societal alternatives should go beyond Agamben and Žižek to include social democracy and its 'other', neoliberalism. The assumption that state intervention is intrinsically regressive is challenged by public health initiatives in which risks are shared and the sick and the potentially sick are cared for. The significance of the social democratic alternative vision, powerfully articulated through public health, has been underestimated in social theory.

COVID illuminates the nature of crisis for social theory. COVID generated not only a health emergency, but an economic recession, and a contested restructuring of the political economy of health; with an ongoing cascade of the crisis through societal domains. Although Agamben is right to understand that the COVID crisis is used to legitimate an extension of state powers, he is mistaken to ignore the real aspects of the crisis in death and sickness. There is no need to create mutually exclusive alternatives of the socially constructed and the real in a crisis; both coexist simultaneously. The setting up of freedom and authoritarianism as the main axis of difference is not appropriate. It is important to contrast the neoliberal and social democratic mobilisation of state power. The crisis is a potential critical turning point between these societal forms, though it is still cascading. Complex systems thinking aids the theorisation of these non-linear forms of social change.

This discussion builds on the debates in political philosophy about COVID and society identified by Delanty, concerning the relationship between individuals and society and the conceptions of justice embedded in these, which contrasted libertarian and authoritarian approaches. This chapter identifies the contestation between social democracy and neoliberalism as a further axis of debate relevant to COVID. Social democracy offers a different way of thinking of the relationship of individual and society; not a zero-sum concept of justice; any one sick we are all potentially sick. Social democracy is missing as a project, form of governance and type of social formation. It is missing in the accounts of science, where contesting approaches are not simply reducible to power. It is missing in the accounts of the variety of forms of governance that contest COVID and its impact on individuals and on society. It is missing in the theorisation of the relationship between individual and society, as a form of political philosophy that does not position the good of the individual and the good of the whole as a zero sum game but rather understands the good of everyone for the good of the whole. The debate between libertarian and authoritarian positions is not the only one of relevance. The contestation between social democratic and neoliberal forms of society and governance in the COVID crisis is also central to debates in social theory.

Acknowledgement: This paper is a shortened and revised version of Walby's 'The Covid pandemic and social theory' published in *European Journal of Social Theory*, November 2020, https://doi.org/10.1177/1368431020970127.

References

Abbott, A. (2001) *The Chaos of Disciplines.*, Chicago: Chicago University Press.

Agamben, G. (2005) *State of Exception*, Chicago: Chicago University Press.

Agamben, G. (2020) The invention of an epidemic https://www.journal-psychoanalysis.eu/co ronavirus-and-philosophers/ (original published in Italian on *Quodlibet,* https://www. quodlibet.it/giorgio-agamben-l-invenzione-di-un-epidemia).

Aradau, C. and Blanke, T. (2016) Politics of Prediction: Security and the Time/space of Governmentality in the Age of Big Data, *European Journal of Social Theory*, 20 (3): 373–391.

Beck, U. (1992) *Risk Society: Towards a New Modernity.* London: Sage.

Beck, U. (2009) *World at Risk*, Cambridge: Polity.

Bellanova, R. (2017) Digital, Politics, and Algorithms: Governing Digital Data Through the Lens of Data Protection, *European Journal of Social Theory*, 20 (3): 329–347.

Berman, S. (2006) *The Primacy of Politics: Social Democracy and the Making of Europe's Twentieth Century*, Cambridge: Cambridge University Press.

Beveridge, W. H. (1944) *Full Employment in a Free Society*, London: Routledge.

Bevir, M. (2010) Rethinking governmentality: Towards Genealogies of Governance, *European Journal of Social Theory*, 13 (4): 423–441.

Bertalanffy, L. von (1968) *General Systems Theory*, New York: George Braziller.

Bruff, I. (2014) The Rise of Authoritarian Neoliberalism, *Rethinking Marxism*, 26 (1): 113–29.

Buzan, B, Wæver, O., and de Wilde , J. (1998) *Security: A New Framework for Analysis*, Boulder: Lynne Rienner.

Cabinet Office (2020) *Our plan to rebuild: The UK Government's COVID-19 recovery strategy* Command Paper number CP 239. https://www.gov.uk/government/publications/our-plan-to-rebuild-the-uk-governments-covid-19-recovery-strategy/our-plan-to-rebuild-the-uk-governments-covid-19-recovery-strategy

Castellani, B. and Hafferty, F. (2009) *Sociology and Complexity Science: A New Field of Enquiry*, Berlin: Springer.

Chase-Dunn, C. and Thomas Hall, T. (1997) *Rise and Demise: Comparing World-Systems*, Boulder: Westview.

Crosland, A. (1956) *The Future of Socialism*, London: Constable.

Delamater P.L., Street E.J., Leslie T.F., Yang Y.T., Jacobsen K.H. (2019) Complexity of the Basic Reproduction Number (R0). *Emerging Infectious Diseases*, 25(1): 1. https://www.ncbi.nlm.nih.gov/pmc/articles/PMC6302597/

Delanty, G. (2020a) *Six political philosophies in search of a virus: Critical perspectives on the coronavirus pandemic.* http://www.lse.ac.uk/european-institute/Assets/Documents/LEQS-Discussion-Papers/LEQSPaper156.pdf

Delanty, G. (2020b) *Critical Theory and Social Transformation: Crises of the Present and Future Possibilities.* London: Routledge.

Delanty, G. (2021) 'Introduction: The pandemic in historical and global context', in Gerard Delanty (ed.) *Pandemic, Society and Politics*. London: Routledge.

Delanty, G. and Rumford, C. (1995) *Rethinking Europe: Social Theory and the Implications of Europeanization*, London: Routledge.

Diamond, J. (2005) *Collapse: How Societies Choose or Fail to Survive*, London: Penguin.

Diken, B. and Laustsen, C. B. (2020) Contingency and Necessity in the Corona Crisis'. Unpublished manuscript.

Dubet, F. (2020) The Return of Society, *European Journal of Social Theory*, https://doi.org/10.1177/1368431020950541

Engelen, E., Ertürk, I., Froud, Sukdev J., Leaver, J. A., Moran, M., Nilsson, A., and Williams, K. (2011) *After the Great Complacence*, Oxford: Oxford University Press.

Esping-Andersen, G. (1990) *The Three Worlds of Welfare Capitalism*, Cambridge: Polity.

Foucault, M. (1977) *Discipline and Punish: The Birth of the Prison*, London: Penguin Books.

Foucault, M., Agamben, G., Nancy, J.L., Esposito, R., Benvenuto, S., Dwivedi, D., Mohan, S., Ronchi, R., de Carolis, M. (2020) Coronavirus and Philosophers, *European Journal of Psychoanalysis* https://www.journal-psychoanalysis.eu/coronavirus-and-philosophers/ (in collaboration with *Antinomie* https://antinomie.it/)

Galtung, J. (1966) *Peace by Peaceful Means: Peace and Conflict, Development and Civilization*, London: Sage.

Gane, N. (2014) Sociology and Neoliberalism: A Missing History, *Sociology*, 48 (6): 1092–106.

Giddens, A. (1998) *The Third Way: The Renewal of Social Democracy*, Cambridge: Polity.

Gilbert, C. (1998) Studying Disaster: Changes in the Main Conceptual Tools. In: Quarantelli, E. L. (ed.) *What is a Disaster?* pp. 3–12. London: Routledge.

Gottfried, H. (2013) *Gender, Work and Economy: Unpacking the Global Economy*, Cambridge: Polity.

Gramsci, A. (1971) *Selections from the Prison Notebooks of Antonio Gramsci*, London: Lawrence and Wishart.

Haas, E. (1958) *The Uniting of Europe: Political, Social, and Economic Forces, 1950–1957*, Stanford: Stanford University Press.

Habermas, J. (1975) *Legitimation Crisis*. Boston: Beacon Press.

Habermas, J. (1996) [1992] *Between Facts and Norms: Contributions to a Discourse Theory of Law and Democracy*, Cambridge: Polity.

Habermas, J. and Günther, K. (2020) What Concerns Me is How Even Lawyers are Now Relativizing the Right to Life"; "No Constitutional Right is Boundless. They can Collide with Each Other, DOI: 10.13140/RG.2.2.22496.10246/1

Haldane, A. and May, R. (2011) Systemic Risk in Banking Ecosystems', *Nature*, 20 January, 469: 351–5.

Hall, P. and Soskice, D. (eds) (2001) *Varieties of Capitalism: The Institutional Foundations of Comparative Advantage*, Oxford: Oxford University Press.

Hanké, B., Rhodes, M. and Thatcher, M. (eds) (2007) *Beyond Varieties of Capitalism: Conflict, Contradictions, and Complementarities in the European Economy*, Oxford: Oxford University Press.

Hay, C. (1996) Narrating Crisis: The Discursive Construction of the 'Winter of Discontent', *Sociology*, 30 (2): 253–77.

Hornborg, A. (2017) Artifacts have Consequences, Not Agency: Toward a Critical Theory of Global Environmental History, *European Journal of Social Theory*, 20 (1): 95–110.

Independent Sage 12 May 2020 *The Independent Sage Report* http://www.independentsage.org/wp-content/uploads/2020/05/The-Independent-SAGE-Report.pdf

John Hopkins University (2020) *Coronavirus Resource Centre*. https://coronavirus.jhu.edu/map.html

Kant, I. (1795) *Perpetual Peace*, San Diego: The Book Tree.

Kauffman, S. (1993) *The Origins of Order: Self-Organization and Selection in Evolution*, Oxford: Oxford University Press.

Keynes, J. M. (1936) *The General Theory of Employment, Interest and Money*, London: Macmillan.

Klasen, S. (2002) Low Schooling for Girls, Slower Growth for all? Cross-country Evidence on the Effect of Gender Inequality in Education on Economic Development', *World Bank Economic Review*, 16(3): 345–73.

Klein, N. (2007) *The Shock Doctrine: The Rise of Disaster Capitalism*, London: Allen Lane.

Klein, N. (2020) Screen New Deal, *The Intercept* https://theintercept.com/2020/05/08/andrew-cuomo-eric-schmidt-coronavirus-tech-shock-doctrine/

Lury, C. (2020) *Problem Spaces: Why and How Methodology Matters*, Cambridge: Polity.

Marshall, T. H. (1950) *Citizenship and Social Class and Other Essays*, Cambridge: Cambridge University Press.

McNeill, W. H. 1998 [1976]. *Plagues and Peoples*, New York: Anchor Books.

Minsky, H. (2008) [1986] *Stabilizing an Unstable Economy*, 2nd edn. New York: McGraw-Hill.

Mirowski, P. (2013) *Never Let a Serious Crisis Go to Waste: How Neoliberalism Survived the Financial Meltdown*, London: Verso.

Morel, N., Palier, B. and Palme, J. (eds) (2012) *Towards a Social Investment State: Ideas, Policies and Challenges*, Bristol: Policy Press.

Penna, S. and O'Brien, M. (2006) What Price Social and Health Care? Commodities, Competition and Consumers, *Social Work and Society*, 4 (2): 217–31.

Perrow, C. (1999) [1984] *Normal Accidents: Living with High-Risk Technologies*, Princeton: Princeton University Press.

Perrow, C. (2011) [2007] *The Next Catastrophe: Reducing Our Vulnerabilities to Natural, Industrial and Terrorist Disasters*, Princeton: Princeton University Press.

Polanyi, K. (1957) *The Great Transformation: The Political and Economic Origins of Our Time*, Boston: Beacon Press.

Ricoeur, P. (1984) *Time and Narrative*. Chicago: University of Chicago Press.

Rose, N. (2001) The Politics of Life Itself, *Theory, Culture and Society*, 18 (6): 1–30.

Scientific Advisory Group for Emergencies (SAGE): Coronavirus (COVID-19) response https://www.gov.uk/government/groups/scientific-advisory-group-for-emergencies-sage-coronavirus-covid-19-response

Schumpeter, J. (1954) *A History of Economic Analysis*, New York: Allen and Unwin.

Shire, K. and Nemoto, K. (2020) The Origins and Transformations of Conservative Gender Regimes in Germany and Japan, *Social Politics*, 27 (3): 432–448

Sunstein, C. and Thaler, R. (2008) *Nudge: Improving Decisions about Health, Wealth and Happiness*, London: Penguin.

Titmuss, R. (1958) [2018] *Essays on the Welfare State*, University of Bristol: Policy Press.

Wacquant, L. (2009) *Punishing the Poor: The Neoliberal Government of Social Insecurity*, Durham: Duke University Press.

Walby, S. (2007) Complexity Theory, Systems Theory and Multiple Intersecting Social Inequalities, *Philosophy of the Social Sciences*, 37 (4): 449–70.

Walby, S. (2009) *Globalization and Inequalities: Complexity and Contested Modernities*, London: Sage.

Walby, S. (2011) *The Future of Feminism*, Cambridge: Polity Press.

Walby, S. (2015) *Crisis*, Cambridge: Polity Press.

Walby, Sylvia (2018) 'Is Europe cascading into fascism? What concepts are needed to address this question?', *Politics and Governance,* 6(3): 67–77.

Walby, Sylvia (2020a) 'Varieties of gender regimes' *Social Politics*, 27(3): 414–431. https://doi.org/10.1093/sp/jxaa018

Walby, Sylvia. (2020b) 'Society and social systems' *Current Sociology*, https://doi.org/10.1177/0011392120932940

Walby, Sylvia, Jo Armstrong and Sofia Strid (2012) 'Intersectionality: Multiple inequalities in social theory', *Sociology*, 46(2): 224–40.

Wenham C, Smith J, Morgan R. (2020) 'COVID-19: the gendered impacts of the outbreak', *The Lancet.* Mar 14;395(10227):846–8. https://www.thelancet.com/journals/lancet/article/PIIS0140-6736(20)30526-2/fulltext?te=1&nl=in-her%20words&emc=edit_gn_20200317

Women's Budget Group (2020) *Covid-19: Gender and other Equality Issues* https://wbg.org.uk/wp-content/uploads/2020/03/FINAL-Covid-19-briefing.pdf

WHO 19 March 2020 *How COVID-19 spreads*
file:///C:/Users/Sylvia/AppData/Local/Microsoft/Windows/INetCache/IE/DN1 A1Z1K/advic-e-for-workplace-clean-19‑03‑2020.pdf

WHO 31 March 2020 *Coronavirus disease (COVID-19) advice for the public.* https://www.who.int/emergencies/diseases/novel-coronavirus-2019/advice-for-public.

Žižek, Slavoj (2020) *Pandemic! Covid-19 Shakes the World.* London: OR Books.

Donatella della Porta
Progressive Social Movements, Democracy and the Pandemic

The Covid-19 pandemic is a critical juncture that deeply affects progressive social movements. While at its onset lockdown policies have constrained collective action in the street, contentious politics spread very quickly with mobilizations in various forms addressing the many and dramatic crises that accompanied the health crises. Protests multiplied on issues such as housing, income, education, but also on participation and repression.

While a pandemic is a rare event, research on social movements has occasionally addressed moments of emergency including, besides other health crises, (more or less) natural disasters, deep economic crises and wars. This stream of research signalled that emergencies present particular challenges – and also opportunities – for contentious politics, their development being linked in part to the nature of the emergency itself and also in part to the political and social context, as well as to the relational dynamics of these intense times.

As these studies indicate, progressive social movements have to face challenges such as the drastic increase in the material needs of a growing part of the population, the scapegoating of marginal groups, and also repression. The centralization of power in the executive branch, increasing censorship, often the deployment of the military, all reduce the space for opposition. Faced with these increasing pressures, social movement organizations are forced to disband or to focus only on their immediate survival with little time for long-term strategizing.

On the other hand, however, there are also new opportunities for protest as emergencies tend to enhance conflicts over scarce and desperately needed resources that often find collective expressions. Faced with the disruption of everyday life, self-organization can bring about self-empowerment. As old social movement organizations encounter new ones that are formed to address the emergency, the shared risks fuel solidarity. Just as sacrifices are demanded, claims for citizens' rights are triggered. The perception of the failure of previous struggles paves the way to the search for alternatives and innovation. The specific balance of challenges and opportunities for progressive social movements during the Covid-19 crisis is the central concern of this chapter. While the development and eventual outcomes of these mobilizations will have to be analysed in depth, some common trends are already visible. First and foremost, progressive movements have pointed to the need to develop social rights. The pandemic has

https://doi.org/10.1515/9783110713350-013

made the effects of social inequalities – including gender, generational and ethnic inequalities – all the more visible and all the more outrageous. Progressive social movements always tend to denounce the lack of accountability and transparency of those in power, sometimes even fighting repression more generally, but as a result of the pandemic they have also begun to focus on the importance of social rights and the lethal effects of social inequalities in a time of pandemic. While radical libertarians and other right wing fringes have criticized constraints on individual freedoms, progressive social movements have privileged calls for new public health and welfare policies, combined with appeals to collective participation.

In what follows, I will first conceptualize the time of pandemic as a specific form of critical juncture, rooted in extraordinary circumstances, that brings about severe challenges to democracy, and I shall consider some expectations about the dynamics of progressive social movements in intense times. Second, on the basis of evidence from documents and reports about protests between March and August 2020, I will analyse the democratic role of progressive social movements as it has played out during the Covid-19 crisis and I will look at their mobilization on social rights and civil liberties, and also at the challenges that are still to be addressed.

Time of Pandemic as an Emergency Juncture

Progressive social movements have been a driving force in the struggle for citizens' rights that are the basis of democracy. In classical sociology theory, democracy is linked to the extension of citizenship rights, which are typically broken down into civil, political, and social rights. In Marshal's influential account (1992), civic rights were the first to be achieved, followed by political rights and, with them, the possibility of creating pressure for social rights as well. However, more recent theorization has considered other possible timings in their development, both for specific social groups and for particular countries. In this sense, they are not necessarily moving in the same direction – in fact, an increase in political rights can accompany a decline in social rights. What is more, the expansion of rights is neither a consolidated trend, not does it proceed at the same pace for different social, gender, generational and ethnic groups (della Porta 2017). In fact, crises such as a severe pandemic can challenge those rights as well as pushing some of them forward in the debate and eventual policy.

Citizens' rights have been key democratic developments, with progressive social movements mobilizing to extend them (della Porta 2013). While democratic states show different achievements on these sets of rights, they are all relevant for democracy at both procedural and substantial levels. As Leonardo Morlino (2012: 197–98) suggests, procedurally, the quality of democracy implies the rule of law, including:

- "Individual security and civil order;
- Independent judiciary and a modern justice system…;
- Institutional and administrative capacity to formulate, implement and enforce the law…;
- Effective fight against corruption, illegality and abuse of power by state agencies…;
- Security forces that are respectful of citizen rights and are under civilian control".

To these procedural dimensions, two substantive ones have to be added:
- freedom (as expressed in political and civil rights)
- and equality (as expressed especially in social rights).

In particular, political rights encompass the right to vote, to compete for electoral support, and to be elected to public office (ibid: 204). Civil rights encompass: "personal liberty, the right to legal defense, the right to privacy, the freedom to choose one's place of residence, freedom of movement and residence, the right to expatriate or emigrate, freedom and secrecy of correspondence, freedom of thought and expression, the right to an education, the right to information and a free press, and the freedoms of assembly, association and organization, including political organizations unrelated to trade unions" (ibid: 206). Finally, social rights include "rights associated with employment and connected with how the work is carried out, the right to fair pay and time off, and the right to collective bargaining … the right to health or to mental and physical well-being; the right to assistance and social security; the right to work; the right to human dignity; the right to strike; the right to study; the right to healthy surroundings, and, more generally, to the environment and to the protection of the environment; and the right to housing" (ibid: 206).

Interactions between these democratic qualities and emergencies are very important because the latter affect the former and, at the same time, these interactions make the achievements and limitations of rights all the more visible. There is also a trade-off between rights. As Baldwin (2005: 247) noted in a comparative analysis of health policies on the Aids epidemic: "attempts to curtail epidemics raise – in the guise of public health – the most enduring political dilemma: how to reconcile the individual's claim to autonomy and liberty with the community's concern with safety… How are individual rights and the public good pursued simultaneously?" This is all the more relevant under exceptional circumstances, such as a pandemic that creates dilemmas not only between individual liberties and public security but also between health protection and other social rights and democratic procedures (see Delanty in this volume's introduction). These dilemmas have been visible during the Covid-19 crisis in the states of emergencies that have been applied, even if they have been applied differently in different countries.

State of emergencies in democracies are justified as extraordinary moments. Jonathan White has singled out some important characteristics of emergency rule, as he observed them in the financial crisis in Europe in the 2010s. As he noted: "Emergency rule is conducted and narrated as the encounter with unfamiliar situations that demand to be handled on their own terms. It is about doing things differently because the situation at hand is different. At least in terms of its own rationale, but also in view of the creations it gives rise to, emergency rule is geared to the singularity of a certain moment" (White 2020: 188). Unconventional arrangements (such as the Troika) are justified by exceptional circumstances: "The political response could depart from existing norms because the problems were unprecedented in nature and scale. ... *necessity* becomes the principle of action. ... they were actions of *last resort*, demanded by the situation rather than the outcome of choice and volition" (White 2020: 22). This is related to an emphasis on speed because: "important decisions in the crisis have to be taken in a rush, at times literally overnight" (White 2020: 21. See also his chapter in this volume).

Exceptional powers break with procedural rules as governance in emergencies tends to be informal and unaccountable (ibid). As Sheppele (2010: 133–34) synthesized: emergencies involve executive centralization, with a reduction in the power of parliaments; militarization, with the military positioned as a key respondent to the threat; procedural shortcuts, with the bypassing of procedural checks; a ban on demonstrations; restrictions on freedom of movement; the inversion of freedom of speech, with censorship and criminalization; the reversal of transparency, with governmental action blanketed in secrecy and increasing surveillance; and anticipatory violence against opponents.

The Covid-19 pandemic has been addressed through emergency measures that have dramatically constrained the rights of movement, expatriation, and freedom of assembly. The duration of these emergency powers is, in most countries, still unknown. While they usually leave space for some emergency powers in extraordinary circumstances, democracies in fact need to set limits to the duration of the emergency. As White noted: "The period of emergency needs to be delimited, so the irregularities it entails do not fatally undermine the polity's norms and procedures more generally" (White 2020: 87).

As seen with the Covid-19 crisis, emergencies affect not only civil rights, but also social rights because they magnify the effects of the unequal distribution of resources within and between countries. In particular, social protection is at stake because living conditions related to primary social rights (such as the right to health, work, housing, education) are jeopardized by exceptional circumstances. As it is during wars or deep economic depressions, the disruption of everyday life hits especially hard some groups of the population, increasing social, gender, generational, and ethnic inequalities. While the pandemic demonstrates the lethal consequences of differential access to public health care in countries that (like the US) have a historically weak welfare state, or countries where neoliberal policies by right wing governments have been more widespread (as in the UK), it is also the case that in other countries (including European ones) the consequences of the commodification of health services, cuts of resources to public institutions, reductions in the numbers and salaries of public sector workers have all been denounced as increasing the spread and potency of the virus. As well as the immediate challenges, the pandemic has made evident the dramatic long term effects of inequalities by hitting especially hard ethnic minorities, old people in overcrowded shelters, poor neighbourhoods. Highlighting the importance of concerns about climate change and the urgency of addressing them, the contagion was particularly intense and the mortality higher in the most polluted areas. Besides the increase in episodes of violence against women, the pandemic also made blatantly clear both the importance of care activities and their unequal gender distribution with the heaviest burden falling on women.

Progressive Social Movements in Times of Emergencies

Social movements can play an important role in these special moments, mobilizing in defence of those rights that they perceive to be at risk or ever more strongly needed. In general, social movements adapt to moments of intense change, mobilizing to turn them to their advantage. In fact, movements might trigger, or at least respond, to what neo-institutionalists call a 'critical juncture': "(1) a major episode of institutional innovation, (2) occurring in distinct ways, and (3) generating an enduring legacy" (Collier and Munck 2017: 2). Different from normal times, critical junctures are periods of "crisis or strain that existing policies and institutions are ill-suited to resolve" and are therefore different from normal politics, when "institutional continuity or incremental change can be taken for granted" (Roberts 2015: 65).

Social movements might play an important role in these sudden breaks in established paths – and in their stabilization – because "usual conventions cease to guide social action and people collectively transcend, bypass or subvert established institutional patterns and structures" (Turner and Killian 1987: 3). As symbolic interactionist approaches have outlined, social movements can trigger social change through the spreading of emergent norms (Turner 1996). A reflection on the relevance of some specific protest moments as catalysts for change points to the capacity for social movements to contribute to emerging norms by breaking routine. So, increasingly, researchers have come to consider protests as momentous events, and in particular they have looked at the way contentious politics can trigger an intensification of the perception of time (della Porta 2017). References to special moments as well as momentous events have been more and more frequent as mobilization for what were expected to be routine protests triggered portentous waves of contentious politics. In the language of political activism, a momentum is now evoked as an act that dares to challenge existing structures, through massive support and at great velocity (della Porta 2000a). Even before the pandemic, recent times have been seen to be characterized by the momentous: a great transformation, a great recession as well as a great regression have been frequently used shorthand to describe the period following the financial breakdown of 2008 which saw quite large mobilization of so called 'movements of the crisis' (della Porta 2015; della Porta and Mattoni 2014). Moments of rupture are recognized as the most important way to define new paths for progressive change.

The capacity of progressive social movements to intervene in the critical juncture of an emergency has been studied, for instance, in research on how important they are during episodes of war. "States make war but war makes states" (Tilly 1975: 42). Political contention is involved in the dynamics of war right from the beginning and this can be seen in the mobilization for or against war, in war making, in support of or in resistance to war efforts, and in the war's wake, because there is an opening of political opportunities to change state politics and even to overturn regimes (Tarrow 2015: 15). So, war – like other extraordinary challenges – "has profound effects on the structuring of strategic action fields across society. This is because such crises undermine all kind of linkages in society and make it difficult for groups to reproduce their power" (Flingstein and McAdam 2012: 101). At the same time, war prompts the "attribution of new opportunities and threats leading to the appropriation or creation of new organizational vehicles for the purpose of engaging in innovative, contentious interaction with other field actors" (ibid).

Moments of crisis, such as wars but also epidemics and pandemics, tend to intensify the pressure for rights. Following Tilly (1992: 10), Tarrow observes that citizens and the state "first bargained over the means of war and then ... over enforceable claims that would serve their interests outside of the area of war; that, in turn, helped to enlarge states' obligations to their citizens" (ibid, 241). When making war, states need soldiers and to restrict freedoms and decrease wellbeing, so wars weaken states from the inside, triggering claims for more rights. Resistance to war develops through anti-conscription riots, tax revolts and refusal to provide food and shelter to the army: "extracting resources from the populace led to conflicts that could be resolved in only two ways: by becoming a coercion-rich state that subjected people to harsher internal rule or by according ... privileges that became the sources of citizenship" (Tarrow 2015: 12). Opposition to government tends to grow during war because: "as states impose higher taxes, armies suffer defeats, and the body bags return from the front, enthusiasm for war dampens. Movements develop in reaction to these costs but also against the constriction of rights that almost always occurs when states go to war" (Tarrow 2015: 24). In the wake of war, rights can be enhanced: "many of the reforms we take for granted today – the citizen army, women's suffrage, and the welfare state – were spurred by war, preparation for war, and contention in war's wake" (Tarrow 2015: 28; see also Starr 2010).

Pandemics are not wars, yet some of the dynamics are similar because they both create major disruption in everyday life. Governments impose various forms of constraints on freedom and, at the same time, are often unable (or unwilling) to address inequalities that are exacerbated by the crisis. Which specific balance of threats and opportunities that emerges for contentious politics in extraordinary moments is related to the characteristics of the exceptional circumstance that triggered the emergency as well as to the general social and political conditions that preceded it. As for the specific challenges deriving from extraordinary events, research on other pandemics indicates the importance of the social construction of the illness. Referring to one of the worst epidemics, Kleres noted that "despite the pervasive dominance of a medico-biological view of illness, from a social and cultural point of view, AIDS – and illness more generally – is the product of social constructions rather than an objective given" (Kleres 2018: 23). While the interpretation of AIDS shifted from a gay disease, to a risk-group disease and then to a threat to the general population, up to its eventual normalization (Kleres 2018: 42), from the social movements' perspective, "the construction of AIDS as gay, thus formed one of the most basic conditions for mobilization" (ibid: 25). From the institutional side, the ways in which different countries addressed the challenge has been linked to general and country-specific evolution in the conception of health and disease, moving historically from the idea of contagion through infectious agents (with quarantine as a remedy), typical in the Middle Ages, to disease caused by unhealthy environments (and therefore, sanitation as a remedy) as promoted in the nineteenth century, to the current conception of illness as deriving from personal dispositions (with appeals to discourage unhealthy habits and encourage healthy ones). Modern public health "entailed an individualization of public health as the new scientific knowledge made individual hygiene focal. The latter involved abandoning coercive means of quarantine in favour of strategies of mass persuasion and education – health education, promotion of domestic hygiene, etc." (ibid). As also noted in the development of the social construction of mental illness (Crossley 2006), epidemiological shifts further contributed to this individualization.

Adding weight to the significance of individual behaviour and personal responsibility, medical knowledge attributed diseases such as obesity, heart disease or some cancers to poor diet, tobacco use, alcohol consumption, insufficient physical exercise, etc. Voluntary individual behaviour changes became focal to public health. What appeared to be a loosening of (coercive) social controls in fact relied on their internationalization by moralizing health (Kleres 2018: 27–28). So, as Baldwin observed, a democratic ethos of good citizens included desirable health behaviour because: "sneezing and suffrage were linked" (Baldwin 2005: 15). In fact, "promotion of health rather than prevention of illness became the focal point, Individual behavior was the concern: overeating, overworking, overdrinking, underexercising, overcopulating. The law was responsible to discourage risky behavior... Democracy could not, however, mandate their citizens' behavior except at the margins" (ibid: 16). Against this vision of individual responsibility, progressive social movements during the Covid-19 crisis have instead pointed at collective responsibility, stigmatizing the neoliberal order for the cuts in public health and also for the many inequalities that have increased the cost of the pandemic in terms of the loss of life.

In sum, while emergency politics is certainly subject to authoritarian tendencies and increased inequalities, social movements can in fact construct spaces of intervention exploiting the crisis for a discourse of change. Emergency moments are populated by movements – and the time of pandemic is no exception. This mobilization is happening during the crisis of Covid-19.

Claiming Social Rights in the Pandemic

Against all the odds, the first stages in the development of the Covid-19 pandemic have been met by what media and activists have already greeted as a new global wave of protest. The fear of contagion and the lockdown measures themselves which seriously constrain physical movement, seem to jeopardize collective actions, but despite this, activists have invented new ways to express their increased grievances and also to spread ideas for change.

Progressive social movements have focused on social injustice, mobilizing in moral shock against the huge disruption the pandemic has caused in the living conditions of the poorest sections of the population. Pot banging, collective performances of protest songs from balconies, live-streamed actions, digital rallies, virtual marches, walk outs, boycotts, rent strikes have all multiplied as ways to denounce what the pandemic made all the more evident and all the less tolerable: the depth of inequalities and their dramatic consequences in terms of human lives (della Porta 2020b; Martinez 2020).

So, since March 2020, all over the world, workers have mobilized for labour rights that they perceived to be under threat. Factory workers and also white collar workers in essential sectors called for strikes – even for general strikes – demanding personal protective equipment and a sanitized environment. So-called gig economy workers, including couriers, Amazon drivers, and call-centre workers, mobilized in wildcat strikes, walked out of work places, called in sick and staged flashmobs to ask for protection against contagion as well as for broader labour rights (Tassinari, Chesta and Cini 2020). They also often criticized their companies' attempts to discourage collective action by firing those who stood up to the lack of security conditions. Workers who became unemployed during the pandemic – from those involved in the tourist sector to those working in the cultural and artistic sectors – also mobilized asking for income support.

In most of the countries that have been hit hard by the pandemic, there were renewed calls for social rights particularly to do with health, but also with social services, housing, public education. Workers in the health care sector called for the immediate provision of life-saving devices as well as resources to be invested in the public health system for their distribution. In Italy, 100,000 doctors signed a petition calling for territorially decentralized organization of health service provision. In the US, nurses staged peaceful protests against the radical right-wing activists who defied public health rules. In Spain, as in many other countries, citizens expressed support for public health systems by collectively clapping hands. Everywhere, health care personnel of private hospitals staged stay-ins (keeping socially distanced) to protest about the deterioration of their working conditions, underfunding of the public health system, and low salaries.

Inequalities have also been challenged by students, calling for reductions in fees and grants. Rent strikes multiply as the loss of jobs makes it more and more difficult to pay for rent which is often very high. Feminist groups condemned the increased burden of care work falling especially upon women after the shutting down of schools and social services.

Within the framework of environmental justice, protests also addressed the increasing deterioration of nature and the effect of this on the force of the pandemic itself. A good example of a digital strike was on the occasion of the fifth global strike against climate change carried out on 24 April 2020 by Fridays for Future with activists geolocalizing themselves in front of highly symbolic places (such as the Italian parliament). Digital assemblies have been virtual places where activists discuss perspectives and build proposals, such as the Back to the Future program, focusing on a socially equitable and environmentally just response to the pandemic. Posters have been put up in squares and on buildings to spread the call for changes to environmental policies.

As with contentious politics in non-pandemic times, disruptive street protests – politics by other means – mix a logic of numbers, to show the spread of support for their proposals (with digital strikes or petitions), a logic of damage, by creating costs for their targets (as in workers' strikes but also in citizens' rent strikes), as well as a logic of testimony, by proving through sacrifice the extent of their commitment (such as the vigil of the nurses standing in front of abusive right wing militants) (della Porta and Diani 2020: chap. 5).

The activities of progressive social movements in the pandemic are, however, not limited to visible protests. Progressive movements have also contributed to a most urgent task in a tragic moment: the production and distribution of services of different types. Faced with the limited capacity of public institutions (weakened by years of neoliberal policies) to support those most in need, activists have built upon a new mutualism that had already been nurtured to address the social crisis triggered by the financial crisis of 2008 and especially the austerity responses to it. Progressive civil society organizations and grassroots neighbourhood groups have distributed food and medicines, produced masks and medical instruments, sheltered homeless people and protected women suffering from domestic violence. The principles of food sovereignty and solidarity have spread through practical examples as an alternative to the disrupted global food chain. In doing this, activists are challenging a top-down conception of charity, supporting instead norms of solidarity that contrast with the extreme individualism of neoliberal capitalism. Through social interventions, they reconstitute relationships that were broken well before the pandemic, but they also politicize demands, shifting from immediate relief to proposals for radical social change.

Empowering Participation in the Pandemic

While progressive movements gave priority to the defence of social rights, concerns also emerged about civil and political rights that they see as at risk. Pandemic times have been times of scapegoating the poor, migrants, homeless people accused by right wing politicians of spreading the virus. They have been times of a lack of transparency and low accountability because the proclamation of states of emergencies have been used, in various ways, to curb dissent. Xenophobic governments have increased forced repatriation and closed borders even to refugees. Even in less dramatic cases, the mainstream media have been focusing on the pandemic, often to spread messages of fear. Progressive social movements have opposed these trends even though they did not criticize lockdown measures per se.

Progressive social movements that mobilized in the pandemic are suggesting that the path to achieve social and environmental justice is not through the centralization of political decision making, and even less through technocratic exercises, but rather by increasing the participation of citizens. Through car caravans (as in Israel) or bike marches (as in Slovenia), progressive groups have protested about government attempts to exploit the crisis to limit political participation and citizens' rights. In Hungary and Poland they have expressed concerns about the restriction of civil liberties by right wing populist regimes. In the US, they have denounced the attempt by Donald Trump to postpone the presidential elections and his attack on the mail system. Especially in countries that were already highly mobilized before the onset of the pandemic, such as Chile or Lebanon, progressive social movements attacked the corruption of politics and called for transparency. Starting in the US after the killing of George Floyd by a police officer, the Black Lives Matter movement spread all over the globe, protesting about racist bias in the police enforcement of public order, about systemic racism within police forces, and demanding defunding of the police.

Faced with decreasing transparency and increasing repression during and after the lockdown, activists called for political and economic powers to be held accountable through the careful collection, elaboration and transmission of information about the effects of the pandemic on the poorest and most disadvantaged groups of citizens – such as prisoners, migrant workers, the homeless – and also on violence against women and the unequal distribution of care work within the family. In fact, activists have produced a lay knowledge that is at least as much needed as the specialized knowledge of the experts. Using digital resources for information sharing as well as online teach-ins, they have helped to connecting different fields of knowledge that the hyper-specialization of science tends to fragment. Intertwining theoretical with practical knowledge, experimenting with different ideas, building on past experience, they prefigure a different future.

Democracy has therefore been enhanced by the very presence of these voices in the public sphere. Different groups of activists – both pre-existing and emerging – are building ties and bridging gaps. In fact, these energies are connecting around a series of central challenges for the construction of post pandemic alternatives. Progressive movements are thus elaborating innovative ideas about how to contrast ever-growing inequalities not only in labour conditions and income, but also between generations, genders, ethnic groups, and different territories. Here the proposed alternatives include a return of the labour rights that neoliberal capitalism had taken away, with consequences that became all the more dramatic during the pandemic, as well as demands for a basic income for those who are excluded from the labour market. They are also elaborating proposals on rights to education, housing, and public health.

In this way, progressive social movements can build upon democratic innovations that they helped to develop as responses to the financial crisis of the last decade. Through deliberate experiments, direct democracy, crowd-sourced constitutional processes as well as the building of movements and political parties, the ideas of the commons (that were developed during the anti-austerity protests) point to public entities that need to be managed with the active participation of citizens, service users and workers (della Porta 2020a). In performing these activities, progressive social movements constitute public spheres in which participation is valued as a vision of solidarity born out of a recreated sense of shared destiny.

Challenges for Progressive Movements

Times of deep crisis can therefore (admittedly, not automatically) trigger the invention of alternative, but possible, futures. As the pandemic changes everyday life, progressive social movements create much-needed spaces for reflection about a post-pandemic world that cannot be conceived to be in continuity with the pre-pandemic one.

There are, however, still many challenges for progressive social movements in their attempts to build solidarity at a very difficult time. Firstly, the pandemic intervened upon an already fragmented class structure, introducing ever new elements of inequality between those who work in a safe environment (or even from home) and those who are instead either occupied in essential services with limited health protection or have lost their precarious jobs due to the crisis. Even within each of those groups, there are differences in terms not only of the degree of job insecurity but also of the gender discrimination in the way in which the work – increased during the pandemic – of caring for young, old or disabled people is distributed. Among those who work in essential services, divisions emerge between those who have more union rights (and can strike or threaten to strike for personal protective equipment) and the growing precariat, with no regular contracts, who are at times even considered to be independent workers.

The pandemic also makes visible – but also fragments around – the different degrees of endowment of other social rights; from the very right to health care and sick leave (or leave to care for others who are sick) to the rights to housing and access to public education or social services. The orders to shelter-in-place increased the impact of unequal living conditions as far as housing rights are concerned, discriminating against those who have insufficient space and no access to increasingly important equipment such as computers and connectivity. The pandemic has especially disrupted the already commodified educational system, with dramatic consequences for students, teachers and other workers. Here as well, inequalities in terms of class, generation, gender and ethnic background tend to add up, growing with the precarious condition of a growing number of citizens – especially in democracies with residual welfare states, such as the US, where losing a job often implies losing health insurance, income and housing.

This fragmentation might be reflected in competing demands, such as from those in secure positions asking for lockdown measures and those in insecure positions fearing the potential consequences – with the former much more vocal than the latter. There is convergence upon shared demands for public health, workers' rights, basic income and universal welfare. As the Black Lives Matter protests demonstrated, when stratified inequalities become all the more visible, specific triggers, such as police violence on ethnic minorities, might provide a symbolic catalyst for the convergence of different struggles. However, they also show the difficulties in overcoming intersectional divisions to mobilize on a shared platform.

In democratic contexts, progressive social movements have, until now, mobilized more around social rights than on civil liberties. Exceptions are visible: first of all, in countries where democracy was already considered to be at risk, and also in movements mobilizing the most powerless groups in the population, such as migrants, the homeless and prisoners. The Black Lives Matter protests pointed at police violence against racialized people; feminist groups condemned societal violence against women. As mentioned above, protests on the left have contested authoritarian measures in Israel, Slovenia and Hungary, whose governments have been accused of exploiting the health crisis to centralize power and repress the opposition. More sporadically, activists have criticized an instrumental and biased use of restrictive measures to selectively repress particular groups such as migrants or sex-workers. By and large however, lockdown and hygiene measures (such as the wearing of masks) have been contested on the right, while the left counter-mobilize in defence of measures of solidarity with the weakest groups in the population.

There have been only limited complaints on the left about the role that democratically unaccountable experts have occupied during the pandemic. They have influenced government decisions, at times on the basis of limited knowledge or contradictory information and expectations. While the economists that supported neoliberal policies were criticized during the financial crisis, the plethora of medical experts that occupied the public space during the pandemic was spared criticism from the left. Instead, when splits emerged among experts, progressive movements tended to rally with those supporting the most pessimistic views about the evolution of the pandemic, as a sort of differentiation from the conspiratorial and 'negationist' narratives of the virus on the other side. Following a recent trend in the movement on climate change, opposition to the anti-science position of the populist right often limits the expression of some critical views of scientific knowledge by the left. It still remains to be seen whether the loss of individual freedom can be challenged as the emergency declines and the repression of collective freedoms, such as rights to protest, become less justified.

More generally, effective protests are still difficult to organize. Even after the end of lockdown, restrictions on street actions are still in place and can be used arbitrarily to repress contentious politics. Online activities selectively involve the most connected, silencing the most powerless. The new mutualism brings about the challenge, noticed in other emergencies, of having to invest limited resources to offer services to supplement insufficient state provisions. In addition, frustration grows with the inability to address fast growing needs along with the limited availability of professional skills and volunteer commitment. Depoliticization emerges as a risk at the collective level, burnout at individual levels, while the power dynamics between those who help and those who are helped are difficult to keep under control.

It is still to be seen how well progressive movements will consolidate some contingent victories not only in terms of more protection at work but also of investment in public health and increased state intervention in social welfare in general. While discursive opportunities have opened up for those concerned with social justice, powerful interests have been strengthened by this crisis – not only from the economic point of view.

Concluding Reflections

While the Covid-19 pandemic is a unique historical event, social science analyses can build upon knowledge that has accumulated about similar events such as other health catastrophes and other exceptionally disruptive events like disasters and wars. Combining insights from this literature, we can single out challenges and opportunities for progressive social movements in emergency-related critical junctures. Among the challenges are increasing inequalities and poverty, mobilization of strong interests, emergency powers and the limitations of freedom, centralization of political power, the increase in repression, the distortion in the public sphere, the development of exclusive identities based on fear with stigmatization of groups such as immigrants or young people. On the other hand, crises also create opportunities for progressive movements, such as a discursive opening on issues of social justice, an increase in public intervention, innovative forms of participation, the building of alternative public spheres, the growth of grassroots solidarity and the broadening of collective identification and global connections.

Risks and opportunities are influenced by the very characteristics of the challenge and by the dynamics of the critical juncture. The social construction of the virus is linked to broader trends in capitalism and also to its political context and the societal resistance to it. The response by progressive movements to the pandemic builds upon a return of the social question that was nurtured by the global justice movement at the beginning of the millennium and by the anti-austerity protests which peaked in the 2010s and, from Lebanon to Chile, mobilized globally in the hot autumn of 2019, culminating just before the official acknowledgment of the pandemic (della Porta 2015).

A typical feature of this pandemic seems to be a relatively short emergency, high contagion but low mortality, a global dimension but with localized dynamics, high public intervention, high ambition (of 'stopping the virus'), the importance of experts. The pandemic has certainly made evident the lethal effects of inequalities; the diffusion of the disease and its mortality increase along with the lack of health, insurance, savings, sick leave, unemployment benefits, housing, income. There is too much pollution, crowding and death; the risk of losing one's job or being infected is too high. Some movements mobilized against these inequalities with demands to broaden citizens' rights. During the pandemic, just as during wartime, citizens mobilized to campaign for the broadening of social rights, including health, work, housing, social services and education. They protested in the streets, when possible, as well as in their work places; they refused to pay rents and used balconies to voice their claims. They also organized self-help initiatives, in solidarity with their neighbours and with those most hit by the pandemic and the measures to contain it. They offered food and shelter, medicines and legal consultations. Progressive movements are also important sources of alternative information about the dramatic effects of class, gender, generation, ethnic inequalities. By building alternative public spheres, they articulate demands for radical changes for post pandemic times.

While more concerned with justice than with freedom, and despite the restriction of individual freedoms, progressive movements mobilized against repression of the opposition and they opposed violence being used against the most marginalized groups. They demanded more transparency and accountability. What is more, they fuelled participation by mobilizing new grassroots groups. They proposed a social construction of the virus that criticized the highest human costs being experienced by the weakest groups in the population. Solidarity was considered a priority while demanding, with some success, that the costs of the lockdown should be paid by public intervention.

While it is still too early to analyse the outcomes of these struggles, their very existence confirms the role of progressive social movements in critical junctures, even of an emergency type. As in any disaster, solidarity is built out of risks, and self-organization nurtures self-empowerment. As it was with Hurricane Katrina in the US or with other extreme weather crises, the recognition of the impact of social injustice pushes people to politicize their claims. Whether the outcome is a garrison state or an expansion of deliberative democracy, as happened after the typhoon disaster in the Philippines (Curato 2020), is therefore an open question for future studies. Research on wars indicates, however (Kier and Krebs 2010; Stern 2010), that the expansion of citizenship rights after disasters is a possible but not a necessary outcome that will depend on the scale of the disaster as well as on the capacity of the opposition to reduce the power of the elites and/or to push them towards compromise.

References

Baldwin, R. (2005) *Democracy and Diseases*, Berkeley: University of California Press.

Collier, David, and Gerardo L. Munck. (2017) Building Blocks and Methodological Challenges: A Framework for Studying Critical Junctures, *Qualitative and Multi-Method Research* 15 (1): 2 – 8.

Crossley, N. (2006) *Contesting Psychiatry*, London: Routledge.

Curato, N. (2020) *Democracy in Times of Misery*, Oxford: Oxford University Press.

Della Porta, D. (2013) *Can Democracy be Saved?* Cambridge: Polity Press.

Della Porta, D. (2015) *Social Movements in Times of Austerity*, Cambridge: Polity Press.

Della Porta, D. (2017) *Where did the Revolution Go?* Cambridge: Cambridge University Press.

Della Porta, D. (2020a) How Social Movements Can Save Democracy, Cambridge: Polity Press.

Della Porta, D. (2020b) How Progressive Social Movements can save Democracy in Pandemic Times, *Interface* 12 (1): 355–358.

Della Porta, D. and A. Mattoni (2014) (eds) *Spreading Protest*, Colchester: ECPR Press.

Della Porta, D. and M. Diani (2020) *Social Movements: An Introduction*, Oxford: Blackwell, 3rd edition.

Kier, E and R. Krebs (2010), Introduction: War and Democracy in Comparative Perspective, In E. Kier and R. Krebs (eds) *In War's Wake*, Cambridge: Cambridge University Press, 1–19.

Kleres, J. (2018) *The Social Organization of Disease*, London: Routledge.

Martinez, M. (2020) Mutating Mobilisations during the Pandemic Crisis in Spain, *Interface,* 12 (1): 15–21.

Morlino, L. (2012) *Changes for Democracy*, Oxford: Oxford University Press.

Roberts, K.M. (2015) *Changing Courses*, Cambridge: Cambridge University Press.

Scheppele, K.L. (2005–6) Small Emergencies, *Georgia Law Review* 40: 835–62.

Starr, P. (2010) Dodging a Bullet: Democracy's Gains in modern War. In E. Kier and R. Krebs (eds) *In War's Wake*, Cambridge: Cambridge University Press, 50–66.

Tarrow, S. (2015) *War, States and Contention*, Cambridge: Cambridge University Press.

Tassinari, A., R. Chesta and L. Cini (2020). Labour conflicts over health and safety in the Italian Covid-19 crisis. *Interface* 12 (1): 128–138.

Tilly, C. (1975) *The Formation of National States in Western Europe*, Princeton: Princeton University Press.

Tilly, C. (1992) Where do Rights Come From? In L. Mjoset (ed) *Contributions to the Comparative Politics of Development*, Oslo: Institute for Social Research, 9–37.

Turner, R. (1996) .The Moral Issue in Collective Action. *Mobilization: An International Quarterly* 1 (1): 1–15

Turner, R., and L. Killian (1987) [1974, 1957] *Collective Behavior.* Englewood Cliffs, NJ: Prentice Hall.

White, J. (2020) *Politics of Last Resort*, Oxford: Oxford University Press.

Sonja Avlijaš
Security for whom? Inequality and Human Dignity in Times of the Pandemic

Popular opinion has been taken aback by the supposed power of the coronavirus pandemic to put capitalism on hold and to bring the state back in. To counteract this maxim, this chapter argues that ongoing state reactions to the pandemic are an inherent feature of capitalism. Responses to Covid-19 do not depart from how the capitalist system of accumulation has historically reacted to crises. There is no capitalism without the state that manages risks and uncertainties of the market economy. Moreover, institutional economists have long recognised that serious economic depressions are not accidental exogenous misfortunes but organic aspects of capitalism (Veblen 1932 in Galbraith 1998: 45). Echoing, many have recognised this pandemic as provoked by the accelerated globalisation and imbalances that have arisen from capitalism's growing encroachment on our natural environment, as discussed by Gerard Delanty in the introduction to this volume.

At the same time, a complex political economy determines who gets access to state sponsored security. Apart from state aid for enterprises, which is indispensable in times of economic downturns, the so-called labour market insiders, usually consisting of the better earning professional classes and pensioners, are generally the most protected. This protection ensures workers' lifetime investment in knowledge and skills, an important input for capitalist production in the era of the knowledge economy, but also political stability in a democratic setting. On the other hand, a growing population of the so-called labour market outsiders (those who have weaker attachment to jobs) are much more likely to experience job loss and not be covered by social security. Such precarity, which often goes hand in hand with the absence of savings or assets such as housing, makes them depend on anti-poverty oriented social safety nets, which have become increasingly residual and conditioned on one's willingness to accept any form of work. Paradoxically, many of the essential workers that have made the lockdown possible in order to save other people's lives belong to these precarious groups for whom socio-economic and health security is out of reach.

Moreover, the all-encompassing state and private sector retrenchment from social reproduction during the pandemic (the shutting down of schools, nurseries, non-Covid-19 related hospital care, care for the elderly) has led to an unprecedented re-familialisation of care. This has generated further pressures on per-

https://doi.org/10.1515/9783110713350-014

sonal and communal resources, already depleted from longstanding interactions with the crises of modern capitalism and the longer term trend of privatisation and commodification of public services which has particularly affected those at the lower end of the income distribution.

Because the pandemic has reinforced these unsustainable aspects of the traditional state-capitalism nexus of security and progress, a possibility for grassroots socio-political transformation is also appearing on the horizon. The pandemic has increased the socio-political visibility of essential and care workers and made us more aware of their indispensability when it comes to providing us all with security. Social countermovements that aim to challenge the traditional structures that reinforce inequality between insiders and outsiders and improve human dignity have also gained momentum and influence. Our appreciation for public and communal resources which facilitate people's ability to survive economic contractions is also increasing, together with our growing awareness of interdependability between different social groups. Could a social revaluation of the traditionally undervalued essential jobs and social roles, which involve care and which are habitually gendered and racialised, take place?

The chapter is structured in the following way. The first section shows that capitalism is at least as motivated by the inclination to protect what one already has, as by the elusive forces of competition. The second section analyses the complex political economy of unequal access to state sponsored security in modern capitalism. The third emphasises this point further, by discussing how social reproduction at household and communal levels often replaces the state and underpins our ability to combat a social challenge such as this pandemic, although the capitalist order continually undermines its value. By way of conclusion, the final section addresses the intersectional countermovement that is expanding around some of these issues, most visibly under the banner of *Black Lives Matter* (BLM).

The Conflict between Security and Capitalism does not Exist

'The conflict between security and progress, once billed as a social conflict of the century, does not exist.'

John Kenneth Galbraith in *The Affluent Society* (1998 [1958]: 94)

The idea that has dominated our understanding of capitalism over the past century has been the classical Marxist view that there is a conflict between competitive market forces, represented by capitalists, and security, epitomised in the welfare state that has been won over by the working class to protect them from the adverse effects of the competitive society (e.g. power resource theory by Korpi 1983). Along these lines of scholarship, the workers' ability to politically counteract market forces has substantially weakened with the advancement of neoliberalism and economic globalisation over the past 30 years, while returns on capital, reinforced by wealth inheritance, have increased. Such circumstances have led to growing socio-economic inequalities and retrenchment of the welfare state across advanced capitalist economies (e.g. Schmidt & Thatcher 2013).

While this interpretation of the relationship between the competitive capitalist society and security is very compelling, it leaves us with an important puzzle. Despite the co-existence of capitalism, which concentrates power and resources, and democracy, which is expected to divide power and resources in an egalitarian manner, the poor have not (yet) soaked the rich.

This has preoccupied political economists for decades. While some scholars focus on understanding how economic interests are aggregated into public policies in a democratic setting in order to find an answer (see Iversen 2008 for overview), others see it as a temporary disempowerment of the social forces under pressures of global capital and the increasing empowerment of the regulatory (technocratic) state, and predict that it is just a matter of time before the 'right type of crisis' ends capitalism and generates a new, more just, socio-economic order. These ideas have gained additional visibility during the coronavirus pandemic, stimulating thinkers such as Žižek (2020) to propose a horizon of hope for a more progressive and socially inclusive post-pandemic world order. In stark contrast, but predicting a similar adverse outcome for capitalism, others have proposed distopian scenarios of further social disempowerment, greater state control and biopolitical securitisation in the post-pandemic world, which would also put capitalism's liberal characteristics on hold (see Agamben 2005 in Gerard Delanty's introduction to this volume).

This section draws on classical and contemporary contributions in political economy to explore what this pandemic tells us about the nature of capitalism and its future prospects. Contrary to both Marxist and libertarian ideological convictions that state efforts to securitise capitalism are anti-capitalist and that they cripple its potency, increasing concern for economic security over the past century has in reality led to unparalleled advances in economic productivity and capitalism itself (Galbraith 1998: 94). Capitalist systems are national, i.e. managed by the state, and this feature allows them to react to external pressures and successfully adapt to challenges and uncertainties (Hall & Soskice 2001).

Galbraith (1998: 83) reminds us that the development of the modern corporation has more to do with the firm's quest for reducing insecurity of its survival through within-firm innovation and reorganisation, than it does with purely competitive forces. Underpinning innovation in modern ICT-driven capitalism, Mazzucato (2013) identifies the state as a key 'de-risker' of innovative companies, and shows that Americans' tax money is a key pillar in the establishment of the Silicon Valley as a global leader in high technology.

Moreover, the state has played a major role in ensuring security for both capital owners and workers during downturns of the business cycle throughout history. For example, the budget was irretrievably out of balance throughout the Great Depression in the US thus allowing the economy to survive (Galbraith 1998: 14). During the more recent crises, including the 2008 one, government spending was widely perceived as necessary, with support for the banking institutions that triggered the crisis justified by the 'too big to fail' motto. Expectedly, when the coronavirus pandemic hit Europe in March 2020, government stimulus for the economy, but also preservation of jobs and salaries was a top priority, together with the epidemiological measures. Also expectedly, the richer EU countries injected more cash into their economies than others from the onset, with Germany accounting for half of all state aid initially approved by the European Commission (Fleming & Espinoza 2020).

Galbraith (1998: 88) further argues that 'the ordinary man' followed the path pioneered by the modern business firm when it comes to seeking protection from insecurity of the competitive system. While historically the poor worried about daily subsistence to a point of not having the time or energy to think about the longer run, as affluence grew, so did the people's desire to protect what they have accumulated. Moreover, Swenson (2002) and Mares (2003) have shown the important role employers played in the early formation of social policies, especially in those sectors and industries that are highly exposed to risk. They showed that it is in the interest of companies to protect their workers enough to motivate them to invest in their knowledge and skills, a trend that has further grown in importance in the era of the knowledge economy. In other words, capital does not always favour welfare retrenchment and liberalisation. The newer generations of political economists have reconceptualised capitalism as a product of interactions and coordination between different stakeholders (e.g. employers, workers, trade unions) who pursue joint interests of increasing their affluence by sharing costs and risks. In this framework, the welfare state emerges as an important tool for managing market risk for all parties (Hassel & Palier 2020).

At the same time, I do not suggest in this chapter that the class conflict is gone, nor do I argue that everybody is protected in modern capitalism. Nothing could be farther from truth. While the politics of who gets to access (state) security in modern capitalism is discussed in the next section, the intention of this section is to dispel the myth that 'able participants' of the competitive society do not need security and protection, while the 'anti-capitalist forces' of security are saved for the poor who are not able to find their way in the competitive society, out of empathy and a sense of justice. Instead, I suggest that management of real life uncertainty is a key concern for all agents of capitalism, as people have long recognised that factors out of one's hand, rather than lack of business ability or hard work, can lead to bankruptcy and loss of all possessions. Farmers, businessmen, workers, politicians – none have wanted to live under the peril of such intrinsic insecurity (Galbraith 1998: 35). This is a key feature of modern capitalism and a prerequisite for the functioning of the competitive society.

Political Economy of Human Security in an Unequal World

'We may be in this together, but that doesn't mean we are in this equally.'

Paul Johnson in *The Times* (2020)

Although security is endemic to capitalism, not everyone who lives in capitalist societies has access to it. This section analyses the political economy of who gets to be protected from the adverse impact of the pandemic (or another crisis) in a system of economic governance that produces stark inequalities in the distribution of property and income, while also being subject to democratic procedures. Politics of redistribution in the modern democracy are multidimensional and increasingly complex. They depend on a myriad of factors, including the national context (Iversen 2008: 608). In an attempt to improve our understanding of the key stakeholders that have been affected by the current situation, I provide an overview of the socio-political context that preceded the pandemic, focusing on Europe and the UK in particular. I then make some observations on how this socio-political context translates into the pandemic politics of redistribution.

Over the past three decades, the number of new actors with political agency has grown and led to major changes along the socio-economic dimension of political competition. Until the 1980s the male breadwinner model of social security was both prevalent and satisfactory to a great number of workers and families whose 'heads' of households were employed in industry or civil service. The thirty years after World War II were characterised by high growth and employment, along with the expansion of the traditional welfare state, which was based on the so-called equivalence principle, i.e. related to workers' former wage levels and contribution records. Following the oil crises of the 1970s, the old economic models of the advanced western economies became increasingly unsustainable. Extensive economic restructuring ensued.

Adjustments to the new trend of internationalisation of production deindustrialised the West, leading to a loss of stable employment for the male industrial workforce. With the service economy expanding, women entered the labour market in growing numbers, leading to a decline in traditional gender roles and division of labour within households. The parallel diffusion of ICT hurled us into a new era of growth where knowledge became a key factor of production, and where economic value is increasingly extracted from tradeable dynamic services, including finance. This transition to the post-industrial economic structure resulted in growing labour market flexibility. One explanation for this trend of weakening labour protection is that a more flexible workforce is needed to boost innovation in the knowledge economy. Yet, we empirically observe that these new regulations have in fact led to labour market dualisation across Europe – the more secure and better quality jobs are preserved for the educated (and often older and white) professional classes in the 'knowledge economy', while the growingly precarious jobs belong to those who provide consumer and personal services to them (see Schwander 2019). In other words, structural changes over the past 30 years have led to a proliferation of the so-called labour market outsiders who do not have traditional labour contracts but exist on the edges of social protection structures from the bygone era.

Intergenerational inequalities have also been exacerbated over the past three decades, as demographic ageing increased the share of public resources that are allocated to pensions, often at the expense of investive social policies that would support youth (this has been especially the case in Italy, France and Greece). In the UK, financialisation has also led to privatisation and marketisation of housing, pensions, education and other social services, further reducing the ability of labour market outsiders who cannot access generous employment contracts and afford these services to secure their wellbeing and livelihoods. New Labour policies in the UK (e. g. no progressive land value tax, no new stocks of social housing), coupled by exorbitant increases in the value of real estate, have also entrenched the strong constituency of homeowners that is heavily and increasingly skewed against youth and towards older generations of workers (and now pensioners) who purchased housing during the Thatcher era.

All these factors have changed the nature of social risks, with women, the young, and low-skilled workers being particularly exposed (Schwander 2019: 17). While there is little research on the racial and ethnic aspects of this phenomenon, we can safely assume that non-whites are also disproportionately vulnerable to new social risks. Although there is cross-national divergence when it comes to adaptation of social security systems to new risks due to the idiosyncrasies of each country's political processes and economic models, most welfare states in Europe (except the Scandinavian ones) can be characterised as status preserving and generally skewed towards supporting the elderly middle class at the expense of youth, children and low earners (for the highly relevant case of Italy, see Kazepov & Ranci 2017). As shown by Avlijaš et al (2020), many policies of European centre-left governments during the 1990s and early 2000s were based on the belief that 'good' welfare reform should serve the middle classes and generate growth and jobs. While these new policies included labour market liberalisation, activation, and social investment, they were often accompanied by welfare cuts and the conditionality of transfer payments for the unemployed, which parts of the electorate did not appreciate. In the UK, this trend has been reinforced by the rise of the knowledge economy, which, on the one hand, places a high premium on education, while on the other expands the domestic demand driven growth model that relies on cheap personal and consumer services (Avlijaš et al 2020).

Therefore, a growing number of actors in advanced capitalist democracies that have been commodified are struggling to obtain protection and security for themselves, whether through the electoral channels or by other means (see section 4). In opposition, a status preserving political push to keep 'outsiders' out of the traditional security-progress nexus of capitalism is also present. The social consensus of the previous era has effectively broken down, generating space for the emergence of new forms of political competition that are attempting to articulate a new one.

While some scholars perceive the pandemic as an opportunity to finally switch from the status preserving tendencies of the European welfare states towards social investment in youth and new social risks, the limited evidence that we have to this date is pointing towards more of the status quo, along with light supplementary measures to support labour market outsiders.

Status protecting public policies, demanded by the middle class electorate and business have expectedly dominated state intervention agendas and budgets since March 2020. While emergency government measures, such as state aid to enterprises, furlough and short-time work schemes have generally managed to deter the negative labour market impact of the pandemic on the European middle classes until now, social scientists are also expecting a strong effect of the longer-term changes in consumer behaviour and economic restructuring, after the initial government interventions wean off.

For whatever the future may hold, a clear distributive profile of the ongoing lockdown related measures has emerged along age, gender and race lines, in interaction with the pre-existing inequalities. The young are being economically hit harder and faster than any other group, both in the short-term but also in terms of having their career prospects severely dented (Costa Dias et al 2020). Across EU27, young men are mostly affected by job loss (Eurofound 2020). People with low earnings (many of whom are young) have also been disproportionately economically impacted (Bourquin 2020), and particularly those of Pakistani, Bangladeshi or black ethnicity (Blundell et al 2020).

Labour markets in Romania, Italy, France, Cyprus and Greece have taken a strong hit, while the Nordic countries have reported fewest reductions in working time (Eurofound 2020). Such geographical distribution of the impact further cements the core-periphery inequalities within the EU. Moreover, existing evidence indicates that countries with a more limited ability to borrow in international markets and less stable budget positions will suffer higher welfare losses and increases in inequality (Clemens & Heinemann 2020).

Given the closure of many childcare and educational facilities that mostly employ female labour, the pandemic is also disproportionately impacting on female paid work. This adverse impact is further reinforced by women's growing informal care responsibilities, as childcare, schooling and housework re-familialises (see next section).

The wealthier income groups are also adversely impacted as they are unable to spend money on many of the recreational activities that typically account for a relatively large share of their budgets. These 'forced savings' will provide them with additional income to spend in the future, while many of the activities they used to spend money on is what provided livelihoods for the low earners in the sectors which have been shut down and for whose products and services demand has substantially fallen (Blundell et al 2020). Such dynamics worsen pre-existing inequalities, but also undercut countries' sources of growth, especially in the UK, whose growth model is largely based on domestic consumption of cheap personal and consumer services. Thus, the pandemic also highlights the interdependency between spending of the wealthier classes and subsistence of the lower earners. Countries will likely be forced to adapt their existing growth models to these new circumstances, while the pandemic politics of redistribution will determine whether we will see a shift towards more inclusive or more exclusive socio-economic models in the post-pandemic era.

The unequal distributive impacts of the pandemic are further complicated by the health inequalities which intersect with the economic ones in several directions, making another dent in the traditional social consensus. While the youth are the most severely impacted economically, they are much more likely to experience milder symptoms of the illness. Yet, they are also driven by the altruistic drive to support their elderly family members. On the other hand, people at the lower end of the earnings distribution are more likely to have the types of health risks that may adversely impact their recovery from the coronavirus, and also be materially affected by the lockdown. There is also the racial and ethnic component to the health crisis, with black and some minority ethnic groups facing a higher risk of dying from the coronavirus (Elwell-Sutton et al 2020). This is an opportunity for new cross-race and cross-generational coalitions, and new interdependent activist networks to emerge.

Additional is the growing awareness that the cost of non-extension of sickness and unemployment benefits to some groups of working persons is too high from the perspective of public health. When those who are not compensated are forced to work even though they have symptoms, they can also endanger others. The numerous supranational and national efforts to monitor the public policies that are being implemented during the pandemic are also generating opportunities for cross-national policy learning. Adaptation of social security is a major policy arena for the EU and beyond, and the coronavirus pandemic has further accelerated and politicised this important policy front. Policy makers might become more aware of the interdependent nature between social security and public health, which would subsequently lead to an expansion of universal access to sickness and unemployment benefits to all types of workers.

Social Reproduction: The Hidden Engine of Capitalism

'If workers' labor produces all the wealth in society, who then produces the worker?'

Tithi Bhattacharya in *Social Reproduction Theory* (2017: 1)

Apart from the role of the state as a key de-risker of the market economy, another de-risker that makes capitalist production possible and that has been long ignored is the daily and generational labour that takes place in households, schools, hospitals, prisons (Bhattacharya 2017: 2). Many people, and especially women, combine employment and unpaid domestic labour to maintain themselves and their households even during times of economic expansion (Bhattacharya 2017: 5). But the role of social reproduction becomes particularly pertinent in times of crisis, as individuals and households fall back on their personal and communal resources to survive the downturn. Social reproduction doesn't stop even when everything else does; people still need to be fed, schooled, nurtured, washed, dressed.

The unprecedented withdrawal of state institutions and the private sector that provide care for children and elderly, including schooling and non-pandemic related health and wellness services, shifted these responsibilities onto the already burdened private individuals (predominantly women), families and local communities. Given that this withdrawal has been all-encompassing, even the wealthier classes have become burdened with care work and subsequently less productive in their jobs, even though these jobs are key sources of material security for them.

But this is not a new trend, the pandemic has simply accelerated it. Despite this important function of social reproduction as an automatic stabiliser of the economy in times of contraction, the past three decades have seen an intensification of its depreciation, as communal and local resources that contribute to the ability of households to care for themselves are being depleted. Through extensive outsourcing of government services to the private sector in an ideological attempt to provide cheaper and better services, the UK has allowed a deterioration of public services including health, while actually spending more of the taxpayers' money (Hood & Dixon 2015; Innes 2018). This growing commodification of care has also resulted in expansion of a strongly gendered and racialised care economy that mostly employs low earning women, non-whites and migrants to offer personal care services for the professional and affluent classes, and their elderly and children. One may legitimately wonder whether the country's inability to better respond to the health aspects of the pandemic could at least partially be attributed to this long term trend of neglecting and undervaluing the role of the public sector in providing quality care to its population, while providing ample profit opportunities for the poorly controlled private monopoly providers of essential services.

The question of migrant domestic workers who fill the 'care gap' in richer countries adds a further layer of complexity to the subject of social reproduction. It brings race and citizenship to the forefront of the care conversation, in an age where anti-migrant and nationalist sentiments are growing while care work is becoming increasingly commodified and the so-called 'global care chains' ever longer (Fraser 2017: 34). The growing visibility of migrant care workers and their situation during the pandemic is also making it increasingly difficult to continue reducing social reproduction to the policy issue of 'work and life balance' for white middle class women.

Apart from this shift towards re-familialisation of care and reliance on the mostly gendered and racialised resources of private individuals, the wider economy of care also includes low-wage essential workers which have had to work in order to sustain the lockdown, from migrant fruit and vegetable pickers that were flown over to the UK from Romania in the height of the pandemic, to food production workers, cashiers in food stores, delivery (wo)men, and so on. These people's labour, and even their lives, as they expose themselves to the virus so that others are able to stay at home, have made it possible to have a lockdown in the first place. Yet, it is precisely these groups who are at the bottom of the earnings ladder, who have the least access to work related social security protection (as discussed in section 2), and who have the least choice in whether to go to work although they may be as scared by the pandemic as anyone else. While this pandemic has made these workers more visible, a key question is whether it will strengthen their agency and whether the perceived value of their labour might increase in the future.

The current British growth model is therefore characterised by a dualisation in the provision of care – it has become commodified for those who can pay for it (via private schooling and healthcare along with the support of private and cheap domestic labour), while at the same time increasing the burden of non-wage domestic labour for the low earners, and especially women. Apart from the diminishing provision and quality of public services such as schools and healthcare, the care burden for low earners has also increased due to their longer and unpredictable working hours and more precarious working conditions. This is a particularly intriguing development for the era of the knowledge economy where investment in human capital is professed as a top priority for new growth models of the digital era, while these families are unable to adequately care for their own children, who are supposed to be future workers. Such system set-up is unsustainable in the longer run. With each new crisis there is less public and communal space to fall back on for the lower income households who are supposed to underpin the economy by 'freeing up' the professional classes to maintain their productivity in the upper echelons of capitalism.

While those who research the economy of care have been long aware of this growing systemic unsustainability of modern capitalism, the pandemic has brought the importance of reproductive labour and the wider economy of care to attention of the general populace. The growing salience of this vital subject of social reproduction may even shift it to the arena of 'noisy' politics.

In sum, this pandemic has brought about a growing awareness of the interdependency between capitalist production and social reproduction, and improved our ability to see how capitalism undervalues the economy of care, although it is an essential engine that underpins its ability to accumulate. This is not only a question of justice for those who are engaged in social reproduction and the economy of care, but a systemic operational error. Without anything to fall back on during downturns, the ability of the system to secure itself against downturns which are endemic to it is being continually undermined and depreciated. Such instability can also stir a socio-political backlash, the subject of the next section. Whether this backlash will reinvent the distinction between production and reproduction and help us to imagine a more progressive gender /race order for the post-pandemic world remains to be seen.

The Rise of the Intersectional Countermovement

'Now, we transform'

Black Lives Matter (2020)

BLM and other progressive socio-political movements, which are challenging the gendered and racialised nature of labour market dualisation and the depletion of public and communal resources necessary for social reproduction, are not a product of the coronavirus pandemic. They have been around for a while. But the pandemic has increased their visibility, since people who would otherwise not be exposed to racial and gender injustices have had more time to follow the news and social media during the lockdown. Moreover, crises tend to magnify pre-existing needs, whether for health, housing, food, employment, social protection, education and care, so more people are driven towards political contestation by a sense of urgency (as discussed by Donatella della Porta in this volume). Crises stir anger, fear, and hope, and propel human agency into action.

The ongoing public health crisis has also shown us that we are all interdependable, and thus further highlighted the importance of collective action. As Lynch (2020) argues, one can only call upon individual responsibility to protect oneself and others from the virus if they are also able to provide people the tools to protect themselves. This is, however, not possible amid existing levels of socio-economic inequality. These inequalities are in turn further exacerbating the effect of the pandemic on all of us. Lynch (2020) outlines three mechanisms through which this interdependency unfolds: i) social inequality makes it more likely that people who get the virus will spread it as they are not able to effectively self-isolate; ii) social inequality burdens the health systems as more people need medical assistance at the same time; iii) social inequality reduces our ability to keep measures in place for as long as they are necessary.

Reflecting this interdependability across different social groups, the social countermovement is growing in diversity and generating new coalitions across race, gender and generations. BLM gathers a lot of youth – a key group of current labour market outsiders that are worst affected by the pandemic. This feature makes it distinct from the US civil rights movement of the 1960s. Other races have also jumped on board, for example Asians who have been targeted as 'carriers of Covid-19' and who were previously in standoff with black communities

(e. g. during the 1992 LA riots), or whites who have learned more about the movement during the lockdown.

This push for progressive socio-economic transformation is going in the direction of redefining market value for outsiders of the modern capitalism's security-progress nexus. Such revaluation is necessary since in the logic of capitalism, access to security is reserved for those who are perceived as having 'enough' market value to be worthy of protection (see section 1). The social counterforces are highlighting the exploitation that their constituents face as a result of undervaluation of their particular economic and social roles. This is a very different argument from the one that we encounter in requests for empathy towards those who are 'not fit enough to survive competitive forces of the market'. It recognises the double standard of the argument that security is anti-capitalist, as well as the essential economic contribution of the 'underclasses' that keeps capitalism and our societies afloat.

Moreover, since most people have multiple roles in their lives – both reproductive and productive – the Covid-19 induced crisis of the care economy has also increased the general population's concern for communal, public and environmental resources that underpin social reproduction, and generated political dissent around this subject. Existing health inequalities that have been made visible during the pandemic have also stirred anger and renewed our concern for human dignity in modern capitalism.

Della Porta (2015) argues that electoral politics has not made much room for these types of contestations, which is why people take them to the streets. Piven (2008) developed an argument about 'interdependent power' to explain why social countermovements are sometimes able to exercise considerable influence and win significant concessions, despite the odds they face against the more powerful preservers of the status quo (Block 2008: 7). Collective refusal to follow standard institutional routines and disruptive protests becomes possible, despite the threat of arrest and legal sanctions, when there is 'an ideological opening that makes a particular injustice appear to be remediable through political action and when there are significant obstacles to a purely repressive response by the state' (Piven 2008 in Block 2008: 7). This takes place when political and economic elites are deeply divided, for example between reformers and conservatives, and unable to resolve the problems through formal political institutions (Block 2008: 7).

While this ideological opening existed prior to the pandemic, as reflected in social polarisation around political phenomena such as Brexit or Trump, the specific conditions of the pandemic, coupled by police murders of several black men in the US during the lockdown, have augmented existing divisions, and reinforced this interdependent power of the people that Piven (2008) describes. Although we have seen most of the confrontation taking place in the US, Europe has also not yet adequately dealt with its race issues, so we can expect the currently ongoing internationalisation of the BLM movement to continue.

While the push to dismantle the exclusionary nature of the traditional security-progress structure of capitalism is becoming stronger due to the pandemic, the status quo is also naturally riddled with vested interests and power relations that are pushing against this intersectional countermovement. We can easily imagine that, in the interest of survival amid economic pressures, firms could be reducing insider workers' rights, e.g. by keeping them working from home in order to reduce costs of renting premises, and by demanding that they pass on their care responsibilities to their families and communities so that they can work uninterrupted. As the academic year starts, higher education workers in the UK are also worrying about the fact that their professional obligation to teach groups of students in person is making it impossible for them to see their elderly parents for the unforeseeable future without taking on the risk of making them seriously ill. Such examples hint that reductions of privilege in exchange for work-related security might reduce the allure of stable jobs for labour market insiders and provoke a restructuring of the labour markets in a direction that is now difficult to imagine. This could perhaps serve the progressive social countermovement by undermining the status quo. Yet, we should also not underestimate the threat of far right social countermovements which are working towards building an exclusionary and divided post-pandemic world. It therefore remains to be seen whether the progressive wing of dissensus politics will succeed in moving us towards greener pastures of a more just and inclusive post-pandemic world.

In sum, the coronavirus pandemic has made a big dent in the already weakened ideology that the 'competitive society' does not need security and protection. It has allowed us to finally admit that it is very human and responsible to want to protect what one already has, and to admit also that we do it all the time, and especially in times of crises. The pandemic has also raised some uncomfortable yet pertinent questions. Who has access to security? And how can one protect themselves while failing to protect another in an interdependent world where our ability to successfully fight the threat depends on the ability of all of us to 'stick to the rules'? And where this ability does not simply depend on personal choice, but on one's socio-economic status.

Moreover, this pandemic shows us that the notion of security is multidimensional and that these multiple dimensions are not always aligned with one another. What may be good for our health may be bad for our economic situation, and vice versa. How do we align these different dimensions of our human experience and how do we use it to articulate a progressive political agenda that will improve our wellbeing? The message of this essay is that taking gender and race relations that underpin modern capitalism more seriously can offer us the much needed critical visions and possibilities for imagining the socio-political reforms that are necessary to reduce the growing social polarisation that is currently making us all worse off.

References

Agamben, G. (2005) *State of Exception*, Chicago: Chicago University Press.

Avlijaš, S., Hassel, A. & Palier, B. (2020) Growth Strategies and Welfare State Reforms in Europe. In A. Hassel & B. Palier (eds.), *Growth and Welfare in Advanced Capitalist Economies. How have Growth Regimes Evolved,* Oxford; New York: Oxford University Press.

Bhattacharya, T. (2017) Introduction: Mapping Social Reproduction Theory. In T. Bhattacharya (ed.) *Social Reproduction Theory: Remapping Class, Recentering Oppression*, London: Pluto Press.

Block, F. (2008) Polanyi's Double Movement and the Reconstruction of Critical Theory. *Interventions économiques,* 38. Available at: http://journals.openedition.org/interventionseconomiques/274 (Accessed 1 September, 2020).

Blundell, R., Joyce, R., Costas Dias, M. & Xu, X. (2020) Covid-19: The Impacts of the Pandemic on Inequality, Briefing Note, 11 June, Institute for Fiscal Studies. Available at: https://www.ifs.org.uk/publications/14879 (Accessed 30 August, 2020).

Bourquin, P., Delestre, I., Joyce, R., Rasul, I. & Waters, T. (2020) The Effects of Coronavirus on Household Finances and Financial Distress, Briefing Note, 29 June, Institute for Fiscal Studies. Available at: https://www.ifs.org.uk/publications/14908 (Accessed 30 August, 2020).

Clemens, M. & Heinemann, M. (2020) *Distributional Effects of the COVID-19 Lockdown.* Discussion Papers 1874, 21 S., DIW Berlin. Available at: https://www.diw.de/documents/publikationen/73/diw_01.c.791516.de/dp1874.pdf (Accessed 3 September, 2020).

Costa Dias, M., Joyce, R. & Keiller, A.N. (2020) COVID-19 and the Career Prospects of Young People, Briefing Note, 3 July, Institute for Fiscal Studies. Available at: https://www.ifs.org.uk/publications/14914 (Accessed 30 August, 2020).

Della Porta, D. (2015) *Social Movements in Times of Austerity: Bringing Capitalism Back into Protest Analysis*, Cambridge: Polity Press.

Elwell-Sutton, T., Deeny, S. & Stafford, M. (2020) Emerging Findings on the Impact of COVID-19 on Black and Minority Ethnic People, Covid-19 Chart Series, 20 May, The Health Foundation. Available at: https://bit.ly/2Ft5T79 (Accessed 30 July, 2020).

Eurofound (2020) Living, Working and COVID-19. First Findings, April, Available at: https://www.eurofound.europa.eu/publications/report/2020/living-working-and-covid-19-first-findings-april-2020 (Accessed 30 August, 2020).

Fleming, S. & Espinoza, J. (2020) EU Members Clash over State Aid as Richer Countries Inject More Cash, *Financial Times*, 1 May. Available at: https://www.ft.com/content/a68bfd0d-47c7-46ec-ac87-20b8b67ddc32 (Accessed 1 September, 2020).

Fraser, N. (2017) Crisis of Care? On the Social-Reproductive Contradictions of Contemporary Capitalism. In T. Bhattacharya (ed.) *Social Reproduction Theory: Remapping Class, Recentering Oppression.* London: Pluto Press.

Galbraith, J. K. (1998) *The Affluent Society* (5th Revised edition; 1st edition in 1958), London: Penguin Books.

Hall, P. A. & Soskice, D. (2001) *Varieties Of Capitalism: The Institutional Foundations of Comparative Advantage.* Oxford; New York: Oxford University Press, U.S.A.

Hassel, A. & Palier, B. (2020) *Growth and Welfare in Advanced Capitalist Economies. How have Growth Regimes Evolved.* Oxford; New York: Oxford University Press.

Hood, C. & Dixon, R. (2015) *A Government that Worked Better and Cost Less? Evaluating Three Decades of Reform and Change in UK Central Government.* Oxford, New York: Oxford University Press.

ILO (2020) 'ILO Monitor: COVID-19 and the World of Work. 5th Edition: Updated Estimates and Analysis', 30 June, Available at: https://www.ilo.org/global/topics/coronavirus/impacts-and-responses/WCMS_749399/lang-en/index.htm (Accessed 15 July, 2020).

Innes, A. (2018) First-Best-World Economic Theory and the Second-Best-World of Public Sector Outsourcing: The Reinvention of the Soviet Kombinat by Other Means *LEQS Discussion Paper 134,* London School of Economics. Available at: https://www.lse.ac.uk/european-institute/Assets/Documents/LEQS-Discussion-Papers/LEQSPaper134.pdf (Accessed 30 June, 2020).

Iversen, T. (2008) Capitalism and Democracy. In: B.R. Weingast, and D. A. Wittman (eds.) *The Oxford Handbook of Political Economy,* 601–623. Oxford University Press, U.S.A.

Johnson, P. (2020) We May Be in This Together, but That Doesn't Mean We Are in This Equally, *The Times,* 27 April. Available at: https://www.thetimes.co.uk/article/we-may-be-in-this-together-but-that-doesnt-mean-we-are-in-this-equally-txtn82tkr (Accessed 24 July, 2020).

Kazepov, Y. & Ranci, C. (2017) Is Every Country Fit for Social Investment? Italy as an Adverse Case. *Journal of European Social Policy* 27(1): 90–104.

Korpi, W. (1983) *The Democratic Class Struggle,* London: Routledge and Kegan Paul.

Lynch, J. (2020) How Does Social Inequality Affect Government's Ability to Deal with Covid-19?, Social Science Research Council, June 18. Available at: https://items.ssrc.org/covid-19-and-the-social-sciences/democracy-and-pandemics/how-does-social-inequality-affect-governments-ability-to-deal-with-covid-19/ (Accessed 20 July, 2020).

Mares, I. (2003) *The Politics of Social Risk: Business and Welfare State Development,* Cambridge: Cambridge University Press.

Piven, F. F. (2008) *Challenging Authority: How Ordinary People Change America,* Maryland: Rowman & Littlefield.

Schmidt, V. A. & Thatcher, M. (2013) *Resilient Liberalism in Europe's Political Economy,* Cambridge: Cambridge University Press.

Schwander, H. (2019) Labor Market Dualization and Insider–Outsider Divides: Why This New Conflict Matters. *Political Studies Review* 17(1): 14–29.

Swenson, P.A. (2002) *Employers against Markets,* Cambridge: Cambridge University Press.

Veblen, T. (1932) *The Theory of Business Enterprise,* New York: Scribner.

Žižek, S. (2020) *Pandemic! Covid-19 Shakes the World,* Cambridge: Polity.

Albena Azmanova
Battlegrounds of Justice: The Pandemic and What Really Grieves the 99%

Two battlegrounds of justice had taken shape in the decade preceding the Covid-19 pandemic that beset the world in the spring of 2020. On the one hand, progressive forces were mobilising under the banner of fighting inequality. 'Tax the rich' had become the rallying cry of the Left, after the *Occupy* movement launched the slogan 'We are the 99 per cent' in the aftermath of the 2008 financial meltdown and academics, pundits and politicians rushed to translate that nebulous grievance into an indignation with unprecedented economic inequality. '[A] dangerous and growing inequality and lack of upward mobility ... is the defining challenge of our time', announced former US President Barack Obama in 2013. Upon receiving the Nobel Prize that same year, economist Robert Shiller declared that 'rising inequality in the United States and elsewhere in the world' is the most important problem faced by society. Most recently, the celebrated economist Thomas Piketty has urged in his panoramic investigation of the history of inequality that unless we radically reduce inequality, xenophobic populism will overtake liberal democracies and demolish them (Piketty 2019). In the run-up to the May 2019 elections for the European Parliament, the Party of European Socialists adopted eight resolutions for equal society as a basis of its electoral platform (PES 2018). Conferences, research centres, and even academic degrees in Inequality Studies have mushroomed over the past decade.[1]

On the other hand, long-standing ecological concerns acquired a novel urgency as youth protests across the globe, inspired by the Swedish high-school student and environmental activist Greta Thunberg, demanded that climate change mitigation become a top policy priority. These efforts culminated in (so far non-binding) policy proposals and commitments such as the European Green Deal policy strategy (Com. 2019) and the Green New Deal, a draft resolution of the U.S. Congress (H.Res.2019).[2]

---

1 In the U.S., the name of the 'Washington Center for Equitable Growth', established in 2013, gives a flavor of the new sensitivities.
2 In March 20202, the European Commission (the EU executive arm with a right of legislative initiative) introduced a proposal for a legally binding regulation – Climate Law (EC Com. 2020).

https://doi.org/10.1515/9783110713350-015

Political Frenemies: Social and Environmental Justice

Although environmental protection and social justice are both valiant creeds of progressive politics, they have stood in long-lasting conflict due to their contrasting relationship to economic growth. Fighting economic inequality via wealth redistribution counts on economic growth to generate the necessary material resources. The insistence on growth is promulgated by a powerful capital-labour alliance hostile to the ecological agenda, as the latter sees growth and consumption as inimical to environmental welfare. This long-standing tacit hostility between the agendas of social and environmental justice was last brought into an explicit conflict when the French government's planned imposition of 'green tax' on fuel in the autumn of 2018 triggered the Yellow Vest protest – a massive civil insurgency that lasted for 45 consecutive weeks. As the grassroots movement voiced grievances against the high cost of living, demanded the introduction of a solidarity tax on wealth and a minimum-wage increase, it evolved into a flagship civil protest for social justice.

While initially the Covid pandemic was expected to have the levelling effect of wars, as the pathogen infects human beings indiscriminately of social status and the containment measures disrupted the economic engines of whole national economies, the public health crisis in fact laid bare existing inequalities and deepened them further. Both in terms of health risks and economic burdens, minority and low-income populations are disproportionally bearing the costs of the pandemic (Blundell et al. 2020; Nassif-Pires et al. 2020).[3] Moreover, as the prolonged lockdown is damaging the chances of the young for entering the labour market, a worsening generational wealth divide risks ushering in a new 'Age of Disorder' (DB 2020). The multiple trajectories along which the pandemic has exacerbated economic inequalities has revived with new rigor the 'class struggle' discourse on the Left, with 'the rich' designated as a class enemy.

The focus on economic inequality as a path of radical politics, however, is fallacious on four grounds – conceptually, structurally, tactically and strategically.

Conceptually, as a matter of ideological framing of grievances of injustice, the departure from neoliberal convention is only apparent, not real. Thinking

---

[3] Racial disparities came into sharper relief as communities of color have been hit hardest by the pandemic in the U.S.: members of the Black, native American and the Hispanic/Latinx communities are, respectively, 3.8, 3.2, and 2.5 times more likely to die from Covid-19 than Whites (Daube 2020).

in terms of inequality engages a logic of comparison between individuals (and the groups they form) and presents the idea of social justice in individualistic terms – as a matter of individual circumstances, of private wealth. Therefore, even as we engage in the worthy struggle against inequality and exclusion, we in fact remain captive of the neoliberal imaginary, which views society as composed by individuals in charge of their lives. This eliminates the notion of collective wellbeing that has always been fundamental for Socialism as it espoused a *solidaristic* economy without emphasizing equality and prosperity. Thus, Marx's formula of distributive justice under communism mandates not equal distribution of existing resources, but sees the economic production of the material conditions of life as a process that follows the logic 'from each according to their ability, to each according to their needs' (Marx 1875:27). A privately-wealthy society, even if not too unequal, can still be publicly poor if essential public services are missing or deficient of funds.

Moreover, constraining the social justice agenda to issues of inequality and exclusion inadvertently entraps us in what I have named 'the paradox of emancipation": we unwittingly validate the social system within which equality and exclusion are being sought, as the very claim for inclusion renders the overall system more valuable (Azmanova 2020a: 12, 129, 139). This de-radicalises struggles against social injustice into attempts to humanise the existing socio-economic system. Defined as a fight against inequality, social policy is thus reduced to 'the safety net' – a mere adjunct to monetary and fiscal policies aimed at sustained economic growth. This is the logic of the post-war 'neo-classical synthesis' in economics, which conceded a managing role to 'Keynesian' policy while reserving social and economic organisation to the so-called 'free market'. According to that logic, a bit of redistribution through progressive taxes, unemployment insurance and the minimum wage is all right, but it must be kept small and not interfere much with the private sector.[4]

Second, impediments of a structural nature stand in the way of reviving the logic of the class struggle fuelled by indignation with inequalities. For a grievance to emanate a social conflict, and then generate a political contention, that grievance needs to be rooted in a structural peculiarity of the social order – in an identifiable institution that enables and structures the unequal distribution of life-chances.[5] At the inception of Socialism as an ideological platform of

---

4 I am grateful to James Galbraith for drawing my attention to the similarity, in this regard, between the post-WWII 'welfare capitalism' and the neoliberal format of the late 20th century.
5 I have suggested that, to achieve their emancipatory ambitions, ideological critique, social criticism and political mobilisation should target all three trajectories of social injustice: (1) relational – regarding the unequal distribution of power (2) structural – regarding the social insti-

the Left in the late 18th century, the institution of the private ownership of the means of production had a decisive structuring effect on the distribution of social status and the articulation of political conflict along the capital-labour divide. In the current context, the proliferation of forms of ownership and professional tenure have reduced the relevance of property ownership on social stratification and political conflict. The fact alone that workers' retirement pensions are invested in the stock exchange makes workers nominally owners of the corporations in which their life-savings are invested, and thus personally reliant on the welfare of these companies. This complicity will only deepen should workers be systematically represented on their companies' boards – an idea that has become fashionable in (self-identified as radical) Left intellectual circles (e. g. in the writing of French economist Thomas Piketty and the policy proposals of US Senator Elizabeth Warren). The fault-lines of conflict currently cut across the capital-labour divide, as the effect of exposure to the global economy largely has to do with type of economic activity and size of the economic actor rather than the form of property ownership. Thus, both capital and labour in high-tech industries are reaping the benefits of the economy of scale, while the old industrial sector, as well as small businesses, are suffering from increased competitive pressures due to exposure to the global market. In other words, there is no straightforward correlation between forms of ownership and impoverishment. Unsurprisingly, the Yellow Vests protest united workers and owners of small businesses in a broad insurgency against impoverishment that cut across the left-right cleavage and across the capital-labour divide. To the extent that there is no distinct structural driver in the articulation of social antagonisms (akin to the role of private ownership of the means of production) the discontent with inequality and poverty are unlikely to foster a significant, radical challenge to the social-economic order and the political rule in liberal democracies in the style of the 'class struggle' of the 19th century.

The focus on inequality is inopportune for tactical reasons, too – it fails to mobilise the social forces that are required to enact radical change. Although economic inequality had become celebrity politics on the Left with authoritative voices proclaiming it to be the gravest social injustice of our times, with the exception of the Yellow Vests protests in France, this had not translated into significant civil insurgencies against inequality and impoverishment. Moral outrage against inequality has proven to be a political loser. Many people, socialised

---

tutions that structure that unequal distribution, and (3) systemic – regarding the constitutive dynamic of the social system – e. g. the competitive pursuit of profit, in the case of capitalism (Azmanova 2020a, 2020c; 2018).

within capitalist democracies, admire the rich; a few expect to get rich themselves, and most of the rest just ignore them. In real-existing socialist societies, excessive *equality*, was just as much of a problem; people hated the drab sameness of their lives. These sentiments remain pervasive. Surveys in the U.S. and Europe have persistently revealed that most people do not care about inequality, even as the evidence about the detrimental effects of inequality are well established and advertised (NPR et al. 2020, Glazer 2005, Lahusen 2020)[6]. In the context of the pandemic, as businesses go bankrupt, livelihoods are being lost and economies are shrinking, a powerful capital-labour alliance is taking shape and anxiously pushing for the return to the pre-pandemic formula of growth, this time with a bigger role given to public authority in the management of the economy – in the manner of post-war welfare capitalism.

Here I come to the strategic reasons against endorsing the anti-inequality platform as a framework of progressive politics. As we noted, a consensus is rapidly emerging on the conviction that we need to return to the growth-and-redistribution formula that provided the inclusive prosperity of the four post-war decades. This, however, would be a mistake. The growth-and-redistribution policy mantra that is gaining popularity in the course of coping with the economic fallout of the pandemic is undercutting the progress made towards ecological sustainability. It is worth recalling that the post-WWII egalitarian affluence was achieved through the (pseudo-)Keynesian formula of stimulating demand to grow the pie and then distribute it. But the foundation of that success – increased production and consumption – eventually wrecked the environment. Four decades of 'inclusive prosperity' also nurtured a shared perception of social justice as an entitlement to being middle-class and increasingly affluent, which is now reflected even in programmatic commitments of the radical left.[7] Such inflated expectations regarding the economic parameters of societal wellbeing not only deviate from the original Socialist vision, but also now stand in the way of plausibly reconciling the agenda of social justice with that of environmental justice.

For the above four sets of reasons, pursuing social justice through policies of growth-and-redistribution would be a mistake – it would undermine ecological justice without altering significantly the socio-economic infrastructure of neoliberal capitalism. On the battleground of fighting inequality through redistribution, even if progressive forces are likely to win the battle against poverty, that

---

6 Europeans are highly sensitive to unequal living conditions between European countries, but not as concerned about inequality within their countries (Lahusen 2020).

7 The Green New Deal resolution, authored by the radical left wing of the U.S. Democratic Party, vouches to 'provide unprecedented levels of prosperity' (H.Res. 109).

victory will come at the price of abandoning hopes for a radical social transformation.

The Epidemic of Precarity

The Coronavirus pandemic, however, is opening yet another battleground of justice – the fight against massive precarity. A paradigmatic shift in the diagnosis of the underlying social malaise is taking place as the societies that have been worst affected by the pandemic – the affluent 'West' – have confronted the following paradox. At the time the epidemic erupted, these societies had reached unprecedented levels of affluence and scientific sophistication. The ability to edit DNA, to detect organic compounds from the moons of Saturn and even detect gravitational waves – minute ripples through the fabric of spacetime – all attest to that fact. And yet, our governments struggled to ensure the basic protective and medical equipment that doctors and nurses needed in order to tend to the sick or to put in place in a systematic way the test-and-trace strategies that the World Health Organization recommends. This paradox has brought to light an overlooked feature of capitalist democracies: their overarching social fragility. This is not the essential frailty we all have as living human beings, i.e. our mortality, but rather a social condition marked by the incapacity of society to safeguard and advance its collective wellbeing.

The economist John Kenneth Galbraith had sounded the alarm for this innate tendency in democratic capitalism (as a socio-political system) already in his monograph *The Affluent Society*, published in 1958, as he traced the co-emergence of 'private opulence and public squalor' (Galbraith, 1998: 191). Importantly, the social condition of precarity has been politically crafted; it is a result of ideas, policies and specific decisions. It is above all rooted in the systemic dynamic of capitalism – the competitive pursuit of profit, which imbues society with risk as the counterpart of profit-generating opportunities. In the late twentieth century, with the adoption of the neoliberal modality of capitalism, social precarity was sharply exacerbated.[8] In the 1980s, governments across the left-

---

8 I deploy a social ontology that views capitalism as a socio-economic order which can be combined with a variety of political regimes (from democracy to autocracy) in forming a distinct socio-political system – a system of social relations, themselves structured through key institutions (such as democratic representation, private property, and the free labour contract). While 'democratic capitalism' has been the predominant socio-political system in the West since the bourgeois revolutions of the 18th century, this system has evolved through four consecutive modalities of capitalism: the 19th century 'liberal' form, the post-WWII 'welfare capitalism', the neo-

right ideological spectrum committed to economic globalisation and fashioned the globally integrated economy on the model of free market capitalism. This intensified competitive pressures, as profit-making in the new context was enhanced through reduced regulation of product- and labour-markets, and technological and financial innovation provided access to countries with cheap supplies of labour. Four decades of 'structural adjustment' and 'austerity policy' – reducing job security and slashing public spending on essential services, including health care – dramatically diminished the governing capacity in democracies and overall weakened societies. These policies were launched in the late twentieth century, allegedly for the sake of ensuring national competitiveness in the global market. After the financial meltdown of 2008, these same structural adjustment policies were further deepened for the sake of financial stabilisation.

Installing the profit motive as dominant logic of social integration has generated precarity along two trajectories – weakening of the commons and destabilisation of personal livelihoods. On the one hand, disinvestment in public services (such as education, research and healthcare) and the imposition of a logic of economic benefit in their running meant that non-profit-generating activities would be marginalised. Thus, the threat, and even the likelihood, of an epidemic was well-known. The European Commission proposed in 2017 that vaccines for pathogens like coronavirus be fast-tracked to allow them to be developed before an outbreak. This was to take place within the Innovative Medicines Initiative – a public-private partnership between the European Union and the European Federation of Pharmaceutical Industries and Associations, with the function of funding health research and innovation. The drug companies rejected the idea as being unprofitable and the project was dropped (Boffrey 2020). While one can expect an economic actor to be driven by considerations of profit, the European Commission, as the executive arm of the European Union, is a public authority with the duty to safeguard public welfare. As it deployed a logic of economic efficiency, it effectively failed to serve the public interest. This instance is illustrative of a pervading tendency, exacerbated under neoliberal capitalism, for *raison d'économie* to not only overtake the old *raison d'état*, putting it to its service, but to replace it altogether (Azmanova 2020a:124).

On the other hand, precarity has been generated on a massive scale by making individual livelihoods insecure – as employment security has all but disappeared, even for the previous labour-market insiders (well educated, well-remunerated, older, typically male employees) under policy reforms of job flexibility

---

liberal capitalism of the late 2oth century, and the 'precarity capitalism' of the early 21st century (Azmanova 2020a).

which center-left and center-right governments have been enacting since the 1980s.

Contemporary capitalism has thus created not just a precarious class what the economist Guy Standing has called 'the precariat', akin to the 'proletariat' (Standing 2016). It has created a precarious multitude, which lives in 'a condition of existence without predictability or security, affecting material or psychological welfare' – as the Collins dictionary defined this neologism when it introduced it in 2016. The social pathology of precarity (economic and social instability) is not a matter of impoverishment; it afflicts rich and poor, men and women, the well-educated workers and the low-skilled ones, irrespectively of employment status – as the very anticipation of a job loss can make us precarious. Precarity is the real affliction of the 99 per cent (Azmanova 2020a).

Social precarity is severely stratified – the insecurity that the poor suffer is a much greater injustice than the financial insecurity of the affluent (whose investments are exposed to the vagaries of global financial markets) but also than the maddening work-related stress of the professional classes trapped in the 'always on economy' (Fleming 2019). On the battlefields of justice in affluent capitalist democracies, there is a 'competition of precarities', as the Bulgarian scholar Milena Katsarska (2020) has put it. The unequal distribution of precarity is unjust and we need to fight it, but the war on inequality should not distract us from the root cause of injustice: the politically engineered social precarity that is the general pathology afflicting our societies.

While the pandemic exacerbated existing inequalities and generated novel ones, it also brought into focus the general fragility of affluent societies: the generalised, all-embracing precarity. We all suffer because the public healthcare system is brittle – because it is underfunded and subjected to pressures of economic efficiency. With this, the pandemic is opening a critical perspective on the inequality debate, a perspective that might enable the radicalisation of struggles for social justice. It does so by inviting us to question *in what sense* inequality is a problem. Indeed, under what circumstances does inequality become a social problem, an instance of social injustice?

This can happen in two ways. The first is when wealth inequality translates into social privilege – into power that is self-serving, exclusive, and predatory, as with the undue influence of money in politics that is ubiquitous in the United States. In such a case we need to undo the mechanisms that transform economic affluence into social privilege (e.g. campaign financing, lobbying). We need to build up countervailing powers: mass organisations, truly democratic political parties, prosecutions and prison for financial fraud.

The second way inequality can become a social injustice is when our livelihoods are so precarious that private wealth becomes the only reliable source of safety. This is, indeed, our current predicament – which the pandemic has brought sharply to light.

The combination of automation, globalisation, cuts in public investment and services, and the failure of social insurance to keep pace with needs in health care, education, public transport and access to utilities and amenities has generated massive economic instability for ordinary citizens. The pandemic was enabled by this massive *social* precarity: not our shared frailty as human beings vulnerable to malicious pathogens, but a state of politically crafted social insecurity that has been in the making for some time. It is above all the demolition of the infrastructure of public service provision – for the sake of pursuing competitiveness in the global market – that is the main reason our societies turned out to be so ill-equipped to fight the contamination by a pathogen which was neither completely unfamiliar, nor terribly deadly. That is why a public health emergency transformed into an economic fiasco and a social crisis comparable to a war-time economic devastation. Indeed, in the assessment of both the European Central Bank and the U.S. Federal Reserve, this is an 'unprecedented crisis' in Western democracies' post-war history (Smialek and Rappeport 2020; ECB 2020). According to the IMF, this is the worst economic crisis since the Great Depression of the 1930s (BBC 2020).

In an effort to mitigate the economic fallout of the pandemic, even conservative-led governments issued substantial payments to shore up (some) workers' depleted incomes. Much as this is a welcome undertaking, fighting inequality cannot be a substitute for a robust public investment in healthcare. Precarity indeed increases the importance of personal wealth (which explains the increased attentions to inequalities), because with the weakening of the commons, one is left to rely on personal resources to secure such essential goods as education and healthcare. But personal wealth (even if it is distributed equally) is a poor substitute for structural stability. No matter how rich we individually are, no one can ensure for themselves a capacious public healthcare service because that needs enormous investment in research, education, culture (for the sake of prevention), and medical service – which is only achievable through substantial and systematic public investment.

This diagnosis of the genesis of the pandemic within processes that have been at work for decades alters the critique of social injustice. It allows us to shift attention from forms of relational injustice (inequality and inclusion) and their structural drivers (e. g. core institutions regulating employment and property relations) to the larger systemic dynamics – that is, constitutive dynamics of the socio-political system. Such a shift will allow us to escape the paradox of emancipation – the risk that we inadvertently glorify and solidify the system within which we seek inclusion and equality.

The systemic sources of the precarisation of our societies are of two related orders – pertaining to political economy and political rule. As a socio-political system (i. e. a system of institutionally structured social relations) democratic capitalism relies on two constitutive dynamics. On the level of the political economy, the competitive pursuit of profit (purportedly) ensures the most efficient generation of material prosperity. On the level of state-society relations, two principles are at play. First, individuals are held responsible for a thriving society. This rule is enacted through the mechanisms of liberal constitutionalism (e. g. individual and collective rights and freedoms, rule of law norms) and democratic sovereignty (e. g. collective self-determination through universal electoral franchise). Second: governments are held responsible for a thriving business environment.

Neoliberalism has sharpened the unadulterated application of these ground-rules that have marked the existence of democratic capitalism since it became the prevalent socio-economic system in the 19th century European societies and their colonial off-shoots. The Covid-19 pandemic has both challenged and sublimated these constitutive dynamics of democratic capitalism. It exposed the neglect of public services (including healthcare) and the autocratic style of rule as mutually necessitating cornerstones of the state-society relation in mature capitalist democracies. A corollary to the precarisation of society which the pursuit of profit engenders is the increased autocratic style of the state's response – because public authority has gradually absolved itself of all social responsibility save for the operation of the economy. Public authority, which has entirely redefined its mandate in terms of serving the economy, copes with the resulting massive precarity through law-and-order tools: social integration is enforced, not nurtured (ergo, the growing importance of the police).

By altering the parameters of our everyday existence, the Covid pandemic triggered a crisis within this socio-political model, fostering its transmutation. First, the narrative that economic activity was the preeminent consideration and undisputed competency of the government suddenly vanished. To much dismay, ruling elites shut down large sectors of the economy for a prolonged period, deliberately triggering a profound economic crisis. Second, the poor management of the public health emergency and the economic meltdown, with ad-hoc, poorly justified, contradictory measures, disclosed that political elites have long abandoned the precepts of accountable rule in the public interest. The facile autocratic measures they adopted (from ordering the lock-down to lifting it for the sake of rebooting the economy) were a way to simulate leadership without engaging in long-term investment for building up public healthcare capacity. Public authority responded to the massive social precarisation through disciplining rather than serving society. To social disintegration, the state responded with security measures – from criminalisation of poverty, to extending the police's domain of operation, to curbing migration and the deployment of federal troops against protesters. Thus, the pandemic fully exposed the direct link between a political economy that generates precarity and an autocratic style of rule.

The remarkable phenomenon of street protests amidst the pandemic – from the George Floyd uprisings in the United States to the anti-lockdown insurgencies across Europe – are indicative of a significant change in the nature of social protest.[9] What these public protests share, beyond obvious differences in the claims they voice to suffered injustice, is a shared quality of the *nature* of that grievance. They could be seen as putting to question the socio-political system as a whole – a system that generates economic precarity and autocratic politics, rather than challenging only the unfair distribution of power within that system, as has been the habit of progressive politics within liberal democracies in the early 21st century. In this way, these insurgencies escape 'the paradox of emancipation'. They could be seen, therefore, as something yet more radical than the calls for equality and inclusion (within the existing system). They can be interpreted, instead, as *systemic disruptions:* a rejection of the political economy, institutional logistics and social dispositions that actuate democratic capitalism as a social and political system. Rather than engaging the logic of the class struggle, these insurgencies are mobilising a great variety of social forces, a multitude of strange bed-fellows, indeed, against the nefarious workings of a socio-political system that generates simultaneously social precarity and political oppression.[10]

Conclusion: from inflammation to insurrection

The 1968 revolts challenged the ethos, institutional foundations and political economy of democratic capitalism – this was the last outburst of political radicalism in Western liberal democracies. Subsequent struggles for justice constrained their demands to pleas for redistribution, recognition, and representation *within* the existing socio-political order – that is, they demanded to equalise relations within the existing system. The economic meltdown of 2008 did not alter the nature of social protest; society reacted to the severe economic

---

9 For a more extensive discussion of the phenomenon of public protest during the pandemic, see Azmanova 2020b.
10 The anti-lockdown protests in the month of August in Germany brought together far-right extremists with people waving peace and rainbow flags, and Hare Krishnas (Sauerbrey 2020).

and social crisis with strange equanimity. The Covid-19 pandemic seems to be a catalyst of novel radicalism – directed at the nature of power, rather than merely at its distribution.

To understand what a significant achievement such a shift in the nature of social protest constitutes, we need to remember that economic insecurity, the destabilisation of livelihoods, tends to foster conservative instincts. Insecurity nurtures an aversion to change – hence, the shift of the vote to the right amidst the economic recession of 2008–2018, disappointing the Left's expectations that the crisis would radicalise voters into an anti-capitalist upheaval. Experiences and perceptions of insecurity had also been fuelling pervasive animosities, bringing our societies to a state of inflammation – much before the eruption of the public health crisis. Regrettably, that predicament was mis-diagnosed and mis-labelled as 'inequality', sending the radical imagination in the wrong direction.

As the pandemic showed precarity to be the real grievance of the 99 per cent, this brings a novel possibility for radical progressive change. It creates the chance to replace the outdated and pernicious growth-and-redistribution idea of social justice with efforts to fight economic insecurity. This will make the social justice agenda compatible with environmental justice – the only way to secure broad societal support for the Green New Deal we so urgently need. By appeasing the toxic anxieties that have been besetting our societies, the alleviation of precarity, in turn, is likely to foster the solidaristic ethos that is needed for effective redistributive policies. Fighting inequality would not eradicate precarity, but fighting precarity might even eradicate inequality in the most radical way – by making inequality politically and socially irrelevant. When our livelihoods and our lives are secured, the fact that others have more and some far too much would be simply beside the point.

References

Azmanova, A. 2020a *Capitalism on Edge. How Fighting Precarity Can Achieve Radical Change Without Crisis or Utopia,* New York: Columbia University Press.

Azmanova, A. 2020b Viral Insurgencies: Can Capitalism Survive Covid?, *Theory and Event,* forthcoming.

Azmanova, A. 2020c Anti-Capital for the XXIst Century (on the metacrisis of capitalism and the prospects for radical politics), *Philosophy & Social Criticism* 46/5: 601–612.

Azmanova, A. 2018 Relational, structural and systemic forms of power: the 'right to justification' confronting three types of domination, *Journal of Political Power* 11/1: 68–78.

BBC 2020 Coronavirus: Worst Economic Crisis since 1930s Depression, IMF Says (9 April): https://www.bbc.com/news/business-52236936

Blundell, R. Joyce, R., Costa Dias, M. and Xu. X., 2020 Covid-19: The Impacts of the Pandemic on Inequality. Institute for Fiscal Studies, U.K. Economic and Social Research Council. 11 Jun. https://www.ifs.org.uk/publications/14879

Boffrey, Daniel. 2020 Exclusive: Big Pharma rejected EU plan to Fast-track Vaccines in 2017. The Guardian, May 25. https://www.theguardian.com/world/2020/may/25/exclusive-big-pharma-rejected-eu-plan-to-fast-track-vaccines-in-2017

Daube 2020 An Epidemic of Inequality. University of California San Francisco Magazine, Vo.9/1: https://www.ucsf.edu/magazine/covid-inequality

DB 2020 https://finance.yahoo.com/news/so-many-young-adults-living-with-parents-will-have-serious-consequences-for-financial-markets-deutsche-bank-203916555.html

ECB. 2020 Committee on Economic and Monetary Affairs Monetary Dialogue with Christine Lagarde, President of the European Central Bank. Brussels, June 8: https://www.ecb.euro pa.eu/press/key/date/2020/html/ecb.sp200608_transcript~43566d31cf.en.pdf

EC Com 2019 The European Green Deal. Communication from the Commission to the European Parliament, the European Council, the Council, the European Economic and Social Committee and the Committee of the Regions. Brussels, 11.12.2019: https://ec.eu ropa.eu/info/sites/info/files/european-green-deal-communication_en.pdf

EC Com 2020 Regulation of the European Parliament and of the Council establishing the framework for achieving climate neutrality and amending Regulation (EU) 2018/1999 (European Climate Law). Brussels, 4.3.2020

Fleming, P. 2017 *The Death of Homo Economicus: Work, Debt, and the Myth of Endless Accumulation*, London: Pluto Press.

H.Res 109 2019 resolution Recognizing the duty of the Federal Government to create a Green New Deal. Introduced in the U.S. House of Representatives on 7 February 2019. Washington, D.C.: U.S. Congress. https://www.congress.gov/bill/116th-congress/house-resolution/109/text

Galbraith, J. K. 1998 [1958]. *The Affluent Society*, Houghton Mifflin Harcourt.

Glazer, N. 2005 Why Americans Don't Care about Income Inequality, *Irish Journal of Sociology* 14/1:5 – 12.

Katsarska, M. 2020 A response to Albena Azmanova. A private email correspondence with Albena Azmanova Suman Gupta, and Frederic Vandenberghe, 19 July 2020.

Lahusen, C. 2020 *The Political Attitudes of Divided European Citizens: Public Opinion and Social Inequalities in Comparative and Relational Perspective*, Routledge.

Marx, K. 1875 *Critique of the Gotha Program*, Worldside Press. 2008.

NPR et al. 2020 "Life Experiences and Income Inequality in the United States", Robert Wood Johnson Foundation, National Public Radio and the Harvard School of Public Health, January 9: (ttps://www.rwjf.org/en/library/articles-and-news/2019/12/survey-shows-starkly-differen-t-life-experience-for-lower-and-middle-income-adults.html

Nassif-Pires, L, de Lima Xavier, L., Masterson, P., Nikiforos, M., and Rios-Avila, F. 2020 "Pandemic of Inequality," Levy Economics Institute of Bard College, Public Policy Brief N.149. New York. http://www.levyinstitute.org/publications/pandemic-of-inequality

Obama, B. 2013 "Remarks by the President on Economic Mobility", Washington, DC. The White House, Office of the Press Secretary, 4 Dec.: https://obamawhitehouse.archives.gov/the-press-office/2013/12/04/remarks-president-economic-mobility

PES 2018 "Equal Societies", Resolutions adopted at the Annual Congress of the Party of European Socialists. Lisbon, 7 – 8 December 2018: https://www.pes.eu/export/sites/default/.galleries/Documents-gallery/Resolutions_PES_Congress_2018.pdf_2063069299.pdf

Piketty, T. 2019 *Capital et idéologie*. Paris: SEUIL:

Sauerbrey, A. 2020 "Meet Germany's Bizarre Anti-Lockdown Protesters", New York Times, 31 Aug:
https://www.nytimes.com/2020/08/31/opinion/germany-covid-lockdown-protests.html

Shiller, R. 2013 Interview with the Associated Press, October 15, 2013. http://www.telegram.com/article/20131015/NEWS/310149727.

Smialek, J. and Rappeport, A. 2020 " Fed Leaves Rates Unchanged and Projects Years of High Unemployment," *The New York Times*, June 10: https://www.nytimes.com/2020/06/10/business/economy/federal-reserve-rates-unemployment.html

Standing, G. 2016 *The Precariat: The New Dangerous Class*, London: Bloomsbury Publishing.

Notes on Contributors

Sonja Avlijaš is a political economist and Marie Sklodowska-Curie research fellow at the Faculty of Economics, Belgrade University. She is also the 2020 Wayne Vuchinich Fellow at Stanford University, California and associate researcher at the Laboratory for Interdisciplinary Evaluation of Public Policies (LIEPP) at Sciences Po, where she was previously a post-doctoral fellow. Sonja holds a PhD from the London School of Economics and Political Science (LSE).

Albena Azmanova is Associate Professor of Political and Social Thought at the University of Kent's Brussels School of International Studies. Her research ranges from critical social theory to democratic transitions, protest politics, and critique of contemporary capitalism. She is author of *The Scandal of Reason: A Critical Theory of Political Judgment* (2012) and *Capitalism on Edge: Radical Change without Crisis or Utopia* (2020) among numerous other publications.

Daniel Chernilo is a Professor of Sociology in the School of Government at Universidad Adolfo Ibáñez in Santiago, Chile, where he is Director of an interdisciplinary doctoral programme in Political Processes and Institutions. Previously, he was a Professor of Social and Political Thought at Loughborough University in the UK, where he remains a visiting professor. His books include *A Social Theory of the Nation-State* (Routledge, 2007), *The Natural Law Foundations of Modern Social Theory* (Cambridge University Press, 2013) and *Debating Humanity. Towards a Philosophical Sociology* (Cambridge University Press, 2017). He is currently writing on questions of secularization, globalization and antisemitism.

Gerard Delanty is Professor of Sociology and Social & Political Thought at the University of Sussex, Brighton, UK. He worked as fellow and visiting professor at York University, Toronto; Doshisha University, Kyoto; Deakin University, Melbourne; Hamburg University; the Federal University of Brasilia; and the University of Barcelona. His most recent publication is *Critical Theory and Social Transformation* (London: Routledge, 2020). Other publications include: *The Cosmopolitan Imagination* (Cambridge University Press, 2009), *The European Heritage: A Critical Re-Interpretation* (Routledge 2018). He has edited many volumes, including the *Routledge International Handbook of Cosmopolitan Studies*, 2nd edition 2019) and, with Stephen P. Turner, the *Routledge Handbook of Contemporary Social and Political Theory* (2011). He is also the Chief Editor of the *European Journal of Social Theory*.

Donatella della Porta is Dean of the Faculty of Political and Social Sciences, Scuola Normale Superiore, Florence, Italy. She is known for her research in the areas of social movements, corruption, political violence, police and policies of public order. Her publications include *Social Movements in Times of Crisis* (Polity Press 2015) and *How Social Movements can Save Democracy* (Polity 2020).

Eva Horn is Professor of Modern German Literature at the Department of German at the University of Vienna. Her areas of research include literature and political theory, disaster imagination in modern literature and film, cultural conceptions of climate, and the Anthropocene. She is the author of *The Secret War. Treason, Espionage, and Modern Fiction* (Northwestern University Press, 2013), *The Future as Catastrophe* (Columbia University Press, 2018), and recently, together with Hannes Bergthaller: *The Anthropocene – Key Issues for the Humanities* (Routledge, 2020).

Daniel Innerarity is a professor of political and social philosophy, „Ikerbasque" researcher at the University of the Basque Country and part-time professor at the European University Institute of Florence (School of Transnational Governance). Former fellow of the Alexander von Humboldt Foundation at the University of Munich, visiting professor at the University of Paris 1-Sorbonne, visiting fellow at the London School of Economics and visiting professor at Georgetown University. His latest books in English are: *Ethics of hospitality,* (Routledge, 2017), *The Democracy in Europe,* (Palgrave-Macmillan, 2018) and *Politics in the Times of Indignation* (Rowmann & Littlefield, 2018).

Helga Nowotny is Professor emerita of Science and Technology Studies, ETH Zurich and former President of the European Research Council. She has received numerous awards such as the rarely awarded Gold Medal of the Academia Europaea, the Leibniz-Medaille of the Berlin-Brandenburgische Akademie der Wissenschaften and the British Academy President's Medal. Helga Nowotny is the recipient of many honorary doctorates, among them from the Weizmann Institute of Science in Israel. Her latest publications include *The Cunning of Uncertainty* (2015) and *An Orderly Mess* (2017), *In AI We Trust. Power, Illusion and Control of Predictive Algorithms* (2021).

Claus Offe is Emeritus Professor of Political Sociology at the Hertie School of Governance, Berlin. He has authored numerous works in social theory and political sociology. He has held chairs for Political Science and Political Sociology at the Universities of Bielefeld (1975 – 1989) and Bremen (1989 – 1995), as well as at the Humboldt-Universität in Berlin (1995 – 2005). He worked as fellow and visiting professor at, among others, the Institutes for Advanced Study at Stanford and Princeton, the Australian National University, Harvard University, the University of California, Berkeley and The New School in New York.

Bryan S. Turner is an emeritus professor of sociology at the Graduate Center CUNY, an honorary professor at Potsdam University, and professor of sociology at the Australian Catholic University (Sydney). He won the Max Planck Award in 2015 and holds a Litt.D. from the University of Cambridge. He was the General Editor of the Wiley Blackwell Encyclopedia of Social Theory (2018).

Stephen Turner is currently Distinguished University Professor at the Department of Philosophy, University of South Florida, USA. His books include *Liberal Democracy 3.0: Civil Society in an Age of Experts* (2003) and essays collected in *The Politics of Expertise* (2013). He has also written extensively on Max Weber, especially on politics, on Carl Schmitt, and on the politics of science and science policy.

Frédéric Vandenberghe is professor of sociology at the Institute of Philosophy and the Social Sciences of the Federal University of Rio de Janeiro. He is an active member of the anti-utilitarian movement in the social sciences (MAUSS) and has recently edited the issue of the *Revue du MAUSS* on the past, present and future of sociology (2020). He has published widely in the field of social theory. His most recent books are *What's Critical about Critical Realism. Essays* *in Reconstructive Social Theory* (Routledge, 2014) and with Alain Caillé *Towards a New Classic Sociology. A Proposal and a Debate* (Routledge, 2021).

Jean-Francois Véran is professor of anthropology at the Institute of Philosophy and the Social Sciences of the Federal University of Rio de Janeiro. He has joined Doctors without Frontiers (MSF) in 2010 as a Health Promotor in Haiti, Guatemala and Honduras and directs the Laboratory of Applied Anthropology (LAPA) in Rio de Janeiro. He co-edited the book: *Médecins sans Frontières and Humanitarian Situations. An Anthropological Exploration* (Routledge, 2020).

Sylvia Walby OBE is Professor of Sociology, and Director of the Violence and Society Centre at City, University of London. She is Fellow of the Academy of Social Sciences, UK; Chair of the Sociology Sub-Panel for the UK's Research Excellence Framework 2021. She has published on rethinking the concept of society and the analysis of societal transformation using complex systems thinking, including *Globalization and Inequalities: Complexity and Contested Modernities* (Sage 2009) and *Crisis* (Polity 2015). Recent work focuses on including violence in a theory of society.

Jonathan White is Professor of Politics at the London School of Economics. His most recent book is *Politics of Last Resort: Governing by Emergency in the European Union* (Oxford University Press, 2019); previous titles include *The Meaning of Partisanship* (with Lea Ypi, Oxford University Press, 2016), and *Political Allegiance after European Integration* (Palgrave Macmillan, 2011).

Jan Zielonka is Professor of Politics and International Relations at the University of Oxford and Venice, Cá Foscari. Zielonka has produced eighteen books including *Counter-revolution. Liberal Europe in Retreat* (Oxford University Press, 2018, awarded the 2019 UACES prize for the best book on Europe and translated into several languages), *Politics and the Media in New Democracies. Europe in a Comparative Perspective* (Oxford University Press, 2015), *Is the EU doomed?* (Polity Press, 2014), and *Europe as Empire. The Nature of the Enlarged European Union* (Oxford University Press, 2006).

Index

https://doi.org/10.1515/9783110713350-017

CPSIA information can be obtained
at www.ICGtesting.com
Printed in the USA
LVHW080505100222
710513LV00001B/1

9 783110 713237